What Should I Read Next?

70 University of Virginia
Professors Recommend
Readings in History,
Politics, Literature, Math,
Science, Technology,
the Arts, and More

What
Should
I Read
Next?

EDITED BY JESSICA R. FELDMAN
AND ROBERT STILLING

UNIVERSITY OF VIRGINIA PRESS
CHARLOTTESVILLE AND LONDON

University of Virginia Press
© 2008 by the Rector and Visitors of the University of Virginia
All rights reserved
Printed in the United States of America on acid-free paper

First published 2008

9 8 7 6 5 4 3 2 1

Library of Congress Cataloging-in-Publication Data

What should I read next? : 70 University of Virginia professors recommend readings
in history, politics, literature, math, science, technology, the arts, and more / edited by
Jessica R. Feldman and Robert Stilling.
        p.   cm.
Includes bibliographical references and index.
ISBN 978-0-8139-2736-7 (pbk. : acid-free paper)
1. Best books. 2. Best books—United States. 3. Books—Reviews. 4. Books—United
States—Reviews. 5. University of Virginia—Faculty—Books and reading. I. Feldman,
Jessica R. (Jessica Rosalind), 1949– II. Stilling, Robert, 1977–
    Z1035.A1W48 2008
    028.1—dc22   2008009234

Contents

2 Mathematics, Science, Technology

3 Literature

4 The Arts

5 Mind, Body, Spirit

Introduction

This book is the result of an experiment and a hope. The experiment: what would happen if we were to ask a number of University of Virginia professors to provide a short list of books they admire, along with a brief essay discussing what makes the list cohere? The hope: that the result would be, not an encyclopedic, systematic, or thoroughgoing volume, but a vibrant album of snapshots of a university at work, a collection that would make some of the passion and expertise of the faculty at that university accessible to those outside its walls. You have before you the result. Like most family albums, it reflects the places, things, and people it just happens to capture, and it suggests the starting place for thought.

Why this particular university? Of course, it happens to be ours, but it's also an institution with a tradition of combining great teaching with successful research. You might even think of each entry as something like the first day of a class, when the professor gives you a reading list and a rationale for the course that will follow. In asking a group of university professors to reach beyond the walls of the university to students and readers from a range of ages and backgrounds, we have challenged them to think of new ways to make the material they love accessible to a wider audience. We also hope to satisfy readers looking for a depth of expertise they might not find so readily elsewhere.

The basic format for each entry is the same. Each contributor provides a short essay to introduce his or her topic with the necessary background to get the reader going, and to make the most of his or her personal enthusiasm for a subject. For the casual browser in search of a place to start, these essays, though brief, will provide their own rewards. After each essay, you'll find a list of five recommended books and a short description of each one, including hints and pointers, highlights of the book's most interesting features, and just enough synopsis to give the book's general flavor.

Because our contributors show such enthusiasm for their subjects, their task—to choose just five representative books—was no easy assignment.

Boiled down, the problem we set before them was to convey their own immense love of learning in a bite-sized amount of space. We find their many solutions to this problem to be simple and elegant, quirky and ingenious, often surprising, and frequently interdisciplinary.

To our delight, the results bubble over academic categories. One entry turns to essays by Sartre and Hergé's *Tintin* comics to show how the French have come to understand (or misunderstand) America. Another demonstrates how Shakespeare and Jane Austen challenge us to think in new ways about illness and inheritance. One list recommends both fiction and nonfiction to get at the contradictions and difficulties of both reading and writing about poverty. Indeed, in these pages, and even within the same lists, the reader will find mention of multiple genres, among them novels, poetry, memoirs, scientific treatises, and environmental meditations, as well as philosophical, liturgical, and critical texts. Here is writing by the powerful and the disempowered, the famous, the obscure, and even the anonymous.

As you'll see, some contributions rethink subjects of perpetual interest: while one list introduces the latest knowledge of infant psychological development, another reconsiders America's time-honored founding. One foray into medieval art history combines great scholarship with primary source material to provide the feel of a hands-on seminar. Others present a cross section of a current debate such as that over climate change, introducing both the science behind the debate and the range of arguments that follows in its wake. In presenting five classics from a particular tradition, such as Hinduism, or a specific time and place, such as pre–Civil War America, our contributors look for ways to offer readers enough traction to get through perennially rewarding works such as the Bhagavad Gita and *Moby-Dick*. While one entry on poetry conveys the ecstatic rhythms of the Persian poet Rumi and of Emily Dickinson, another follows the slow path of mourning in William Butler Yeats and Seamus Heaney. In combining critical and fictional work as typified by W. E. B. Du Bois and Toni Morrison, another list gives shape to the complex emotional, historical, and philosophical landscape left by the troubling legacy of slavery in America.

As this small sampling shows, in addition to the wide range of subjects found in this volume, the reader will find an equally wide range of approaches. With a quick glance at the table of contents or by perusing the index of authors and works at the back of this volume, readers can design their own approach, discover how these separate lists speak to each other, and thread their own way through the books and topics presented here. Or, one can flip through this volume and, without going deep into the booklists, find something new that might be worth returning to later. For those who like to discuss what they read with others, in book clubs for example, we hope some of these lists might provide a resource.

Lists themselves, of course, have a rich cultural history. Old Testament genealogies are lists that help us understand both the passage of time and the concept of community. When we come to a catalogue of great ships in Homer's *Iliad,* it slows down the story, but it also helps us to see in our mind's eye and feel more vividly the events and people that it refers to. Perhaps *this* short list of examples points to what we think you'll find within: reflections on a wide and deep cultural heritage by a generation or two of scholars at a leading public university, and lists that will slow us down and help us to enjoy books that we're now thinking of reading next.

We thank Ed Ayers, former Dean of Arts and Sciences, for his support for this project. For their advice as we began, we thank Christine Taylor, Adena Siegal, Colleen Lanick, and Kristen Taylor.

Bibliographical note: Whenever it was possible, we have listed recent paperback editions of the recommended books.

What Should I Read Next?

History

Memory

Politics

ALON CONFINO

The Past as Memory and Oblivion

All societies have been in different ways attentive to the past, that protean and essential factor of life: we depend on it and seek it, yet at times we cannot stand facing it. Our sense of individual and collective identity requires it, whether we decide to repress, embellish, or just lie to ourselves about it. My topic is how people in modern society, ordinary people but also historians, construct images of the past to give meaning to their world, and what it says about us.

The five books deal with the different ways people remember the past. They are concerned not so much with finding the true tale, the way things really were. Instead, they are concerned with the ways a given past shaped our identity. Remembering is not about getting the past right; it is often about getting it wrong, thus making the present bearable and meaningful. These books are about the process of remembering, and the self-consciousness gained during the journey.

To approach the topic, I selected five books: three novels (by Cercas, Khoury, Guttfreund), one history book (by Nora), and one essay written in a literary style by an anthropologist (Augé). Together they cover two foundational representations of the past, a literary and a historical one, that are connected but are not identical. Reading these books with this in mind enhances our understanding of the power of historical memories to shape, for good and bad, one's life.

The novels by Cercas, Khoury, and Guttfreund evoke how foundational pasts—the Spanish Civil War, the Palestinian Nakba (the 1948 dispossession and the loss of Palestine), and the Holocaust—continue to disturb identities generations later. They are particularly suitable to describe the messy process by which individuals remember, for the novels can legitimately commingle past and present, mix dreams and traumas, and jump from the individual to the collectivity without hesitation. Novels thus evoke the haphazard and unpredictable process of remembering precisely because they are not limited by the disciplinary rules of history such as anachronism, chronology, and relations of cause and effect. They describe the process of remembering by, for example, using literary flashbacks, and being expressively written and overtly nostalgic. They touch us when they possess a moral core and humanism, as these books do.

If novels, as an artistic representation, are important to describe the process of remembering, they are also insufficient, for some insights into the process can be captured only by the historical discipline: it is crucial to understand the experience of a given past and how and why we remember it. Thinking with history is rewarding because it makes us aware of the similarities and differences between history, as a discipline whose role is to think about the past, and memory, as a cultural production about individual and collective images of the past. The historian's role is to illuminate the construction of memories as cultural, social, and political phenomena: who wants whom to remember what and why? How and why do people internalize a given past? The historian's aim, when it is properly done, is not to invent pasts (although this does happen at times), but to explain the reasons for and consequences of the emergence of certain memories and not others. Reading a history book about the process of imagining a past makes us aware of the elements of power, intention, and agency, as well as of unintended consequences and irrational motives, that are part of the construction of memory.

Reading about recollection means keeping in mind that memory is shaped by forgetfulness, as Augé reminds us. The very act of remembering is often also an act of repudiation, denying and erasing the past of others. In this respect, what some of these books tell us is that memory should not be sanctified: it is not always good to remember, and not all memories are innocent.

Why should we read about memory and history? Not in order to learn from the mistakes of past planning to avoid making them in the future.

History does not provide an easy-to-use instruction manual of how to act in the future; had this been the case, our world would have been perfect long ago. We read about memory and history to gain the wisdom and self-consciousness that come with doubt and a sense of perspective. What emerges from these books is the limits of ideology to offer answers and the inadequacy of black-and-white moral judgments. Some questions do not have answers, some stories have no happy ending, and sometimes the journey traversed by people to understand the past is the true illumination about their identity, about memory and history. A final thought: Tell me what you remember and forget—and what you read—and I'll tell you who you are.

 Marc Augé, *Oblivion,* trans. Marjolijn de Jager (University of Minnesota Press, 2004)

The argument of this short and expressive essay is that memory needs forgetfulness: "Memories are crafted by oblivion as the outlines of the shore are created by the sea." Marc Augé, a French anthropologist, describes forms of forgetfulness and how they influence the way we remember.

 Javier Cercas, *Soldiers of Salamis,* trans. Anne McLean (Bloomsbury, 2004)

In the dying moments of the Spanish Civil War (1936–39), Rafael Sanchez Mazas, a writer, fascist, and founder of the Spanish Falange, is found by a Republican militiaman who instead of killing him simply looks him in the eyes, turns away, and leaves. Mazas becomes a minister in Franco's first government; the soldier disappears from the annals of the Civil War. The novel, told by a journalist also called Javier Cercas in contemporary Spain, is about what happened at that moment when the eyes of Mazas and the soldier met. Cercas begins with Mazas as the protagonist, but comes to understand it is the unknown solider who is the key to the story. Who was he? Why did he save Mazas's life? Is he still alive? The questions open up a journey to the memory of the war.

 Amir Guttfreund, *Our Holocaust,* trans. Jessica Cohen (Toby Press, 2006)

In a small neighborhood in northern Israel there is a community inhabited mostly by Holocaust survivors. Guttfreund imaginatively describes their lives and nightmares through the eyes of a boy who is a second generation to a family of survivors. The boy, together with a girlfriend named Efi, attempts to understand what actually happened there in the Holocaust. Yet the book is not about the historical event, but about the multitude of personal Holocausts that each survivor carries, and about what it wrought in the life and memory of these survivors as seen through the eyes of the children. This is described with humor and empathy that endow the topic with a powerful truth.

⮞ Elias Khoury, *Gate of the Sun,* trans. Humphrey Davies (Archipelago, 2005)

Yunes, a veteran Palestinian fighter, lies ill and unconscious in a hospital in the Shatila refugee camp near Beirut. By his bed sits Dr. Khalil, who attempts to bring him back to consciousness by remembering their lives. What emerges is the Palestinian past from 1948 to the 1990s through a splendid patchwork of memories that give this past humanity, longing, and pain. At the center are two love stories: of Yunes, who fled to Lebanon in 1948, and Nabila, his young wife whom he hardly knew and who stayed behind in the Galilee, as well as a love story for Palestine. Elias Khoury, born in 1948 in Beirut, based his fiction on interviews he conducted with 1948 refugees. He interweaves these tales into a narrative that has no clear beginning or end, and that is human while being critical, and nostalgic without being sentimental.

⮞ Pierre Nora, ed., *Realms of Memory: Rethinking the French Past,* ed. Lawrence D. Kritzman, trans. Arthur Goldhammer (Columbia University Press, 1996)

The project of the French historian Pierre Nora, *Les lieux de mémoire,* on the construction of the French past, was made a generation ago, and has since received a classic status in memory studies. Scholars of memory have by now gone beyond it in terms of method, interpretation, and subject matter, but it remains a cornerstone in modern thinking about memory and history, and therefore is a good starting point for thinking of these relations.

ALON CONFINO, Professor of Modern German and European History, has written extensively on memory, nationhood, and historical method. His new book, *Germany as a Culture of Remembrance: Promises and Limits of Writing History* (University of North Carolina Press, 2006), is a collection of ten essays that explore the ways laypersons and scholars use the notion of memory as a tool to understand the past.

HERBERT TICO BRAUN

Human Connections: History and the Latin American Novel

It is Sunday, May 28, 2006, and I am writing this introduction to five Latin American historical novels that tell us about the ties among human beings. The newspapers are filled with book reviews today. "We all like the sensation that we're taking in something useful, or at least informative, but fiction's news is ultimately about interiors, not exteriors," writes the reviewer of *Come Together, Fall Apart: A Novella and Stories,* by the Panamanian novelist Cristina Henríquez. Interiors indeed. This is why as a historian I also read novels. We practice something we call social history, and also cultural history, and even psycho-history, but it is still so very difficult for us to get inside of our subjects' hearts and heads.

And also today there is a review of *La Malinche,* by Mexican writer Laura Esquivel, who is well known here in the United States for her somewhat magical realist *Like Water for Chocolate.* Esquivel tells the story of the young Mexican woman who by learning a smattering of Spanish words comes to serve as the conqueror Hernán Cortés's interpreter and mediator. She has a child with him, a son who is one of the land's first mestizo offspring in a joining of bloods from which the Mexican people have descended. La Malinche resides, ambivalently, at the core of Mexican nationhood. She turns powerful in a man's world. "It was a confusing time," Esquivel writes, "in which her time and Cortés's were ineluctably interconnected, laced, tied together."

Tied together? Indeed. This is the other reason why I also read novels. More than a few of us historians brush the connections away. For many of us the Spanish conquest was harsh, bitter, brutal, and decisive. It was all that, of course, but it was also much else and less. We tend to be better at seeing the fallings apart than the comings together, the contradictions than the connections, the revolutionaries than the conciliators, the failures than the successes, the rape of la Malinche than the supple lacing of two human beings who not so long before could hardly have imagined that anyone like the other one even existed on this earth. Might these not have been moments of intense intimate curiosity? Imagine such a joining! These conquest encounters were so filled with interior conflicts on all sides that we historians have a hard time coming to grips with all the messiness.

Fiction works precisely because it deals with the interior needs of its created characters. Historians can place the lives of Hernán Cortés and la

Malinche, and of, say, Thomas Jefferson and Sally Hemings, on a broad canvas, but it takes the novelist to put them in bed. An imagining of such private relationships, both vicious and convivial or more often somewhere in between, can tell us much about people's exterior relationships, about the public comings and goings of the emerging conquest culture in Mexico, and of an established political culture in the slave South.

Should I study novels and ask my colleagues in the Department of Spanish, Italian, and Portuguese to receive me? Should I move into the ugly modernist bowels of Wilson Hall, leaving the stately and historical Randall Hall that houses the History Department behind? No. I spend many of my working moments unraveling the extensions of time, delving then into moments, and then diving into the imagined worlds of characters that may certainly have lived their lives pretty much as the fiction writers suggest they did. With novelists by my side, I inquire into the human condition. I have learned that the histories of Latin Americans are a continuous search for human ties, and that the voyage is both gratifying and not. Conversations abound in Latin America.

⊷ Carlos Fuentes, *The Campaign,* trans. Alfred MacAdam (Harper Perennial, 1992)

Spanish America's independence was a falling apart. Historians look down on it. In the pages of Carlos Fuentes, we live it from the inside. Our hero is an idealistic, young urban liberal yearning for equality. In battle he confronts an inscrutable Indian who should be his fellow citizen. "I realized that if I was in fact going to kill an enemy, he couldn't be my equal, my fellow man, my real enemy brother, not because he was fighting in the ranks of the Spaniards, but because he really was different, other, Indian." He kills him. Our protagonist suffers this intimate conflict, this uncertain moment, this separation, when he seeks to connect with the lives of others. We don't want to understand this violent urge, but we do. Can there be liberty without equality? our Mexican author asks. This question haunts us still, in Latin America and beyond, and we have been trying, although fitfully, to build from this harsh beginning ever since.

⊷ Mario Vargas Llosa, *The War of the End of the World,* trans. Helen R. Lane (Penguin, 1997)

Antonio Conselheiro was an actual rural mystic of the northeastern backlands of Brazil in the late nineteenth century. Around him a movement at Canudos evolved that was so seemingly millenarian that it was brutally destroyed. For Euclides da Cunha, in his celebrated firsthand account, *Os Sertoes* (*Rebellion in the Backlands*), Conselheiro, the thin, robed man who walked for years from town to town, was the product of rural recidivism and national abandonment. This might well be true. For most historians thereafter, Conselheiro is the logical result of failed political, economic, and cultural structures, which could also be true.

In Vargas Llosa's long and evocative novel populated by multiple characters, some more invented than others, only the main character does not speak. But through all those who surround him, we come to walk right next to him. Antonio wants to be accepted and to live a moral life together with his followers. He (probably) feels that there is plenty of space in Brazil for everyone. He is not a revolutionary. Others above him, whom we also credibly meet in these pages, want to be rid of him more than he wants to be rid of them.

↬ Gabriel García Márquez, *One Hundred Years of Solitude,* trans. Gregory Rabassa (Harper Perennial Classics, 2006)

Latin American novels about the countryside often exaggerate the exotic. In this one, butterflies circle over a beautiful girl and people are born with a tail of a pig. Time stands still, or works in circles. The author is attracted to his rural tropics in which this epic is set, and he claims a disdain for the cold highlands and its stuffy sorts. Publishers turned the book down time and again, but the Nobel laureate's colorful characters are forever curious, eyes open, welcoming gypsies, looking afar for fun and innovation, science and alchemy. Even self-serving urban politicians and that damn American banana company are a marvelous mystery, at least at first. The Buendíase do not want to live in solitude. This masterpiece is understood mainly as a work of rural isolation, of breakings apart, but it is more powerfully about the human effort to be with others. The inhabitants of Macondo exude a self-evident respect toward their highland compatriots that the author himself may not have recognized. We need only read his joyful autobiography, *Living to Tell the Tale,* to feel how he radiates in the company of his fellow Colombians, urban and also rural.

↬ Julia Alvarez, *In the Time of the Butterflies* (Algonquin, 1994)

↬ Mario Vargas Llosa, *The Feast of the Goat,* trans. Edith Grossman (Picador, 2002)

These two books are political thrillers. Rafael Trujillo ruled over the Dominican Republic from 1930 until he was assassinated in 1961. Julia Alvarez, who was born there, tells the story of the Mirabal sisters, who conspire against the dictatorship. This is no simple story of frontal opposition. Many an adolescent girl seeks to dance with the dictator, and to become his mistress. Gossip reigns. Trujillo's power digs deeply into people's hearts. Power seduces. And not all of the sisters are equally committed to the struggle, for personality counts too. Intimate reasons for political action, we learn, are often more pressing than ideology. Power enrages.

So too in Vargas Llosa's telling is erotic power the dictator's allure. But here when it counts he can't perform sexually. And alas, the aging Trujillo is forever in fear of a small stain appearing on his carefully pressed trousers. We feel for him. Better still, as his body betrays him and he feels his power draining away, we are emboldened. We too can fight against the oppressors above us, for they are also weak.

Like the dictator in his waning years, the writer is a bumbling politician. When he lost the presidency of his native Peru, he declared that he no longer could be a citizen of such a place. He would return to mother Spain, as though our desperate liberal had not already slain the inscrutable Indian. But his fictional travel into the human psyche, into our attraction to power, is without parallel in Latin America's letters. Fiction exceeds reality, if not history. The protagonist is a woman who refuses to bed down with him. Urania Cabral is her name, and she is unforgettable.

HERBERT TICO BRAUN is Associate Professor of History and writes in different voices about the strains in our human connectedness. In *Our Guerrillas, Our Sidewalks* (University Press of Colorado, 1994), he seeks the voice of his brother-in-law, of the Colombian guerrillas who kidnapped him, and his own, as the family's negotiator. Neither history nor fiction, it is an almost intimate memoir, one filled with bumbling steps all around. He often recalls that liberal who in an intimate moment in the vortex of independence suddenly felt the need to kill.

DENISE WALSH

Your Culture or Your Rights? Women and the Multicultural Dilemma

What is "death by culture"? Is it *sati* (widow burning), a barbaric Indian custom that violates the most fundamental of women's rights? Or is *sati* a Hindu woman's highest, definitive expression of religious faith? Is dowry the marriage price a groom pays for a bride, equivalent to trafficking in women? Or is it the material expression of families joined in a mutual alliance of care and commitment? Is marriage an exclusionary rite that unjustly privileges heterosexual couples over single women, men, and same-sex relationships? Or is it a sacred covenant underpinning the moral foundations of society? What should governments do when immigrants bring controversial cultural practices with them? Must immigrants reject their culture to claim their rights?

At its worst, this polarized quandary over culture and rights has led conservatives to label feminism a threat to social morality, while feminists have attacked culture as irredeemably retrograde. No doubt elite cultural conservatives have promoted traditions that enhance their power at the expense of women. And liberal feminists have occasionally been at odds with the women they aim to liberate. It appears that neither culture nor rights alone provides a just or sufficient solution.

The problem has been particularly intense in postcolonial countries with free speech and a civil society, and in liberal democracies with sizable immigrant and/or indigenous populations. Postcolonial states must grapple with the imperial legacy of denigration and suppression of "native" beliefs and practices. Cultural revival becomes an expressive act of national pride, independence, and freedom. In contemporary liberal democracies, respect and toleration for different customs lie at the bedrock of their governing philosophies and are crucial to the peaceful coexistence of their diverse populations. In both sites the result is contestation that crosscuts women's lives as they become markers in a struggle that pits tradition, family, and faith against individual rights.

Women's status and well-being are also at the contentious center of academic debates over identity and freedom. While liberal feminists have aggressively defended the autonomy of individual indigenous and minority women, immigrant and minority rights champions argue that *group* identity is the fountainhead of personal dignity. Scholars thus debate about how to conceptualize human beings: as group members, individuals, or both? If both, are human beings first group members and then individuals seeking autonomy and freedom—or vice versa? Must either group *or* individual rights always trump? Who should have the power to make this decision? What should the role of government be? Should society regulate group practices that threaten individual autonomy? Promote cultural diversity? Practice neutrality? Solutions are neither obvious nor simple, yet the need for answers is pressing.

The best and most accessible work in the field raises questions, forcing us to think beyond the culture-rights binary. Admittedly, this does not make finding answers easier, but it vastly enriches our understanding of the problem. Too often, discussions about culture and rights are not only dichotomized, but also abstracted in a way that ignores women's complex, varied interests. The first book on the reading list thus showcases the autobiography of one Indian woman's struggle for survival. Neither culture nor rights is offered as causal problem or solution. Instead, the reader must sift through the evidence, forming her own opinion. She can then turn to Uma Narayan, an Indian feminist and U.S. academic, who integrates her personal history while exploring the clash of women's rights with culture. Read together, the two books reveal that the stark choices offered by the culture versus rights debate are misleadingly simple.

The next two books on the list address culture and women's rights in the United States. Mary Shanley's anthology and Linda Hirshman's contributions are contentious, offering views guaranteed to provoke readers. They are included not because they provide definitive answers, but because of their clarity, directness, and willingness to face the problems equality raises for mainstream Americans. American readers might compare their reactions to Hirshman's controversial proposals with their views on India. In teaching these books, I have found that most of us tend to recommend dramatic cultural transformation for others while resisting it ourselves.

The last book on the list is now a staple in academic circles. A veritable who's who of political thinkers, *Is Multiculturalism Bad for Women?* initially poses the culture-rights dilemma in binary fashion, but generates a host of thoughtful critiques rewarding for those interested in investigating the challenges liberal democracies now face as home to peoples from across the globe. A timely concern, it is likely to be with us throughout the twenty-first century.

↦ Baby Halder, *A Life Less Ordinary,* trans. Urvashi Butalia (Zubaan; Penguin, 2006)

A blockbuster Indian novel, the autobiographical tale *A Life Less Ordinary* is an unblinking account of one Indian woman's saga of tragedy and determination that has been likened to Frank McCourt's *Angela's Ashes.* In simple, searing prose, Baby Halder recounts being a child bride at twelve, a mother at thirteen, and a survivor of protracted, brutal domestic violence. The novel was a sensation in India in part because poor, runaway wives like Baby are silenced by social ostracism and shame. Halder's unlikely literary success was facilitated by her employer, Prabodh Kumar, who encouraged Baby to write her life story and sent her manuscript to publishers. Halder continues to work for Kumar as a maid. *A Life Less Ordinary* puts a compelling face on female, impoverished India, illuminating women's multiple vulnerabilities. Can women's rights ameliorate the situation of women like Baby Halder? The next book on the list explores this question.

✧ Uma Narayan, *Dislocating Cultures: Identities, Traditions, and Third-World Feminism* (Routledge, 1997)

The essays in this collection—forays on rights, culture, and gender politics—are witty and personal. In one chapter, Narayan recounts a woman's opening line at a cocktail party: "I have heard that many Indian women are burned by their families for dowry." How, Narayan wonders, might she respond? "Nice to have met you. I think I need another drink!" The essay that follows is her search for a more thoughtful answer. In the chapter titled "Eating Cultures," Narayan investigates food, gender, and politics, noting along the way that curry powder was a British invention, that her grandmother had a "visceral repugnance" for "beef-eaters," and that "eating cultures" might be one small way to transcend difference. The essays are ruminations, the literary equivalent of dining with Narayan. Entertaining, thought-provoking, and voracious, she raises far more questions than she answers, but nevertheless leaves you sated, relishing the taste of something new.

✧ Mary Lyndon Shanley, *Just Marriage,* ed. Joshua Cohen and Deborah Chasman (Oxford University Press, 2004)

Nowhere in the United States does culture clash more contentiously with women's rights than in the private sphere. The provocative contributions in this compact, lively collection interrogate marriage, inequality, caretaking, and the family. Modeled on the highly accessible, diverse format of *Is Multiculturalism Bad for Women?* Shanley's highly praised volume makes clear that the private is public in ways we often overlook. Who should be allowed to marry? What does government gain from regulating marriage? Should marriage have a special legal status? Can marriage be a relationship among equals in a society that remains highly unequal? The authors, far from being in agreement with one another, ask difficult, compelling questions, prompting us to think about domesticity, love, and relationships through the lenses of public policy and individual rights. Moreover, the authors powerfully illustrate how cultural practices in the United States come into conflict with equality, dignity, and liberty.

✧ Linda R. Hirshman, *Get to Work: A Manifesto for Women of the World* (Viking, 2006)

Based on Hirshman's intensely debated article "Homeward Bound," which presumed to offer young women a set of rules for avoiding the cultural trap of domestic inequality, this little volume packs a wallop. Critics of "Homeward Bound" lambasted Hirshman's recommendations, such as "find a spouse with less social power than you . . . marry down." Energized by the debate she ignited and not to be outdone by her opponents, Hirshman promptly published *Get to Work,* an elaboration on her assertion that American women's "choice" to stay at home "cleaning bodily waste" is an ethical mistake that prevents talented, highly educated women from fulfilling their personal goals and meeting their social obligations. While Shanley's volume prompts us to think deeply about why such choices are made, Hirshman forces us to squarely face the professional costs of caretaking in a society that rewards status and power far more than its lip service to family values suggests.

⮐ Joshua Cohen, Matthew Howard, and Martha C. Nussbaum, eds., *Is Multiculturalism Bad for Women?* (Princeton University Press, 1999)

If people with different beliefs and norms deserve our respect, what should we do about repugnant cultural traditions practiced here at home? Should polygamy, genital cutting, or purdah be tolerated in liberal countries? In direct and accessible prose, this slim book contains a range of philosophical answers. It opens with Susan Okin's biting rejection of cultural claims that limit women's rights. In response to her now classic essay, fifteen distinguished scholars plumb the depths of the dilemma. In extremely pointed briefs, contributors explore the philosophical underpinnings of contemporary liberalism and its capacity to integrate diversity while guarding individual rights. Each response can be savored on its own for the insights and questions it raises about rights, diversity, and toleration. When read in its entirety, the volume impresses as a singular example of the freedom of thought that liberalism cherishes yet finds so challenging in an era of multiple, hybrid identities.

DENISE WALSH is Assistant Professor of Politics and Studies in Women and Gender. Her dissertation, "Just Debate: Culture and Gender Justice in the New South Africa," won the Hannah Arendt Award for best politics dissertation from the New School for Social Research. She was the lead editor and authored two articles for the March 2006 issue of the *Journal of Southern African Studies.* Walsh is writing a book about democratization and gender politics in South Africa.

FARZANEH MILANI

Best Sellers and Half-Truths: Misreading Iran in America

"Americans read only American literature," regrets Maryam, the Iranian American protagonist of Anne Tyler's novel *Digging to America*. On the face of it, the statement seems implausible. Strictly speaking, it isn't even true. The Iranian poet Jalal-ed-Din Rumi has been a best-selling poet in America for the last two decades. Iranian studies is a thriving field, producing an avalanche of books from a variety of perspectives and disciplines. Yet, and this is where Maryam has a point, while some poets and academics and a small number of books translated from Persian reach a narrow and ghettoized audience, popular books on Iran reach millions of people. They wield much power by touching the hearts and souls of the American public.

Despite a long history of friendship and cooperation with the United States, Iran is now seen as a purveyor of aggression by many Americans. Persia, "the Land of the Rose and the Nightingale," is now Iran, the vanguard of a terrorist apocalypse. It is a member of the "Axis of Evil," a rogue state, a "greater challenge" to the United States than any other country, according to President Bush's 2006 National Security Strategy.

The genesis of this hostility can be traced back to November 4, 1979, when a group of militant students stormed the American embassy in Tehran, taking fifty-two Americans hostage for 444 days. On that day, a sense of anguish etched itself into the collective consciousness of a justifiably outraged nation. "America in Captivity" was the headline that captured the mood of a country in psychic pain. Twenty-eight years later, Iranians still find themselves hostages of their own hostage-taking. Although they are currently the most pro-American people in the Islamic world, their image as a dangerous enemy dominates the American imagination.

There are several reasons for this misreading of Iran. The two countries have had no official relations since 1980. With scarce diplomacy, a dearth of intercultural communication, and restrictions on travel and tourism, opportunities to reach a better understanding have been few. There are also precious few books translated from Persian into English. Indeed, the number of translations into English from any language is startlingly low in America. The not-so-lucrative business of translation, a cornerstone of intercultural communication and better understanding between nations, barely interests the $25.1 billion U.S. publishing industry.

The paucity of translated books is further complicated by the increasing politicization of the popular books published in the United States about Iran. Consider the *New York Times* best-seller list, established in 1931. Even though America was intimately involved with Iran at the time, no book about Iran appeared on the list during its first fifty years. The hostage crisis quickly changed that. A slew of books was ushered into print with a fanfare of publicity. In less than two decades, at least five novels— *On Wings of Eagles, Whirlwind, Sword Point, Shadows of Steel,* and *House of Sand and Fog*—and three nonfiction books—*Under Fire, Not Without My Daughter,* and *Reading Lolita in Tehran*—scaled the list.

The two most popular books ever written in the United States about Iran depict the country as an angry sea of chest-pounding, fist-shaking mobs that burn effigies of the American president, trample on the American flag, and scream "death to America" like a mantra. Part reality and part imagination, with a splash of concern for national security thrown in for good measure, *Not Without My Daughter* and *Reading Lolita in Tehran* offer engaging stories, but fan the flames of antagonism between the two countries. The Muslim woman, held captive in segregated spaces and trapped underneath her veil—a prison shrunk to the size of her body—is a central and indispensable character in the unfolding plot of both books.

We need not entertain any illusions about the Islamic Republic. Repression, autocracy, political and religious purges, censorship, and gender inequity are facts of life in Iran. These issues should be written about, inside and outside of Iran. And they have been. Authors like Shahrnush Parsipur, Marjane Satrapi, Shirin Ebadi, and many others have recorded the diminution of civil rights in the Islamic Republic, but they have also described a culture of resistance. They have portrayed the ongoing battle between clerical rule and the people's will. It is this complex mix of defiance and submission, of resistance and acquiescence that most accurately reflects the literary scene and the political climate in postrevolutionary Iran.

⊖ Betty Mahmoody with William Hoffer, *Not Without My Daughter* (St. Martin's Press, 1993)

This memoir claims to be an accurate account of a mother and daughter held hostage in an alien land. The author is an all-American housewife whose idyllic life in the United States ends when, accompanied by her husband and four-year-old daughter, she travels to Iran. Suddenly, a two-week vacation turns into an endless nightmare. Betty's doting husband becomes a monster who wants to keep his wife and daughter locked up in Iran against their wishes. This "true story of a desperate struggle to survive and to escape from an alien and frightening culture" constructs a fictional Iran, a country at once primitive and repressive. It concentrates on binary opposites—oppressed/liberated, barbaric/civilized, bad/good—and depicts Iran as a "backward nation" where women have no rights and "are slaves to their husbands." Indeed, the whole country is beyond redemption. Even Iranian citizens think extinction is all they deserve. Quoting her despairing spouse, Mahmoody writes: "The only thing that could ever straighten out this screwed-up country is an atomic bomb! Wipe it off the map and start over."

↝ Azar Nafisi, *Reading Lolita in Tehran: A Memoir in Books* (Random House, 2003)

Reading Lolita in Tehran is the story of seven "girls" and their teacher caught in the clutches of repression and evil. The students meet once a week at the Tehran house of their devoted teacher, the author, to discuss "forbidden" works of Western fiction. While ostensibly championing women's rights, the book actually denigrates Iranian women and belittles their subversive activities. The author confirms prevailing stereotypes about Iran, selectively describing social and historic realities, confounding fact with fiction. She either ignores or reduces the resistance and self-assertion of women to their silent suffering, their passive-aggressiveness, their secret meetings, their wearing of makeup, and their wayward strands of hair. But even these paltry triumphs are contradicted by the overall message of the book, which emphasizes Iranian women's helplessness, their dependence, their invisibility, and above all, their incarceration. Iran is depicted as a giant gulag, an open-air detention facility, and all Iranian women, like Vladimir Nabokov's Lolita, are entrapped little mistresses.

↝ Shirin Ebadi with Azadeh Moaveni, *Iran Awakening: A Memoir of Revolution and Hope* (Random House, 2006)

In her memoir, Ebadi, the first Iranian citizen and the first Muslim woman to win a Nobel Prize and Iran's first female judge (who was demoted soon after the Islamic Revolution to the position of a clerk), describes her betrayed hopes for a revolution she supported. While Ebadi's meticulous record of the atrocities she suffered before and after the Revolution calls on the reader's sense of outrage, her memoir is ultimately a story of resolve and a declaration of victory. It debunks powerful stereotypes. It calls attention to the unprecedented presence of women as teachers and students in institutions of higher education in Iran, the sharp increase in women's literacy rates across the country, their attainment of leadership positions, their active participation in nongovernmental organizations, their vigorous involvement in art, politics, publishing, and sports. Refusing to give in to vengeance or hostility, Ebadi focuses on nonviolence and dialogue as the two central tropes of her memoir.

✎ Marjane Satrapi, *Persepolis: The Story of a Childhood* (Pantheon, 2004)

Marjane Satrapi believes Iran "has been discussed mostly in connection with fundamentalism, fanaticism, and terrorism. As an Iranian who has lived more than half my life in Iran," she argues, "I know this image is far from the truth." Thus, Satrapi focuses on "those Iranians who lost their lives in prisons defending freedom, who died in the war against Iraq, who suffered under various repressive regimes, or who were forced to leave their families and flee their homeland to be forgotten." *Persepolis* celebrates the Iranian people's history of resistance, subversion, and rebellion, and bears witness to the injustices caused by political and religious dogmatism. The story is told from the perspective of a sassy, intelligent, and wide-eyed child. Mixing inky black-on-white graphic designs with Persian miniatures, Satrapi documents the reality of life in pre- and postrevolutionary Iran. She depicts a complex web of paradoxes, a vibrant mix of contradictions, ultimately capturing the intricacies of a society in transition.

✎ Shahrnush Parsipur, *Women Without Men,* trans. Kamran Talattof and Jocelyn Sharlet (Feminist Press, 2004)

Large-scale access to the public sphere by Iranian women and their unfettered and uninhibited freedom of movement are relatively new developments in Iranian society, defining moments in Iranian modernity. Indeed, women's entry into previously all-male territories in the last 150 years has reorganized the cultural landscape of Iran. *Women Without Men* charts the difficulties, but also the exhilaration of these changes. It is the story of five women and one man explored through a multivocal narration. The theme that connects all thirteen chapters and all five female protagonists (who feel frustrated with their societal roles) is their desire to be on the road, to be free, to come and go as they please. Eventually, the women manage to escape the past and their confinement and transform their lives. As intruders into masculine spaces, as trespassers who disturb the age-old arrangements of femininity, they reject the exemplary paradigms of ideal womanhood. They remap the cultural geography of Iranian society.

FARZANEH MILANI is Professor of Persian Literature and Women Studies. She is the author of *Veils and Words: The Emerging Voices of Iranian Women Writers* (Syracuse University Press, 1992), and cotranslator, with Kaveh Safa, of *A Cup of Sin: Selected Poems of Simin Behbahani* (Syracuse University Press, 1999). Currently, Milani is a Carnegie Scholar and completing a manuscript on the cultural geography of Iran.

WILLIAM B. QUANDT

How to Understand 9/11, Iraq, and Bush's War on Terrorism

Most Americans will readily remember where they were when they learned of the attacks on the World Trade Center on September 11, 2001. But many fewer understand why those attacks happened and how we ended up at war with Iraq as a result. Although I have devoted most of my professional life to studying the Middle East, I will not pretend that I have all the answers, but I can steer a willing reader toward some excellent sources that will open eyes, raise many questions, and answer some of them. Where to start?

A bit of history is always useful, and in the case of figuring out where Osama bin Laden and the 9/11 attacks came from, we need to revisit Afghanistan in the period of the Soviet occupation of the 1980s. This little-remembered era saw the United States actively involved with others in the region—especially Pakistan and Saudi Arabia—in creating and supporting a band of Afghan fighters—the *mujahideen*—who wanted to free their country from Soviet occupation. One of the ideological motivations came from a heavy dose of Saudi-financed Islamic education in schools and training camps in Pakistan. From there came the fighters and eventually the Taliban regime that took over in Afghanistan after the Soviets left, and then gave sanctuary to bin Laden in the mid-1990s. No book will tell you more about this than Steve Coll's *Ghost Wars: The Secret History of the CIA, Afghanistan, and bin Laden, from the Soviet Invasion to September 10, 2001,* a remarkable piece of investigative journalism that reminds us of our own country's role in sowing seeds of Islamic extremism.

Next, the patient reader should dig into *The 9/11 Commission Report: Final Report of the National Commission on Terrorist Attacks upon the United States.* I would not normally suggest that any reader spend a lot of time with a government report. But this one is different. It is well written, filled with remarkable information, and full of real lessons in how government does—and does not—work. Just don't waste much time on the conclusions and recommendations for further action—they are predictable political compromises drafted by committee, and even they have mostly not been acted on.

If you are still with the program, you will have a pretty good idea of how and why 9/11 occurred, but there is a yawning gap between the tragic events of that unforgettable day and the decision to invade Iraq in spring 2003. To understand that policy choice by the Bush administration you need to go to George Packer's *The Assassins' Gate: America in Iraq*, a superb account of the background to the decision, the mistakes made early in the post-Saddam era, and the reactions of Iraqis across the political spectrum to the American presence. But as good as Packer is, Anthony Shadid, *Night Draws Near: Iraq's People in the Shadow of America's War*, is even better on Iraqis' views of the occupying American army and of their own future. The sad fact seems to be that Saddam's prolonged and harsh rule had a devastating impact on many Iraqis, depriving them of the most elemental capacity to trust one another and to work toward rebuilding their society along more decent lines. Shadid may seem pessimistic to some readers, but he has the advantage of being fluent in Arabic, unlike most American reporters, so he can talk to people from all walks of life. And he does just that, and he listens. Both of these Pulitzer Prize–winning journalists have a lot to tell us about Iraq—and ourselves.

Finally, the new medium of the blogosphere has yielded up an amazing book by an amazing Iraqi. I wish I could tell you her name, but she goes only by the pseudonym Riverbend, and her blogs have been collected in a book entitled *Baghdad Burning: Girl Blog from Iraq*. Shortly after the onset of the American occupation, this young Iraqi woman began to write about her everyday life, as well as her political opinions. She wrote in English, which she had apparently acquired while with her family in England. She is secular, well educated, from a mixed Sunni and Shii family— and she writes beautifully. I have had my students read her blog, and most of them are deeply impressed. You will be as well. She dislikes American policy, fears the rise of religious extremism and sectarianism in her country, but manages somehow to keep a humane and at times humorous view of daily life. We rarely get such an intimate view from the people who are at the other end of our foreign policy. This one is worth reading.

↬ Steve Coll, *Ghost Wars: The Secret History of the CIA, Afghanistan, and bin Laden, from the Soviet Invasion to September 10, 2001* (Penguin, 2005)

The *Washington Post* reporter Steve Coll charts the trail from the efforts to build up the Afghan *mujahideen* movement in the 1980s, to the rise of the Taliban and bin Laden in the 1990s, to the eve of 9/11. It is a tragic story of unintended consequences.

↬ *The 9/11 Commission Report: Final Report of the National Commission on Terrorist Attacks upon the United States* (Norton, authorized ed., 2004)

No commission has ever had better access to intelligence information. Led by University of Virginia professor Philip Zelikow, a team of academics and analysts details the story of how the 9/11 plot unfolded and how it managed to succeed. Read it and weep. It would seem that we had ample warning, but of course it is always easier to see the patterns in hindsight.

⊕ George Packer, *The Assassins' Gate: America in Iraq* (Farrar, Straus and Giroux, 2006)

The *New Yorker* writer George Packer sees the invasion of Iraq as stemming from ideas that had taken root, largely among neoconservative thinkers, in the 1980s and 1990s. The decision to go to war in Iraq was about much more than just Saddam and his alleged weapons of mass destruction. Packer originally sympathized with the argument for war because of his distaste for the Saddam Hussein regime, but he became disillusioned when he saw how little the Americans understood about the harsh Iraqi reality that they encountered.

⊕ Anthony Shadid, *Night Draws Near: Iraq's People in the Shadow of America's War* (Henry Holt, 2005)

The *Washington Post* writer Anthony Shadid uses his knowledge of the Middle East, his fluency in Arabic, and his patience to let Iraqis talk about Saddam, about their hopes and fears in the aftermath of the American occupation. He finds Iraq a complex and hard-to-fathom country, but no one does a better job of helping to lift the veil. There is not a lot of analysis here, but there is a great deal of empathy for Iraqis and the tragic circumstances that they have been forced to live through, first under Saddam and now under occupation.

⊕ Riverbend, *Baghdad Burning: Girl Blog from Iraq* (Feminist Press at CUNY, 2005)

This young Iraqi woman with a gift for words may not be typical—she lives in Baghdad and is from a middle-class professional background—but no voice from Iraq more deserves to be heard. Hers is heartfelt, sometimes angry, and always eloquent. Her descriptions of the insecurity of everyday life in Baghdad are chilling. She also has an eye for detail and a way with words that are truly impressive.

WILLIAM B. QUANDT is Edward Stettinius Professor of Politics; he teaches courses on the Middle East and American foreign policy. Among his publications is *Peace Process: American Diplomacy toward the Arab-Israeli Conflict since 1967*, 3rd ed. (Brookings Institution Press, 2005). In the 1970s, he twice served on the staff of the National Security Council with responsibility for the Middle East. He recently won an All-University Teaching Award.

ELLEN V. FULLER

Writing Self and Society: East Asian Women Authors

When Westerners consider the roles of women in East Asia, stereotypes often come first to mind. Adjectives such as "meek" and "submissive" are used to characterize the women, and "Confucianism" is taken to serve as one primary vehicle for explaining the necessity of these adjectives. In fact, women in all three countries of China, Japan, and Korea have a long history of asserting themselves in numerous contexts both inside and outside domestic life, all the way up to and including public acts of both individual and large-scale rebellion, and Confucianism at best has limited power as an explanatory model.

To understand better the women of China, Japan, and Korea, it is necessary to differentiate among the three countries, and to consider the writings of the women themselves as they seek to represent their lives and their worlds in different historical and social settings. An added benefit to this inquiry is that in the process of deepening our understanding of women in East Asia, we also gain a richer perspective on the countries they represent. Rather than regarding the category "woman" as a separate and independent field of inquiry, it is integral to analyses of all forms of cultural, economic, political, and social life.

As a social scientist, I read anthropology, economics, history, politics, and sociology, but I also read a great deal of literature in both the original and in translation. Besides enjoying literature, I find that it offers me insights that enrich my understanding of social science texts. I do not read literature as a literary critic; I read it as an observer of social life. I look for clues to women's thoughts and feelings, note which themes surface more than others, and try to visualize the microcosms being represented. Literature written by women thus provides me with opportunities to "compare notes" with historical records that have been written predominantly by elite men.

Though you will find some exceptions in the recommended readings, the production of literature, too, is primarily an elite endeavor, and must be understood as such. However, the topics that women in the reading list choose include but stretch well beyond their personal concerns as elite women. For example, you will find Japanese women presenting in their short stories commentaries on politics, reflections on the state of the poor, opposition to war, and interest in socialism, even when it was exceedingly dangerous for them to do so in the years leading up to World

War II. Korean women point out the drawbacks of rapid modernization despite the fact that support for this type of development was positioned by the government as an act of patriotism and national pride; they also write about the problems associated with authoritarian government as well as the wrenching effects on families coping with members on either side of the North-South divide. And Chinese women wrestle with feminism, expansion of educational opportunities for all women, Western imperialism, and national weakness in the early part of the twentieth century, which for some authors resulted in their beheading. All of this is in addition to the authors' portrayals of the trials and tribulations of women who seek personal autonomy while filling a variety of roles within families, communities, and countries.

I teach a course called "East Asian Women: (Self-) Portrayals in Social Context" that includes parts or all of the following six texts (two from each country) and places autobiography alongside fiction. I present the historical and social circumstances that surround each work; for your own reading, some of this contextual information can be found in the introductions to the texts, and I have added a few points to the description of each book. Once we engage the stories directly, students in the course tend to be quite surprised by what they read. In addition to learning the history and sociology represented by each piece, they discover that the numerous stereotypes they have held about East Asian women must be dismantled one by one. This leads to the realization that the stereotypes themselves are the products of historical circumstance rather than objective points of fact. Literature provides an opportunity to come to this realization in a profound way.

⇄ Ida Pruitt, *A Daughter of Han: The Autobiography of a Chinese Working Woman* (Stanford University Press, 1990)

> Ida Pruitt was born in China, the daughter of missionaries, and had a long and intimate relationship with the country, feeling more at home there than in the United States. She spent two years interviewing the subject of the book, Ning Lao T'ai-t'ai, a woman whose family had fallen from its more elite status by the time of her birth, leaving her to marry poorly and learn increasingly to fend for herself and her children. Her circumstances required that she become mobile despite the bound feet that marked her parents' class aspirations. Because Ning lived in a variety of worlds over the course of her life, including becoming a beggar at times, the book is a wonderful opportunity to see the multiple roles and attendant survival strategies of women and to understand the effects historical circumstances, societal beliefs, and foreign presence both did and did not have on them.

⊷ Amy D. Dooling and Kristina M. Torgeson, eds., *Writing Women in Modern China: An Anthology of Women's Literature from the Early Twentieth Century* (Columbia University Press, 1998)

China was forcibly opened by Western powers beginning in the nineteenth century. In the early twentieth century, Western and Japanese interests semi-colonized numerous parts of China, and Chinese intellectuals increasingly engaged in analyses of the value of Chinese culture, appropriate paths to modernization, the meaning of nationalism, and the role of women in a new society. Contrary to popular conceptions of docile women, female intellectuals struggled with ideas of independence and self-actualization; many of them cohabitated with men, chose not to have children, sought educational and employment opportunities for all women, and viewed the expansion of women's roles as crucial to the future success of the Chinese nation and culture. Though influenced by writings from the West, their ideas were by no means simple adoptions of Western thought; as these stories show, women challenged both Chinese and Western thinking.

⊷ Makiko Nakano, *Makiko's Diary: A Merchant Wife in 1910 Kyoto,* trans. Kazuko Smith (Stanford University Press, 1995)

Japan was comparatively free of Western intrusion and successful at modernization (and militarization) beginning in the late nineteenth century, and its citizens enjoyed a fairly liberal atmosphere through the 1920s. This diary provides a detailed look at both family and community life in this time period, and is accompanied by Kazuko Smith's explanatory notes and analysis of the representative nature of Makiko's life as a Japanese woman living in 1910. Makiko, having married into her husband's family, lived in an extended household that also functioned as a pharmaceutical store. The diary goes a long way in dispelling many of the stereotypes we hold about East Asian women in traditional contexts—she got along well with her mother-in-law and had an enjoyable life despite her many responsibilities. Smith's adept translation makes for a very pleasant read.

⊷ Noriko Mizuta Lippit and Kyoko Iriye Selden, trans. and eds., *Japanese Women Writers: Twentieth Century Short Fiction* (Sharpe, 1991)

Japan's modernization efforts included territorial expansion into other parts of Asia alongside the West. Wars with China and Russia eventually led to colonization of Korea and Taiwan, and to control of parts of Manchuria and China proper. Such imperialism and militarism characterized Japan from the late 1920s to the end of World War II. Lippitt and Selden provide fluid translations of fourteen stories that cover a range of engaging themes. I recommend that you turn to the brief biography of each author before reading her short story. Alongside political statements against Japan's forced expansion into Asia you will find intense explorations of the conflicts between women's sexuality and their social roles; the varied collection also highlights a type of literature that is unique to Japan: atomic fiction, which explores the aftermath of the World War II atomic bombings. This volume goes a long way toward demonstrating the capacities of Japanese writers who happen to be women.

⇨ Young-Key Kim-Renaud, ed., *Creative Women of Korea: The Fifteenth through the Twentieth Centuries* (Sharpe, 2004)

Although I have yet to come across a Korean woman's autobiography or diary similar to those listed above for China and Japan, Kim-Renaud's edited volume serves as an excellent substitute and is worthy in its own right. Focusing on an analysis of both literary and artistic works by women, Kim-Renaud does an admirable job of outlining the nature of Confucian society in Korea, often considered the most Confucian of the three countries, and its specific effects on women. She then goes on to address women's self-determination within this Confucian context and provide fascinating accounts of how women negotiated their autonomy through their artistic endeavors.

⇨ Bruce Fulton and Ju-Chan Fulton, eds. and trans., *Wayfarer: New Fiction by Korean Women* (Women in Translation, 1997)

This is another collection produced by the prize-winning Fulton team, with contributions from some of Korea's most renowned writers. There is a brief but important introduction to the struggles of Korean women writers to gain recognition for their craft. Historically, Korea suffered invasions by both China and Japan, was colonized by Japan from 1910 to 1945, and then occupied by the American and Soviet armies that divided themselves along Korea's thirty-eighth parallel immediately after World War II. Government authoritarianism and social protests marked postwar development until the 1990s. The stories encompass the psychological effects of modernization, the strife generated by a divided Korea, and Korean immigrant life in the United States, to name but a few themes. Excellent translations convey the passionate and lively writing of the originals.

ELLEN V. FULLER is Assistant Professor of East Asian Languages and Cultures and of Studies in Women and Gender. She teaches courses on China, Japan, and comparative East Asia, focusing on culture, social movements, and social change. Her first book, *Going Global: Culture, Gender, and Authority in the Japanese Subsidiary of an American Corporation* (Temple University Press, 2008), is an ethnography of the men and women who work for an American corporation in Japan.

BRANTLY WOMACK

Approaching China: Philosophy, History, and Politics

For most Americans, China is a vast unknown that became more distant with the tragic events in Tiananmen Square in 1989 and has become more frightening with its rapid rise in the first years of this century. While it is clear that coping with China will be one of the major world tasks of the future, our image of China is more a cloudy mirror of our own hopes and fears than it is a result of understanding China's situation and dynamics. We react to our American impressions and preconceptions of China; we rarely try to go behind them.

Most of our experience as Americans ill prepares us to go beyond those impressions. No other language seems less intelligible: no alphabet, no cognate words, no fixed direction of text, tones as parts of words. Furthermore, China grew up in a different international neighborhood, and so its experiences and priorities in foreign affairs are different. It was the world's most successful traditional society, while we (led by Mr. Jefferson!) were the world's first modern one. It experienced a total crisis in the first half of the twentieth century, and what for us was the threat of radical politics became China's solution. We are and have been the world's most prosperous and powerful society; China has had to cope with abject poverty and the turbulence of transformation. Even China's recent economic growth raises an enigma for us. China's reforms validate the importance of the market and the failure of command economies, and yet China is the most successful Communist country.

Yet, with effort, we can begin to understand the situation of the Chinese and put ourselves in their shoes. As we attempt to grasp some Chinese philosophy, history, aesthetics, and politics, we will extend our own horizons as human beings. Despite political problems, Chinese and Americans have felt considerable empathy for each other for the past hundred years. But should that empathy falter, knowledge of one's enemy is the key to both military victory and to avoiding wars, as the military strategist

Sun Zi (Sun Tzu) pointed out long ago. Whatever our relationship with China may be, if we do not understand the complexities of this nation, we will be misled by our often simplistic impressions.

The challenge of understanding China has called forth the best of Western scholarship, and many of the ancient and modern Chinese classics have been translated into English. Unfortunately, many of the finest works deal only with specific aspects of China and presuppose more general background. The selection here, therefore, is not "the best of the best," but rather a collection of first steps in a number of different but basic directions. To the person who reads these five books, China will seem more complex—a bigger problem to understand—than it was before. Like a ship approaching from the horizon, the closer the reality, the more complicated. And thanks to globalization and Chinese economic success, the ship is approaching quickly and it behooves us to understand it.

The five books introduce four basic dimensions of Chinese reality: philosophy, history, politics, and current affairs. The classics of Chinese philosophy are perhaps even more important for understanding Chinese thought and action than Western philosophy is for the West. Classical Chinese philosophy's major theme is how to behave in society, and although Daoism (Taoism) and Confucianism give opposite answers, they have created a field of ethical discourse that has defined Chinese high culture and has penetrated to the roots of Asian civilization. Happily, these classics are not abstruse. They read more like Plato than like Aristotle, and their intellectual impact is vivid and personal even for contemporary Western readers.

Chinese history deserves two books, for two reasons. First, Chinese history is not usually a part of our general cultural background, and so we have to hear a general narrative in order to make sense of the pieces. If the Kangxi emperor is less familiar to you than Queen Victoria or Frederick the Great, you need a coherent mental map for the events and personalities that you will encounter. Second, political history is not made in a vacuum. China's social and economic context has been and remains radically different from our own, and it sets the parameters for what a political community feels it must do. Thus an understanding of China's material transformation is as important a history as the narration of its politics.

Chinese politics is a much more difficult topic to introduce. For the past hundred years, Chinese politics has been so turbulent that the best attempts to capture its essence are too abstract for introductory reading. Here we focus on a concrete account of the axial event of modern Chinese history, the rural revolution that culminated in the founding of the People's Republic of China in 1949.

Current events are where our images and concerns start, and so a reading that puts these in order and evaluates the evidence is a good starting place. But it should be remembered that getting a better look at China is not the same as getting inside of China. Attention to China that is defined by our current concerns satisfies our curiosity, but it does not address the questions of what China thinks, or where it is coming from. The wise reader will seek to understand these questions more deeply in order to perceive where China is going.

Of course, the best way to get inside China is to go there. It is an unforgettable experience. Reading any or all of these books will make the trip more memorable and more worthwhile.

↶ Arthur Waley, *Three Ways of Thought in Ancient China* (Stanford University Press, 1982)

> This short book has long been appreciated as an introduction to Chinese classics. Although Waley is clearly more sympathetic to Daoism than to Confucianism, and more stimulated by Legalism, his translations are enticing entries into the world of Chinese thought. Just as importantly, his presentation of three very different ways of thought subverts the impression that all Chinese think alike.

↶ Jonathan Spence, *The Search for Modern China,* 2nd ed. (Norton, 2001)

> A number of excellent histories present the broad reach of modern and contemporary Chinese history, but Spence's is the best. It is a massive book, but well written, and it covers Chinese history from the decline of the Ming Dynasty to Tiananmen, or, to mark it on a Western time frame, from Columbus to the collapse of the Soviet Union. Think of it like a trip to the Metropolitan Museum of Art—it can't be digested in a day, but every visit is worthwhile.

↶ Lloyd Eastman, *Family, Fields, and Ancestors: Constancy and Change in China's Social and Economic History, 1550–1949* (Oxford University Press, 1988)

> Eastman's social history of China synthesizes a vast reach of social science research into a readable overview. Although not as titillating as the stories of emperors and revolutionaries, this book presents the social conditions that shaped their horizons. Since the reality of China is as different from American reality as its political story, this is required reading.

↶ William Hinton, *Fanshen: A Documentary of Revolution in a Chinese Village* (1966; University of California Press, 1997)

> Bill Hinton was a Pennsylvania farmer who went to China in 1947 as an agricultural expert and ended up on a land reform team in the village

of Long Bow. It is an enduring classic of how Long Bow "turned over" from a village dominated by landlords, the local Catholic Church, and the Japanese to the kind of village that made the Communist revolution possible. It is a long book, but full of notable peasant characters, and after the first hundred pages it becomes a page-turner.

✣ C. Fred Bergsten, Bates Gill, Nicholas Lardy, and Derek Mitchell, *China: The Balance Sheet* (Public Affairs, 2006)

This brief book is a collective effort by notable scholars to assess the evidence regarding current American concerns about China: politics, economics, and security. Like all balance sheets, it will need to be redrawn, and the bottom line is American attitudes regarding China, not China from the inside. However, it is considerably more balanced and more expert than many other publications aimed at current American concerns, and issues such as China's political dynamics, the imbalance of trade, and environmental and security concerns are treated carefully and comprehensively.

BRANTLY WOMACK is Professor of Foreign Affairs and the author of *Foundations of Mao Zedong's Political Thought* (University Press of Hawaii, 1982) and, with James Townsend, *Politics in China* (Little, Brown, 1986), both of which have been translated into Chinese. His most recent book, *China and Vietnam: The Politics of Asymmetry*, was published by Cambridge University Press in 2006. He has been named an honorary professor at two universities in China.

SYLVIA CHONG

Asian America: Studying Culture and Ethnicity

Although Asian Americans make up only a small part of the American population (4.2 percent in 2000), they have had a disproportionately large impact on American history. Even before the Civil War, Asian laborers began to change the racial landscape of America, becoming a "problem" that was difficult to fit into the black-white binary. When sociologists coined the term "melting pot" in the early 1900s, Asians were excluded because they were assumed to be unassimilable. As a result, Asians were the only group ever to be explicitly barred within U.S. immigration law. Over 120,000 Japanese Americans were forced into internment camps during World War II as suspected traitors—the largest racial removal in American history, and a lesson in the fragility of civil rights. Finally, many of America's wars during the twentieth century were fought in and over Asia, and the legacies of those wars changed not only Asia but America as well. Thus, even from this brief historical overview, one can see how Asian Americans played a central role in defining what we now know as America. The books on this list tell the fascinating story of how Asian Americans entered into the heart of American history, politics, and culture.

A common misconception about Asian Americans is to confuse them with Asians—with foreigners or outsiders. But a study of Asian Americans begins not with Asia but with an examination of America. Prior to the civil rights movement, the term "Asian American" was unheard of. Instead, individual ethnic groups such as Koreans and Japanese thought about themselves as separate, even antagonistic, entities. But in the 1960s and 1970s, students and activists began to conceive of this broad, pan-ethnic category of the Asian American as a way of acknowledging their shared past, present, and future. That is, they recognized how a common history of racial discrimination and violence linked these Asian ethnicities together in America, and felt that their goals would be best achieved by forming a coalition with each other and with other racialized groups such as African Americans, Latinos, and Native Americans. This formative era is an important touchstone in all of the books below, ending one era of Asian American history for Mae Ngai and Henry Yu, while inaugurating another for Vijay Prashad and Yen Le Espiritu.

Thus, it is not culture or geography, but rather the peculiarities of American history that have thrown these disparate Asian ethnicities together under the name "Asian American." The category of Asian American has now grown to encompass not only the first Asian groups to immigrate to America in the late 1800s—Chinese, Japanese, Koreans, Filipinos, and Asian Indians—but also newer immigrants from Vietnam, Thailand, Laos, Cambodia, and Pakistan, as well as Pacific Islanders such as native Hawaiians, Tongans, and Samoans. (Terms such as "Asian Pacific American" [APA] or "Asian Pacific Islander" [API] attempt to reflect the widest margins of this group.) This is not meant to imply that Asian Americans are a distinct group separated from other "races" by essential biological or cultural differences. Many Asian Americans themselves do not use this label, preferring instead to identify with their nationality or religion. Recent immigrants, who arrived after the reforms of the 1965 Immigration and Naturalization Act and who often identify with their country of origin, may not share the attitudes of the first Asian American activists, many of whom were second-, third-, and even fourth-generation Asian Americans and had few ties to their reputed "homeland" in Asia. Older Asian Americans, having come of age before the term was available, may prefer to identify as purely American, since they struggled to be accepted into

American society. Today, we employ this term not primarily as a label for differentiating people, but more as a category for analysis and reflection.

The books below reflect the best in their fields—history, literature, law, sociology, politics—and provide fascinating details on how Asian Americans relate to other races and ethnicities and to America as a whole. They are a great accompaniment to the standard textbook histories, most notably Ronald Takaki's *Strangers from a Different Shore: A History of Asian Americans* (1989) and Sucheng Chan's *Asian Americans: An Interpretive History* (1991). Reading these cultural studies will also deepen your appreciation and understanding of Asian American literature by writers such as Maxine Hong Kingston, Chang-Rae Lee, Bharati Mukherjee, and Carlos Bulosan. I hope you will recognize in these works something familiar rather than exotic—something that deepens your own understanding of what it means to be an American.

⊘ Gary Y. Okihiro, *Margins and Mainstreams: Asians in American History and Culture* (University of Washington Press, 1994)

Along with Ronald Takaki and Sucheng Chan, Gary Okihiro is one of the first major Asian American historians, and his work and mentorship have helped shape the field. This set of essays represents his recent work in popular history, written in a lively style and directed at a nonspecialist audience. First delivered as a series of lectures at Amherst College in 1992, these essays approach the history of Asians in America through a variety of unusual perspectives, as evidenced by their surprising starting point: fifth century BCE, when Asians first entered European consciousness through the writings of Hippocrates and Aristotle. Okihiro quickly moves into the modern era, confronting the division of American racial politics into a limiting black-and-white binary, the omission of women from early Asian American historical record, and the difficulty of narrating the history of an oppressed people through a "great man of history" model.

⊘ Henry Yu, *Thinking Orientals: Migration, Contact, and Exoticism in Modern America* (Oxford University Press, 2002)

Yu tells the neglected story of the "Oriental Problem," or how sociologists at the beginning of the twentieth century made sense of the earliest Asian immigrants to America. These immigrants posed a problem to "melting pot" theories of assimilation that were used to incorporate new southern and eastern European immigrants into the American body politic. In explaining the differences between these "Orientals" and white and African Americans, the social scientists of the Chicago school—named for their concentration at the University of Chicago—formulated the concepts of culture and race that we still use today. Yu doesn't just explain these theories, but narrates the story of individual sociologists and their experiences in gathering and interpreting this data. Some of these sociologists were the first Asian American academics, recruited by their mentors first as native informants, and later turned into participant observers interpreting their own communities for outsiders to understand.

↬ Mae Ngai, *Impossible Subjects: Illegal Aliens and the Making of Modern America* (Princeton University Press, 2005)

Ngai's sprawling work chronicles the period between two great migrations: the pre-1924 immigration of mostly Europeans, and the post-1965 immigration from Asia and Latin America. In between, a series of restrictive immigration laws based on race and national origin created the impossible situation of the illegal alien—a person who should not exist from the perspective of the law, and yet presents a pressing social reality that cannot be ignored. Looking at two groups that were most racialized by these laws—Asian and Latino Americans—Ngai confronts the rosy picture of America as a "land of immigrants" with hard questions. Why are some citizens considered "forever foreigners" no matter how many generations their ancestors have been in this country? Do noncitizens have any rights if they are exploited outside their country of citizenship? Why do we have immigration at all, instead of completely open or completely closed borders?

↬ Yen Le Espiritu, *Asian American Panethnicity: Bridging Institutions and Identities* (Temple University Press, 1993)

This highly accessible work of social science explains the reasoning behind the category of "Asian American." In the process of showing how this panethnic coalition formed in the wake of the civil rights movement, Espiritu also gives an excellent overview of modern sociological theories of culture and ethnicity. Her case studies are both heartening and sobering: the rise of anti-Asian violence reminds Asian Americans of what they have in common as people of color in America, while the practicalities of electoral politics, census data collection, and social services funding show the need to be critically aware when one uses such categories. Espiritu's analysis highlights the problem of allowing a few ethnicities to speak for the entire panethnic group, especially with the "bimodal distribution" of the Asian American population, in which data on those groups who are doing relatively well obscure information on those who are more disadvantaged.

↪ Vijay Prashad, *Everybody Was Kung Fu Fighting: Afro-Asian Connections and the Myth of Cultural Purity* (Beacon Press, 2002)

Taking aim at our cherished ideals of multiculturalism, Prashad argues convincingly that post–civil rights society has replaced "race" with "culture" as a basis for division, and in doing so, has pitted peoples of color against one another for socioeconomic advantage. As a corrective, he offers the concept of polyculturalism, in which there is no such thing as a "pure culture." Instead, all cultures are inherently hybrid and mongrel. Prashad proceeds to outline one important strain of hybridity, that of radical anticolonialist and antiracist ideas from both Africans and South Asians. Like Okihiro, Prashad expands the boundaries of Asian American studies in both time and space— the history of modern racism does not begin with the slave ships of the New World, but rather with Vasco da Gama. Likewise, events in India, Japan, the Caribbean, and Ethiopia are as significant to Asian and African Americans as those happening in America.

SYLVIA CHONG became interested in Asian American studies through her research on how America imagines its foreign others. She is Assistant Professor of English and of American Studies, and a cofounder of the new Asian Pacific American Studies minor. Her forthcoming book explores how Americans understood race relations during the Vietnam War through violent genres such as the war film and the martial arts film.

PETER S. ONUF

Improvising America: Rethinking the Founding

In a global perspective, the founding of the United States seems much more important now than it did in 1776, when rebellious colonists declared their independence, or in 1783, when independence was recognized at the Peace of Paris, or in 1787, when delegates from twelve of the then thirteen states met at Philadelphia (Rhode Island skipped the meeting) to draft a constitution for a "more perfect union," or when state ratifying conventions subsequently debated the document (at first, North Carolina refused to ratify), or in 1789, when the First Federal Congress convened. Had the union collapsed, as seemed likely on several occasions before 1861, or if it had not been reconstructed after it finally *did* collapse in the Civil

War, the "founders" would not be seen now as such visionary law-givers and nation-makers. History is a work in progress, an ongoing negotiation between the present and the past, between where "we" are now and where we were then. The most fundamental questions pivot on our collective identity as a people. This largely imaginary genealogy connects us with previous generations and enables us in turn to imagine ourselves as a nation (the wars that have punctuated our history reinforce that sense of solidarity). Historians like to think that we can think "objectively" about our national beginnings, but they know that no one would care if the American "experiment" had failed and if the United States did not now dominate the modern world.

If historians can never hope to transcend their own times, we can aspire to fresh perspectives—if not finality—on familiar topics. The American founding is an unusually revealing mirror for our own "postmodern" times, at "the end of history" when progress no longer seems inevitable, when nationhood has been demystified and deconstructed, and when dark, dystopian images of globalization prevail. Bad news for the world is good news for historical understanding. For one thing, historians are much more sensitive to "contingency" now than they were during the heyday of the (once) "new social history" when "deep" social structure trumped the political history of "great men"—and when historians fancied themselves "social scientists." Under the emerging disciplinary dispensation, everyone matters (the signal contribution of the social historians), but the exercise of unequally distributed power leads to unpredictable, highly contingent outcomes. The American Revolutionaries knew their revolution could fail; their motives—to secure their rights *as* overseas Britons, to gain easier access to foreign markets, to shirk tax burdens, and only belatedly, after fifteen months of fighting, to secure their independence— were ambiguous if not contradictory; and their loyalties—to what or to whom?—were volatile. The Revolution was a civil war and only in retrospect a war of national liberation, for there was no nation to liberate until Americans declared themselves to be one—or, rather, to be a union of state republics—on July 4, 1776. Union was both means and end: if the Revolutionary new states failed to act together, they would be destroyed; acting together, they could offer war-torn Europe a model of peaceful and prosperous coexistence, "a new order for the ages."

The Revolutionaries were confused about who they were and what they were doing. They improvised constitutions and invented a nation as they stumbled through the "fog of war." These complexities are resonant for modern historians who are similarly perplexed about the future of their world. They are less inclined than their patriotic predecessors to discern providential purposes in the contingent and unforeseeable circumstances that produced the new nation. But that disenchantment raises the interpretative stakes for early American historians: the "nation" is not a predicate—its existence cannot be taken for granted—but rather a problem, an outcome to be explained. Given the central importance of the idea of the nation—and the reality of the nation-state—in contemporary world (that is, international) history, the historians' challenge is now to show how the United States became a nation, however inadvertently and accidentally, and barely survived subsequent decades of world war before dividing into two warring nations in the American Civil War.

The direction of scholarship on the founding is moving inside out, from celebrating the achievements of heroic, larger-than-life founders toward a better appreciation of the contexts, at home and abroad, within which they acted. Their constitutional experiments shaped the history of succeeding generations, and constitutional continuity has sustained the myth and therefore the reality of American nationhood. They are "our" founders, warts and all, and understanding their world as much as possible on their own terms will help us make better sense of our own.

↪ Alan Gibson, *Interpreting the Founding: Guide to the Enduring Debates over the Origins and Foundations of the American Republic* (University Press of Kansas, 2006)

Gibson, a political theorist, provides an elegant and concise introduction to the vast literature on the founding produced over the last half century. Progressive historians and their heirs focused obsessively on the founders' material interests, suggesting that the ratification of the Constitution contained and suppressed the radical, democratic potential of the revolution. In response, historians of political thought countered with "thinking"—or ideologically driven—revolutionaries whose ideas made the crucial difference, then and now. These historians in turn divided over the sources of these ideas in classical republicanism, liberalism, the Scottish Enlightenment, or common-law constitutionalism. Gibson also offers a generous review of the work of the new social historians who have raised fundamental questions about evolving definitions of the "people."

↪ Gordon S. Wood, *The Creation of the American Republic, 1776–1787* (1969; University of North Carolina Press, 1998)

Wood's landmark 1969 study reveals the interpretative possibilities—and limits—of the study of political thought as "ideology." The "classical republicanism" of the founders shaped Americans' view of their world, defining threats and promising civic renewal through virtuous citizens' devotion to the public good. Wood traces the Americanization of republican thinking through debates over state constitutions in the decade before the drafting of the Constitution, concluding that the new federal charter marked a decisive turn away from "republicanism" and toward "liberalism." Critics have shown that Wood exaggerates the "classical" elements in revolutionary republicanism, overemphasizes the Federalist reaction to the "democratic" excesses of state governments under the Confederation, and fails to recognize the central importance of the problem of union for the founders. For all its interpretative shortcomings, however, *Creation* remains the point of departure for students of the founding.

↪ Edmund S. Morgan, *Inventing the People: The Rise of Popular Sovereignty in England and America* (Norton, 1989)

Morgan's wonderful book is an intellectual history of the "fiction" of popular sovereignty, illuminating the idea's pre-Constitutional antecedents in English and American political thought and culture. *Inventing* is less interesting on the founders themselves. Morgan follows Wood's argument in *Creation* that the Federalists had succeeded in creating an energetic national government by persuading voters in state ratifying conventions that the "people," not the states, were "sovereign" and that it was in their primal power to delegate authority to all levels of government. Morgan thus embraces the "fiction" of nationhood—that Americans understood themselves as a single people—that his book so persuasively deconstructs; like Wood, he fails to grasp the alternative and contested conceptions of the "people" that flourished in the new United States. Morgan nonetheless illuminates the central problem of legitimacy, showing how loyal subjects of King George III could so suddenly see themselves as their own sovereigns.

↪ Max M. Edling, *A Revolution in Favor of Government: Origins of the U.S. Constitution and the Making of the American State* (Oxford University Press, 2003)

Edling, a young Swedish historian, shows that the founders were focused on the national security dilemma: how could their fragile union survive in a dangerous world? The scope of national governments in the founders' world was, by today's standard, very limited: central governments collected taxes in order to prepare for and make war. The Federalists' great achievement was to service the Revolutionary War debts by establishing the central government's authority over import duties as well as other forms of direct taxation. The results of their "revolution" were ironic: the new regime provided instant tax relief for overburdened state governments that were now able to extend their authority into new areas of governance; meanwhile, the success of the federal government within its own limited ambit of authority made it increasingly irrelevant to most Americans and therefore vulnerable to future challenges.

↷ David C. Hendrickson, *Peace Pact: The Lost World of the American Founding* (University Press of Kansas, 2003)

Hendrickson's important book restores the founding to its original geopolitical context. The founders sought to achieve a precarious balance between the threat of anarchy—the war of all against all famously described by Thomas Hobbes—and the danger of the kind of despotic central government that had led the Revolutionaries to bolt the British Empire. As they created a federal government strong enough to protect the United States from foreign threats, they also sought to secure the sovereignty of their new state-republics and therefore the liberties of Americans generally. The result of their efforts, Hendrickson argues, was a "peace pact," a new order for the new world that would banish the threat of war that characterized the Old World balance of power. Optimistic Americans hoped they could have it both ways, enjoying the benefits of both liberty and power. They still do.

PETER S. ONUF is the Thomas Jefferson Foundation Professor in the Corcoran Department of History. His scholarship focuses on Thomas Jefferson and his age, with specific interests in federalism, geopolitics, nation-making, and world order. Onuf's works include *Jefferson's Empire: The Language of American Nationhood* (2000) and, with his brother Nicholas G. Onuf, *Nations, Markets, and War: Modern History and the American Civil War* (2006), both published by the University of Virginia Press.

DANIEL R. ORTIZ

Discerning Constitutional Meaning

Unlike a poem, a constitution should mean, not be. It must provide answers to hard questions like who decides a particular issue—a judge, the legislature, an executive officer, or a private individual—how the actor should make the decision—by majority vote of preferences, by recourse to preexisting rules, or by no rules at all—and when to decide it. The United States Constitution, for example, allocates some decisions to the

Congress, some to the president, some to courts, and still others to states and to private individuals; it sometimes says how they should decide them (think of the Byzantine rules governing the election of the president), and when such decisions can or must be made. Sometimes the Constitution speaks directly and specifically to issues; other times it speaks in majestically broad and allusive terms. It very specifically requires, for instance, that a candidate for president be at least forty years old, a natural-born citizen, and a resident for fourteen years. On the other hand, it defines some of the most important protections of individual liberty quite generally. States cannot "abridge the privileges and immunities of citizens," "deprive any person of life, liberty, or property, without due process of law," or "deny to any person . . . the equal protection of the laws."

How should we find meaning in the Constitution, particularly in these more general provisions? Should the constitutional text control? If so, how can its broader provisions give helpful guidance? Should the original intentions of its framers and ratifiers trump instead? If not their specific intentions, then their values and general understandings? Or should the values and understandings of those who live today control the document's meaning? If so, in a culture as pluralistic as ours, which particular groups' values and understandings should matter, and how should we determine them? Or should deep background assumptions of our political culture, like majority rule, fill in meaning when the text and original intentions are unclear? More radically perhaps, should constitutional meaning be a more pragmatic project enlisting all these interpretive strategies to different degrees in different circumstances to further some vision of social well-being?

This debate is a lively one, and much hangs on it. Scratch nearly any hot-button social issue—race, religion, sex, abortion, and crime, to mention only a few—and disputes about constitutional meaning quickly appear. It is no accident that the recent confirmation hearings of Chief Justice John Roberts and Justice Samuel Alito seemed briefly to provoke more public interest than even the continuing Iraq war. Over the last fifty years, in fact, constitutional meaning has become one of the central battlefields in the culture wars. When the Supreme Court decided in *Brown v. Board of Education* that "separate but equal" schools for white and black children violated the Constitution's guarantee of equal protection, it signaled a willingness both to enter some of the most contentious fields of social conflict and to rest constitutional meaning at least in part on contemporary social attitudes.

Since then, the Court has intervened in many fractious social debates, and its decisions have created as well as settled social conflict. In determining what the Constitution means, it has created backlash among some social groups and changed the dynamics of American politics. Some, for example, point to the Supreme Court's decision in *Roe v. Wade*, which limited the state's ability to criminalize abortion in the early months of pregnancy, as the cause of the recent ascendance of the "religious right" in American politics. In their view, *Roe v. Wade* so energized those against it that it led to the election of conservative politicians who would seek the appointment of judges to overrule it. These judges, of course, could be expected to follow a broader conservative agenda as well, as could the politicians who appointed them. The result, in this view, is not just the likely retrenchment of *Roe* itself, but the setback of progressive politics more generally, as both the courts and the political branches come to stand ever more firmly against it.

The debate, of course, will not end soon. One side or the other may temporarily win—but never completely. There is just too much at stake to allow one side total victory, and as issues change, different ways of finding constitutional meaning may become attractive to different groups. But perhaps that's the true significance of constitutional meaning. In the end, our debates over how the Constitution means may tell us more about ourselves than about the Constitution itself.

⤷ Alexander M. Bickel, *The Least Dangerous Branch: The Supreme Court at the Bar of Politics* (Yale University Press, 1986)

> Bickel, a law clerk on the Supreme Court during the time of *Brown v. Board of Education,* revived the field of constitutional theory. Asked while a clerk to research how the original intent of the Equal Protection Clause bore on the constitutionality of "separate but equal" schools for black and white children, Bickel found that the intent did not clearly condemn the practice. Yet, he believed *Brown,* which did condemn it, was correctly decided. In this book, he argues why original intent should not strongly limit constitutional meaning. The early sections, where he defends resting constitutional meaning in part on contemporary social values, are particularly interesting. His argument is direct but in some places also ambivalent.

⤷ Antonin Scalia, *A Matter of Interpretation: Federal Courts and the Law* (Princeton University Press, 1998)

> This book contains a lively essay by Justice Scalia advocating a return to original meaning in legal interpretation, especially in constitutional interpretation. By "original meaning," Justice Scalia does not mean "what the original draftsmen intended" but rather "how the text of the Constitution was originally understood." His approach grants primacy to text but allows evidence of what people at the time of its adoption

would have thought it meant. Most importantly, however, his approach gives no weight to current social values; in fact, Justice Scalia recently referred to those who would give weight to current social values as "idiots." Several legal theorists and a prominent constitutional historian respond in brief essays of their own. This book offers a range of countercutting arguments for how best to find constitutional meaning.

↶ John Hart Ely, *Democracy and Distrust: A Theory of Judicial Review* (1980; Harvard University Press, 2006)

This brisk and clearly written book takes on both nonoriginalism (think Bickel) and originalism (think Scalia) at the same time. To Ely, both methods of finding constitutional meaning fundamentally disrespect democracy. The former replaces the judgments of the people's democratically elected representatives with those of unelected judges; the latter—at best—with a democracy of the dead. Ely proposes that courts interpret constitutional meaning against a strong background norm of representation-reinforcement. In other words, courts should strike down the outcomes of the political process only when they have reason to believe that some structural flaw prevented that process from operating democratically. Ely's approach proves powerful and controversial and commits him to a set of positions that looks puzzling from the usual ideological perspectives. He would, for example, find racial affirmative action constitutionally permissible but overrule *Roe v. Wade* and the Supreme Court's current approach to gender discrimination.

↶ Richard A. Posner, *The Problematics of Moral and Legal Theory* (1999; Harvard University Press, 2002)

Judge Posner, one of the stars of the federal judiciary, makes the provocative argument in this book that constitutional meaning should never rest on moral theory. Moral theory, he believes, cannot even well answer moral questions, let alone legal ones, and judges are even less well equipped than moral philosophers to employ it. His views have angered people on both the left and right and, to some, leave the Constitution without sufficient grounding. If law does not ultimately rest at least in part on moral theory, what, they ask, does it stand on and from what can its legitimacy spring?

↶ Michael J. Klarman, *From Jim Crow to Civil Rights: The Supreme Court and the Struggle for Racial Equality* (Oxford University Press, 2006)

Michael Klarman asks a somewhat different question: What difference does the Supreme Court's constitutional work make? Klarman asserts two important claims. First, the Court generally does not move outside of cultural consensus. Although some of its decisions, like *Brown*, may deeply anger some people and appear courageous to others, they are at most bringing cultural outliers into line with a broad social consensus. Second, and more controversially, constitutional decisions do not themselves directly effect social change. Against the views of many others, Klarman argues that *Brown* did not really lead to the civil rights revolution. Rather, it led directly to a powerful and violent backlash in the South, which in turn led to an ultimately more powerful political counterbacklash, when people elsewhere saw for themselves the brutal southern police attacks on civil rights demonstrators. Their revulsion, not the Supreme Court's pronouncement in *Brown*, revolutionized civil rights.

Daniel R. Ortiz is John Allan Love Professor of Law. He teaches constitutional law, election law, and legal theory. He has also taught at the law schools of the University of California, Berkeley (Boalt Hall), and the University of Southern California.

LAWRIE BALFOUR

The Life and Afterlife of Slavery

"Modern life," observes Toni Morrison, "begins with slavery." The same might be said of American life. Intertwined with celebrated stories about the birth of freedom are stories of millions of Africans and their descendants whose American experience began in forced transport and enslavement. This is not news. Yet despite the centrality of slavery to the making of the nation, Americans generally remain reluctant to acknowledge its ongoing significance. For many of us, born in the twentieth century, perhaps raised in the North or descended from recent immigrants to the United States, it is hard to acknowledge the force of slave history as *our* history and even more difficult to understand why it has any bearing on life today. For white Americans, this is particularly true. These five books offer a powerful rebuttal. They indicate the dangers of relegating slavery to another time, or banishing it to somewhere else. Beginning with W. E. B. Du Bois's exploration of the ways in which denial of the slave past abetted the establishment of Jim Crow, they probe the connections between the persistence of racial injustice and the suppression of the past. They insist that no experiment in democratic life is really possible so long as Americans disavow slavery's importance in its own time and its lingering legacies in ours.

It may seem far-fetched to insist on the urgency of coming to terms with slavery today. After all, the Civil War amendments, which promised slavery's abolition and the reconstruction of citizenship, were passed over a century ago; the landmark civil rights legislation of the twentieth century, now nearly fifty years old, aimed to eliminate the vestiges of racial caste; and Americans by and large endorse the principle of racial equality. Nevertheless, these authors probe the limits of those laws and the subconscious associations that have outlasted changes in racial philosophy and policy. Their inquiries into the ways that race is lived help readers to understand more fully the ferocity of contemporary debates about affirmative action or reparations or the response to Hurricane Katrina, and they illuminate the stakes of ongoing arguments about the meaning of Confederate symbols.

Du Bois, Baldwin, Butler, Morrison, Williams. This list includes three of the best-known names in the American canon, as well as two authors—Butler and Williams—whose writing deserves a wider readership. Spanning the twentieth century, there are two novels, two collections of essays, and Du Bois's assemblage of what he called "fugitive pieces," which range from essay, to elegy, to biography and fiction. Difficult though it was to winnow a group of five books from the rich tradition of African American literature—or even to choose from among the writings of the authors included here—these books stand out. They are all strikingly beautiful. Further, they do as much as any books I know to make vivid the ways in which American life is haunted by the slave past. Gifted moral psychologists, these authors lay bare Americans' interior lives; their object, in Baldwin's words, is "to examine attitudes, to go beneath the surface, to tap the source." In doing so, they provide luminous portraits of the complex humanity of African Americans, both under slavery and in its aftermath; and they retain sympathy for white Americans, even as they offer keen criticism of white efforts to preserve an illusory "innocence."

Despite the conviction that defines their writing, these authors resist the temptation to moralize, to provide pat lessons about how the past is to be used. None of them contends that simply knowing what happened will set anyone free. All of them eschew easy distinctions between the innocent and the guilty, painting instead a more complicated picture of what it might mean to act responsibly in the shadow of injustice. By stretching the imaginations of their readers, they indicate how engagement with the past might allow us to understand the present, and, maybe, they can enable us to envision more capacious and democratic forms of citizenship.

↬ W. E. B. Du Bois, *The Souls of Black Folk* (1903; Bedford, 1997)

The Souls of Black Folk begins with a promise to introduce the reader to things that "lie buried," and the fourteen short pieces that follow are replete with images of ghosts and silences and haunting. Writing at the moment when the hopes of Reconstruction were eclipsed by the development of Jim Crow in the South and the abandonment of the former slaves and their descendants by the North, Du Bois explores the imprint of slavery on American cultural, political, and economic life. *Souls* is probably best known for its prophecy that "the problem of the Twentieth Century is the problem of the color-line" and its account of African American "double-consciousness." Yet it is equally keen in its depiction of the inner turmoil of white Americans who believe in the principle of equality and yet cannot acknowledge the full humanity of their black fellow citizens. I recommend the Bedford Books edition for its wonderful introductory essay and excellent footnotes.

↬ James Baldwin, *Notes of a Native Son* (1955; Beacon Press, 1984)

Baldwin's essays are similarly concerned with the ways that the disavowal of the past inhibits the possibility of democracy in the present. All of the essays are worth reading and rereading, but I particularly recommend three. "Many Thousands Gone" challenges the idea that Americans can simply transcend the horrors of the past by asserting that race no longer matters, and it does so ingeniously by playing with the narrator's racial identity. "Notes of a Native Son" examines the interconnections between the private hurts and public effects of racial injustice through the simultaneous telling of three stories: of his father's bitter and impoverished life and death, of the Harlem Riot of 1943, and of Baldwin's own experiences of discrimination in New Jersey. Finally, in "Stranger in the Village," Baldwin transforms a recollection of time spent in Switzerland into an extraordinary meditation on whiteness and democracy in the United States.

↬ Octavia Butler, *Kindred* (Beacon Press, 2004)

Variously described as science fiction, "grim fantasy," and neo–slave narrative, *Kindred* is a novel that follows the travels of an African American writer named Dana Franklin as she is repeatedly transported from twentieth-century Los Angeles to antebellum Maryland. Dana's trips to the past are occasioned by the appeals of a self-destructive white boy who calls on her to rescue him. As Dana becomes increasingly entangled in life on the plantation, she uncovers buried truths about her heritage and attempts to reconcile the tensions between her own implication in the crimes of the past and her desire to get on with life in the present. Not only does Butler tell a gripping story, but she deftly traces the lingering traces of slavery in contemporary life and raises provocative questions about the making of history.

⤸ Toni Morrison, *Beloved* (Vintage, 2004)

In a 1989 interview, Morrison remarked about *Beloved*, "I thought this has got to be the least read of all the books I'd written because it is about something that the characters don't want to remember, I don't want to remember, black people don't want to remember, white people don't want to remember. I mean it's national amnesia." While Morrison's prediction about the fate of her novel has not been borne out, her insight into the desire to bury the past remains instructive. Even with the recent explosion of books, movies, and exhibitions about slavery, it is not clear that simply acquiring new knowledge equips us to grapple with its ongoing effects. Morrison helps us to understand why. Examining the struggle of an African American community to build new life after bondage and to come to terms with a fugitive mother's decision to kill her daughter rather than allow her to be returned to slavery, *Beloved* intimates both the necessity and the difficulty of confronting the past.

⤸ Patricia J. Williams, *The Alchemy of Race and Rights: Diary of a Law Professor* (Harvard University Press, 1992)

This is the most expressly "academic" of the books on the list, but it rewards the careful reader. A stunning blend of memoir, social criticism, and legal theory, Williams's book addresses the ongoing significance of race in contemporary American law and culture. At its heart is an account of Williams's ambivalent relationship to her great-great-grandmother Sophie, a slave, and to the white lawyer who bought and impregnated her when she was only eleven. Williams uses this twin inheritance, of ownership and dispossession, as the basis for illuminating discussions of such wide-ranging topics as poverty, university politics, affirmative action, shopping, contract law, and the Rockettes.

LAWRIE BALFOUR teaches political theory in the Department of Politics, where she is Associate Professor. She is the author of *The Evidence of Things Not Said: James Baldwin and the Promise of American Democracy* (Cornell University Press, 2001) and articles on race and democracy. Her current projects include essays on reparations for slavery and a book on the political thought of W. E. B. Du Bois.

RISA L. GOLUBOFF

Ongoing Struggle: The Deeper History of the Civil Rights Movement

For many of us, the civil rights movement of the 1950s and 1960s and the laws it produced hardly count as history. They are part of our memory, our own lived experiences. They are too current to call history. They involved struggles still ongoing today.

All that may be true. In fact, that is precisely why understanding civil rights history is so important today. The history of civil rights protest and civil rights law informs so much about current political, social, and cultural debates. And the way historians tell their stories influences how we understand not only the past but also the present.

Over the last several decades, historians have quite thoroughly documented, revisited, argued about, and interpreted the history of the civil rights movement and civil rights law. These histories have varied wildly. Some more popular books recount events familiar from television coverage and popular lore: the Montgomery bus boycott and the Supreme Court's 1954 decision in *Brown v. Board of Education;* Martin Luther King Jr.'s "I have a dream" speech in front of the Lincoln Memorial and the sit-ins at lunch counters and on segregated buses across the South; the murders of civil rights workers in Mississippi and the passage of the Civil Rights Act of 1964 and the Voting Rights Act of 1965.

Exhaustive, readable, and even gripping histories of such events are widely known and readily accessible. They include Richard Kluger's history of *Brown,* entitled *Simple Justice;* Taylor Branch's trilogy about Martin Luther King Jr., *Parting the Waters, Pillar of Fire,* and *At Canaan's Edge;* and Anthony Lukas's *Common Ground,* which narrates the lives of three families through the 1970s busing crisis in Boston.

In books tailored more specifically to audiences of serious students and teachers of history, historians have delved deeper and further than these popular accounts in a variety of ways. They differ in both focus and scope. Some historians emphasize political activism, others litigation in the courts, and still others the kinds of economic protest involved in joining a union and going on strike. Scope varies both temporally and geographically. Some take a long view of the civil rights struggle, pointing out African American resistance to Jim Crow decades before the civil rights movement of the 1950s and 1960s. They suggest that that movement was merely the continuation of a plethora of older movements through new means and methods.

Other scholars move from the national to the local level, bringing to life not the leaders of major organizations but the everyday people who made civil rights change possible. Still other historians have moved in the opposite direction. They point to the international dimensions of the civil rights struggle—the role war has played in democratizing American life, the effects of the Cold War on civil rights activism, and the connections between racial protest at home and the struggle against colonialism and imperialism abroad.

The books that follow go well beyond the traditional stuff of civil rights history to provide a smattering of these approaches. Reading these five books will not tell you all you could ever know about the history of civil rights. But it will, I hope, do three things. First, taken together, these books will suggest that what you know already about civil rights history is only the most visible tip of a very deep and wide iceberg. They will reveal the immense variation of arenas, tactics, goals, personalities, fissures, conflicts, and outcomes of civil rights history. Second, they will reveal the ways in which history shapes our sense of what is possible today and in the future. Racial inequality is still very much a part of the fabric of American society, and the stories we tell about civil rights history mold our imaginations about the potential for continuing change. Finally, I hope these readings will represent the beginning of a long-term project rather than a fixed and finite endeavor. Once you begin reading these selections, you will see references to other books and other authors. Do as professional historians do, and take those references as your cues for further reading. Just as I hope you will see civil rights history as the necessary origins of our civil rights futures, I hope you will see these readings as the inauguration of your own future as a civil rights historian.

↜ Michael J. Klarman, *From Jim Crow to Civil Rights: The Supreme Court and the Struggle for Racial Equality* (Oxford University Press, 2006)

As the title suggests, Klarman takes as his subject the role of the Supreme Court in creating racial change in the twentieth century. Beginning with the infamous case of *Plessy v. Ferguson* and continuing through the southern backlash against *Brown v. Board of Education*, Klarman skillfully weaves together the internal deliberations and decision-making processes of Supreme Court justices with the litigation strategies of lawyers who brought civil rights cases and the large-scale social forces that shaped both the legal cases and their real-world effects. Klarman's is a masterful and readable account of the development of civil rights law. It is also an accessible yet sophisticated introduction to some central questions of constitutional law. In particular, he challenges the reader to think about how judges decide cases and to what extent such cases are the product of social change, spurs to social change, or both.

↪ Charles M. Payne, *I've Got the Light of Freedom: The Organizing Tradition and the Mississippi Freedom Struggle* (1995; University of California Press, 2007)

Like Klarman, Payne takes the long view of civil rights history. Payne's focus could not differ more from Klarman's, however. Payne describes the roots of some of the most famous episodes in civil rights history in what many would think was an unlikely place: among poor and working-class African American men and women in rural Mississippi. In moving and revealing prose, Payne recounts the struggles of everyday resistance that provided the groundwork for the more visible freedom struggles of the 1960s. By the time you have finished the book, you will realize that people you might have thought unable to struggle against forces more powerful than they, people you might once have deemed passive followers of national leaders, were in fact indispensable to both the existence of the civil rights movement and its success.

↪ Carol Anderson, *Eyes Off the Prize: The United Nations and the African American Struggle for Human Rights, 1944–1955* (Cambridge University Press, 2003)

Where Payne delves deeply into a single locale, Anderson moves outward from the United States to consider the relationship between American civil rights and contemporaneous international developments. Anderson suggests that American civil rights activists, especially the National Association for the Advancement of Colored People (NAACP), saw deep parallels between domestic struggles and those occurring elsewhere in the world. She shows how they tried to harness international human rights protections, like those in the United Nations, for the benefit of American blacks. Ultimately, Anderson laments that these efforts were stymied by the repression of black activism during the Cold War of the 1950s. She argues that had American civil rights integrated the central ideas of international human rights, civil rights organizations might have more successfully attacked the economic dimensions of racial oppression than they did. Had that occurred, Anderson suggests, African Americans, and indeed all Americans, might be better off today.

✑ Eric Arnesen, *Brotherhoods of Color: Black Railroad Workers and the Struggle for Equality* (Harvard University Press, 2002)

> With a clean and commanding style, Arnesen offers a civil rights history both narrower and broader than those discussed above. It is narrower in that Arnesen zeroes in on one particular group of African American workers—those employed in a number of capacities on American railroads. But it is broader in critical and enlightening ways. Like Klarman and Payne, Arnesen takes the long view. He begins with the rise of the railroad in the nineteenth century and ends as recently as the 1990s. Moreover, in documenting the protests of this group of workers, Arnesen represents an important and growing strand of civil rights history that includes not only voting rights and sit-ins but labor and economic issues as crucial parts of civil rights history. Moving easily between the hopes and struggles of the workers themselves, the efforts of their leaders and lawyers, and the benefits and drawbacks of judicial decisions and legislative enactments, Arnesen reminds us of the significance of work to civil rights and to the structures of American society.

✑ Nancy MacLean, *Freedom Is Not Enough: The Opening of the American Workplace* (Harvard University Press, 2006)

> While the focus of this list is on the African American freedom struggle, MacLean offers the perfect ending by broadening out beyond black and white. MacLean focuses in particular on the contributions of Mexican Americans and white women to civil rights progress. She explores the extent of change in the workplace and in society in the last forty years through the lens of workers' complaints under the Civil Rights Act of 1964. Although the book centers on the federal laws prohibiting workplace discrimination, MacLean's emphasis on the workers themselves makes the read anything but dry. She brings to life the way law can work in action, and the ways in which ordinary people can change society by channeling law to their own ends.

RISA L. GOLUBOFF is Professor of Law and History. Her scholarship focuses on the history of civil rights, constitutional law, and labor. Goluboff's *The Lost Promise of Civil Rights* (Harvard University Press, 2007) explores the development of civil rights law in the era before *Brown*.

GRACE ELIZABETH HALE

"The Cruel Radiance of What Is": Poverty in America since 1945

The most important fact about poverty in America is that people live their deprivation surrounded by plenty. Poor people, of course, do not need to turn to books to learn about their plight. It is the rest of us, the nonpoor, who most often read about poverty. The act of reading confirms the very class divisions most people who write about poverty are trying to bridge. Nothing is simple. Context contradicts text. Class difference is acknowledged and then denied. The best books about poverty push and pull and press their readers, urging them to see a common humanity and yet requiring them to acknowledge their great privilege.

What kinds of writing, then, can make poverty real for people who are not poor? No writer in English thought more about this problem than James Agee, who traveled to rural Alabama in 1936 with the photographer Walker Evans to study the plight of sharecroppers during the Great Depression. On assignment for *Fortune* magazine, which rejected the article that became the basis for the classic book *Let Us Now Praise Famous Men* (1941), Agee and Evans spent several weeks with three poor white families, finding that "The communication is not by any means so simple." Agee wonders how he can write about oppression while he, as a member of society but also more directly as a writer, oppresses his subjects: "These I will write of are human beings, living in this world, innocent of such twistings as these which are taking place over their heads; and that they were dwelt among, investigated, spied on, revered, and loved, by other quite monstrously alien human beings, in the employment of others still more alien; and that they are now being looked into by still others, who have picked up their living as casually as if it were a book." Agee continues, "If I could do it, I'd do no writing at all here. It would be photographs; the rest would be fragments of cloth, bits of cotton, lumps of earth, records of speech, pieces of wood and iron, phials of odors, plates of food and excrement. . . . A piece of the body torn out by the roots might be more to the point." How, he wonders, can he convey the reality of their poverty in writing, in prose that itself distances and dehumanizes his subjects even as it informs his readers?

Still, Agee does write. And in his writing, he struggles to atone for the fact that to make the families he is writing about real for his readers, he has to put the Woods and the Ricketts and the Gudgers on display in all their misery and humanity. Tensions profoundly permeate Agee's work: the impulse to document unflinchingly and yet also to turn away in shame, the realism (this is what it is like here) that cannot escape idealization (the poor are better than the rest of us). Such tensions continue to shape worthwhile writing about poverty, even when authors tell of their own poverty.

Idealizing or romanticizing in some form, in fact, seems indispensable. The poor cannot simply be. While it is true that poor people live on the margins, often doubly and triply so (not middle class, not white, not married or living with both parents, not men), the best writing about the poor over the last half century portrays this outsider status as something to admire. Poor people, writers often tell us, are more moral, more hardworking, more aware of life's gifts—in short, *more real*—than the nonpoor.

American authors have tried many genres in their efforts to depict what Agee called "the cruel radiance of what is": novels and autobiographies, journalistic accounts, and studies in history and other disciplines. They have provided facts and provoked emotions. They have seduced readers with the power of narratives and characters both real and fictional. But they have not been neutral. Neutral books on recent American poverty do not exist. Since the mid-twentieth century, every author starts, whether consciously or unconsciously, by confronting the question of how the problem of extreme deprivation can persist in a nation of such wealth. Since poverty is not now a material problem in the United States—we have the resources to eliminate all economic deprivation—every writer, even the academics, offers an explanation, a political point of view that tells us where poverty comes from and why. The causes are structural (due to racial segregation or deindustrialization, for example) or individual (people take too many drugs or have too many babies, among other reasons)—or some combination of the two. And the solutions are political and moral. How do we dismantle the structures that promote poverty? How do we get people to behave differently?

So, dear readers, beware. Often beautifully written and always engaging, the best books about the last half century of American poverty are demanding. They will trouble and haunt you. They will ask you to change. They will chase you with questions. What are you going to do about the problem of poverty in our time?

↵ Ann Moody, *Coming of Age in Mississippi* (Delta, 2004)

Not just a strong account of what it was like to grow up poor in post–World War II America, *Coming of Age* is also among the finest autobiographies written in English in the twentieth century. Moody shows us how living in segregated, class-divided rural Mississippi while knowing about the larger world turned her and others of her generation into the activists who made the modern civil rights movement.

↬ Dorothy Allison, *Bastard out of Carolina* (Penguin, 1993)

This book is one of the most gripping novels about poverty written in America since John Steinbeck's *Grapes of Wrath* and Richard Wright's *Native Son*. Allison depicts with beauty, realism, and grace a child's view of growing up poor in the American South in the 1960s and 1970s and the sexual abuse that poor children suffer all too often.

↬ J. Anthony Lukas, *Common Ground: A Turbulent Decade in the Lives of Three American Families* (Vintage, 1986)

Lukas gives us a brilliant nonfiction portrait of an American city, Boston, as its residents struggle with poverty, racial oppression, race riots, and busing in the aftermath of the civil rights movement.

↬ Barbara Ehrenreich, *Nickel and Dimed: On (Not) Getting By in America* (Holt, 2002)

This book smartly investigates not just the monumental problem of the working poor in contemporary America but also the fact that most nonpoor Americans fail to see this form of poverty. Paradoxically, by putting herself at the center of her story—the book describes her undercover efforts to survive on low-wage work in three different towns—she depersonalizes the condition of poverty. It is not the person, *Nickel and Dimed* tells us—even the talented Ehrenreich could hardly make it—it's the system. And I guarantee you will never think about vacuuming again without conjuring up an image of maid Barbara and the strap-on vac.

↬ Jason DeParle, *American Dream: Three Women, Ten Kids, and a Nation's Drive to End Welfare* (Penguin, 2005)

This must be the only book on poverty praised by both the *Nation* (on the left) and the *National Review* (on the right). DeParle, learning more than a little from Lukas, follows three families (African American single mothers and their children) across both time and space, back to their roots in the Mississippi Delta and forward to their present lives in Milwaukee as they try to live through the Clinton-era drive to end welfare. An amazingly skilled writer, DeParle makes the partisan and bureaucratic battles over the scope and nature of welfare reform as interesting as his deep and rich portraits of the families' everyday struggles.

GRACE ELIZABETH HALE is Associate Professor of History and American Studies. Her publications include *Making Whiteness: The Culture of Segregation in the South, 1890–1940* (Vintage, 1998) and *Rebel, Rebel: Outsiders in America,* forthcoming. She teaches and writes about twentieth-century American culture, poverty, race in America, and popular music.

CINDY ARON

Sex in the United States: Some History

Sex has a history. While people have been having sex since—well, since the beginning, the meaning, experience, context, and consequences of sex have changed across the centuries. The history of sex includes topics like courtship, marriage, prostitution, contraception, abortion, and het-ero- and homosexual love. But the history of sex also offers a window onto other important stories—such as the changing standards of personal behavior and the ways in which the state has affected the most intimate aspects of people's lives.

The books in this list will, I hope, make the reader think about both history and sex a little differently. History concerns more than the public acts of public men; besides war, politics, and diplomacy, it also encompasses the everyday lives of everyday people. And sex is about more than reproduction or pleasure; it involves more than the personal and the intimate. Sex is also about power, property, religion, and race. The readings suggested here reveal the struggle between the sexual conventions of any specific time and how American men and women have chosen to behave when it comes to sex.

Many of us share misperceptions about America's sexual history. One, for example, is that the Puritans were extremely "puritanical" sexually. In fact, the Puritans have gotten a fairly bad rep with regard to sex. They believed that sex was a good thing—as long as it was confined to marriage. They forbade sex only on days when they would have prohibited other earthly pleasures, such as fast days and religious holidays. And while Puritan ministers and magistrates did what they could to inhibit nonmarital sex, the historical record reveals large numbers of bridal pregnancies and numerous court cases for adultery and fornication. Clearly, everyone did not obey the rules.

It was, rather, the Victorians who earned a well-deserved reputation for their "puritanical" sexual attitudes. Nineteenth-century arbiters of morality, proclaiming that sex should be solely for reproduction, attempted to persuade men that sexual indulgence could lead not only to financial ruin but also to physical breakdown. The Victorians also enshrined a new conception of womanhood, one that altered (rather than dispensed with) the long-standing view of women as the lusty daughters of Eve and established the ideal woman as pure and nonsexual. Women's role was to submit stoically to their husbands' sexual demands and dutifully to bring forth children. While it was primarily white women of the emerging middle class who were held to such standards, these norms in fact affected women of all classes and races, particularly as the local, state, and federal governments became increasingly involved in the regulation of sex. For example, abortion before quickening (the moment when the pregnant woman feels the fetus move, usually in the fifth month) was legal until the mid-nineteenth century, when states began to pass laws regulating and prohibiting it. Similarly, an 1873 federal statute made it a crime to send obscene materials through the mail and labeled any references to sex, reproduction, or contraception as obscene. In the wake of this legislation, many states passed their own laws cracking down on purveyors of "obscene" devices or literature. Yet despite the legal and social restrictions on sex during the nineteenth century, "misbehavior" persisted: prostitution flourished, abortionists continued to practice, and—legal constraints on the sale of contraception notwithstanding—the birth rate fell.

America's sexual history reveals not only the struggle women faced to control their lives, but also the ways in which race and sex were closely linked. Anglo-American colonists who imported Africans in the seventeenth century quickly devised certain conceptions about the men and women they enslaved. Particularly important was the notion that slave women were lascivious and wanton. Such ideas offered a convenient rationale for the sexual abuse that slave women, as chattel, routinely suffered at the hands of their owners. No rape laws protected slave women. While the image of the black woman as "Jezebel" persisted throughout the late nineteenth and into the twentieth century, the post–Civil War years brought sex and race together in increasingly violent ways. Black men's alleged sexual "insults" to white women provided the pretext for a wave of lynchings in the Jim Crow South. And yet, the story of sex and race is more complicated than simply a tale of violence and exploitation. Interracial sex—even between white women and black men—was, as some of the readings on this list reveal, at times not only recognized but tolerated.

The readings suggested below offer a glimpse into how Americans not only constructed systems of sexual regulation but also continually negotiated, challenged, and flouted those systems.

↤ John D'Emilio and Estelle Freedman, *Intimate Matters: A History of Sexuality in America* (University of Chicago Press, 1998)

This book offers an overview of the history of sex in America, beginning in the early seventeenth century and taking us to the 1980s. The authors see America's sexual history divided into three chronological periods: the colonial period, when sexuality was focused on reproduction and the family; the nineteenth century, when romance and intimacy flourished but when sexuality also became ever more fraught and suspect; and the modern, post-1920s era, when sexuality became increasingly commercialized. The book asks questions about who has regulated sexuality and who has been regulated; about men's efforts to control female sexuality and women's efforts to resist that control; and about the class and race tensions that infused issues of sexuality throughout our history. *Intimate Matters* gives you the whole picture and does so in an engaging and lively manner.

↤ Joshua D. Rothman, *Notorious in the Neighborhood: Sex and Families across the Color Line in Virginia, 1787–1861* (University of North Carolina Press, 2007)

Rothman shows that Virginians engaged in a lot of interracial sex in the period from the late eighteenth century to the beginning of the Civil War. Virginians cared more, according to Rothman, about maintaining social stability than about strictly enforcing laws that prohibited miscegenation. As a result, interracial sex was "tolerated if not accepted." Rothman finds that interracial sex existed around the state and at all social levels. Beginning with an analysis of Thomas Jefferson's putative relationship with his slave Sally Hemings, Rothman then introduces us to a long-standing interracial community in the small town of Charlottesville, to an underworld of interracial sex in the city of Richmond, and to divorce cases throughout the state that rested on charges of interracial infidelity.

↤ Leslie J. Reagan, *When Abortion Was a Crime: Women, Medicine, and the Law in the United States, 1867–1973* (University of California Press, 1998)

Looking at the history of abortion in the century before *Roe v. Wade*, Reagan shows the reader how abortion was a well-established part of women's world. In the late nineteenth century, women embraced a "popular ethic" that differed from the codes and norms of the legal, religious, or medical establishments. Reagan's book charts the efforts to make legal restrictions against abortion more stringent and the efforts of those who chose to circumvent such restrictions. While some physicians pushed for strict anti-abortion laws, others were willing to exploit legal loopholes and to provide women with safe abortions—especially during periods of economic depression, when feeding another mouth meant real hardship for many families. Given the heat of our current debate about abortion, an examination of the history reveals that questions about the "right to life" or the viability of the fetus have only recently come to public attention.

◈ George Chauncey, *Gay New York: Gender, Urban Culture, and the Making of the Gay Male World, 1890–1940* (Basic Books, 1995)

Chauncey uncovers the gay male culture that flourished in New York City from the end of the nineteenth century through the 1930s. Gay men were neither isolated nor hidden, but participated in an open and lively urban community that was widely recognized and visible. Chauncey's book demonstrates that our current ideas about sexual identity—particularly our insistence that people be either gay or straight—are of quite recent origin. In the early twentieth century and especially among the working class, choosing a male sexual partner would not have necessarily classified a man as homosexual. More important would have been his gender behavior—specifically whether he assumed masculine or feminine characteristics and mannerisms. Chauncey's book suggests how sexual identities are as much a product of culture as of biology.

◈ Marge Piercy, *Sex Wars: A Novel of Gilded Age New York* (Morrow, 2006)

Piercy's most recent novel offers a fictionalized account of the conflicted, hypocritical, and varied sexual world of post–Civil War America. Based on good historical research, *Sex Wars* interweaves the stories of four characters—three of them real and one fictional—whose lives overlapped and whose agendas sometimes conflicted: Anthony Comstock, the extremist enemy of all things sexual and the architect of the federal anti-obscenity law; Elizabeth Cady Stanton, the most famous and most intellectually far-reaching feminist of the nineteenth century; Victoria Woodhull, the notorious advocate of free love and the first woman to run for president; and a fictional Jewish immigrant woman named Freydeh Leibowitz, who brought her family from poverty into the middle class by manufacturing and selling condoms. A really good read, this novel shows both the extreme hardship that strict Victorian sexual codes exacted on women and the teeming world of illicit sexuality that existed despite such codes.

CINDY ARON, Professor of History, teaches the history of American women as well as courses in the history of the family and the history of sexuality. Her books include *Ladies and Gentlemen of the Civil Service: Middle-Class Workers in Victorian America* (1987) and *Working at Play: A History of Vacations in the United States* (1999), both published by Oxford University Press. She is currently working on a book on the history of prostitution in the United States since World War II.

CHRISTIAN W. MCMILLEN

New Histories of the American West

The American West occupies a unique place in popular culture (there are, after all, no southerns, just westerns). The West of the imagination remains a place where rugged individualism and unbridled independence still reign. That lone explorers discovered and settled the West in service to no one but themselves is a central myth in the history of the American West. The notion that these explorers discovered an empty, virgin land accompanies this myth. Neither notion is true—and in the last generation, historians of the American West have worked hard to demonstrate just how untrue they are.

Historians have been most successful in demonstrating that the American West was never a place of lone pioneers carving a living out of free land. Rather, the West was a place where settlement was made possible only by the largesse of the federal government and large-scale capital investment on land wrested from Indians. Indeed, without the aid of the federal government, the vast majority of the arid West could not have been settled, much less made profitable. Liberal land policy, massive subsidies for such things as irrigation projects, treaties with Indians designed for dispossession, and the creation of national parks and forests all became the essential building blocks of the West. Without the role played by the federal government, none of these developments would have come to pass. In the past twenty-five years, historians have made a steady, sustained, and successful effort to rewrite the history of the American West.

For the most part, this work has been carried out by historians who care deeply about the West, and whose main concern has been to interrogate the past in an effort to confront the future. This was the revisionist school I attended; its curriculum, loosely gathered under the term "the new western history," has marked me indelibly. In the early and mid-1990s, while working for the National Park Service and U.S. Forest Service, I began to read the new western history. It changed how I saw and thought about the West. Donald Worster, whose work is most responsible for convincing me to leave my life as a ranger, go to graduate school, and become a professional historian, summed things up as follows: "Perhaps the single most important, most distinguishing characteristic of the new western history is its determination not to offer cover for the powers that be—not to become subservient to them, by silence or consent. A rising generation of historians insists that it is their responsibility to stand apart from power and think critically about it. . . . This new western history is now setting the agenda of the field."

In this vein, a recent raft of excellent work on American Indians and national parks has made clear that those sacred places of the American West were not always the empty symbols of wilderness that we now take them to be. On the contrary: from Yellowstone to Yosemite, from the Grand Canyon to Glacier, almost all National Parks were once home to American Indians. Indians, of course, have known this all along, but now that historians have begun documenting the processes of dispossession, Indians have gained a powerful voice helping them make claims to land that was once theirs.

The list below presents a sampling of the new western history that has helped us to see the West anew. In different ways, these books all address two of the areas where the new western history has been most eye-opening: Indians and the environment. Some aren't even history: one is a novel, and another is a brilliant ethnography. They all, however, adhere, in some fashion, to Worster's dictates quoted above: they both subvert dominant myths and offer news ways of seeing the western past, its people, and its places.

↪ Donald Worster, *Under Western Skies: Nature and History in the American West* (Oxford University Press, 1994)

> This is the single best introduction to the field. The eleven essays are essential reading. Throughout his work, but most especially here and in *Rivers of Empire: Water, Aridity, and the Growth of the American West* (Oxford University Press, 1985), Worster explores the ways in which the large-scale manipulation of land and politics has served powerful interests at the expense of the environment. He has mostly done this by exploring western water development. If you have seen and enjoyed Roman Polanski's classic neo-noir film *Chinatown*, then read Donald Worster—both lay bare the politics of water in California.

↪ Rebecca Solnit, *Savage Dreams: A Journey into the Landscape Wars of the American West* (1994; University of California Press, 2000)

> Solnit's book explores two different places, separated by very little distance in space, but by immeasurable distance in perception: Yosemite

National Park and the Nevada Test Site. In the section on Yosemite, Solnit uses landscape painting and photography to demonstrate, quite elegantly and convincingly, that our interest in places like Yosemite comes from "a wholly cultivated taste for nature." In writing about Yellowstone, and by extension many other "natural" landscapes, Solnit shows that such places have long been acted upon and interpreted by people.

By arguing that photographs and paintings misleadingly "suggest a place in which nothing has ever happened and which no human has ever touched," Solnit was one of the first historians to point out how changing ideas about landscapes erased Indians from the western past by inventing the idea of a virgin land. By contrast, Solnit discusses the Nevada Test Site as Yosemite's antithesis; it is a sacrificial landscape, bombed to oblivion because it does not satisfy the "cultivated taste for nature."

↪ D'Arcy McNickle, *Wind from an Enemy Sky* (University of New Mexico Press, 1988)

Published posthumously, McNickle's fictional account portrays life on a northern Montana reservation in the 1920s and 1930s. As an employee of the Bureau of Indian Affairs in the 1930s and 1940s, and a founder of the National Congress of American Indians, McNickle offers a rare insider's view of both the reservation and the bureaucracy responsible for directing most aspects of Indian life. No novel I know of has captured, with such fidelity to history, life on an Indian reservation in the first decades of the twentieth century. McNickle's novel, like much of the new western history, strives to give Indians a historical voice and a measure of agency in deciding their lives in the face of great power. In this way, *Wind from an Enemy Sky* is an ideal fictional companion to much historical writing.

↪ Keith H. Basso, *Wisdom Sits in Places: Language and Landscape among the Western Apache* (University of New Mexico Press, 1996)

Basso's ethnography of the Western Apache has become a staple in western and Indian history classes; my students have loved it. The informal tone and the focus on story and anecdote mask the real accomplishment and density of this book. Only someone with Basso's experience—close to thirty years of fieldwork—and knowledge of the Western Apache language could have written this book. By closely examining the ways in which the Apache talk about landscapes, Basso discovered that the Western Apache have embedded their history in the land. (Of course *they* already knew this!) The Apache are more concerned with *where*, not *when*, events occurred, and thus have a very different conception of history than do most non-Apaches. As Basso puts it: "Weakly empirical, thinly chronological, and rarely written down, Western Apache history as practiced by Apaches advances no theories, tests no hypotheses, and offers no general models. What it does instead . . . is fashion possible worlds, give them expressive shape, and present them for contemplation as images of the past that can deepen and enlarge awareness of the present."

↪ Mike Davis, *City of Quartz: Excavating the Future in Los Angeles* (1992; Vintage, 2006)

The historiography of Los Angeles has exploded in the last decade, and this book must take responsibility. Davis writes about many things in his books (one of his latest is on the avian flu), but he is at his best when analyzing L.A. This is not a book for those looking for a tour of a land of happiness, health, and sunshine. Rather, it is, among other things, an acerbic exploration of planned segregation, the aesthetic poverty of much of the built environment in L.A., and the construction of myths about L.A. via fiction and film. *City of Quartz* is a highly readable look at all the ways L.A. has been imagined and planned during the twentieth century. Like all of the new western history discussed here, *City of Quartz*, like its follow-up, *The Ecology of Fear: Los Angeles and the Imagination of Destruction*, debunks myths and offers a critical, not laudatory, history of a particular western place.

CHRISTIAN W. MCMILLEN, Assistant Professor of History, teaches courses on the American West and American Indians. His *Making Indian Law* was published by Yale University Press in 2007. With a course development grant from the University Medical School's Center for Global Health, he has begun work on a new project looking at Indian health and disease in a global context.

LARRY SABATO

Political Power: How to Get It, Use It, and Avoid Losing It

The headlines scream scandal: bribery, lobbying excesses, congressional junkets, wiretapping, and political greed and intrigue of all sorts. All true, all worrisome. But is it really news? Since America's founding—and eons before—ambitious people have been positioning themselves to get power, use it, and avoid losing it, sometimes going outside the bounds of ethical behavior to do so. The business of power has always attracted or developed fascinating individuals. In turn, these characters have generated timeless literature.

Where should one start? Machiavelli's *The Prince* is a savvy beginning for amateurs and professionals alike. One of the most politically influential books of all time, this work was the first to formulate some sense of ethics for the political process while justifying, in practical terms, the idea that the end justifies the means. While not the stuff of the U.S. Constitution, Machiavellian tactics have nonetheless better encapsulated the actual practice of American politics as it has existed from the Republic's early days. From Tammany Hall to Huey Long to George W. Bush, the sly exercise of political power, overt and hidden, to achieve one's goals has been a constant. Tammany Hall, for example, was one of the most powerful, corrupt political machines in American history. One of its most prominent players was New York state senator George Washington Plunkitt, a practitioner of the oxymoronic brand of politics he called "honest graft." In *Plunkitt of Tammany Hall,* the "good" senator explains how his self-serving practice of graft also held benefits for those he governed, a paradoxical update of Machiavelli's assertions. (Former congressman Randy "Duke" Cunningham of California, recently sent to prison as the all-time champion bribe-taker in House history, could have used some of Plunkitt's rationalizations.) Governor and Senator Huey Long was a southern version of Plunkitt, of course, and the "Kingfish" of the Bayou State served as the basis of Robert Penn Warren's *All the King's Men.* One of the great classics of American political fiction, the novel chronicles a Long-esque character's rise to power, and his inevitable fall, once undone by corruption, overreaching, and the abandonment of ideals.

Of course, there is much more to American politics than the seamy ruthlessness exhibited by Tammany Hall and Huey Long. Three founding giants of American politics were proponents of a very different theory of political success. In the *Federalist Papers,* Alexander Hamilton, James Madison, and John Jay penned a manuscript that served as the basis for the Constitution of the United States. Their design, while drawing on John Locke's principles, was remarkably original and shrewd, a workable combination of idealism, pragmatism, and suspicion of the concentration of power. These constitutionalists orchestrated a symphonic composition of individual liberty and social contract by dividing power, separating governmental authority into branches, adding a dozen major checks and balances, and further complicating the exercise of power by means of a federal system. More than two centuries later, the *Federalist* essays are still the starting point of debate and discussion for a nation that is now continental in scope and global in impact.

From the start of the Republic, public people have pondered their proper role. Should they be a delegate, a pure mirror of the opinions of their constituents casting votes and making decisions as the electorate desires, or is it better to serve as a trustee, someone who studies the issues and tries to make choices in the best long-term interests of the people and the nation—even if, short-term, a majority of the population may disagree? There is never an easy, all-purpose answer, though it is obvious that most elected officials are mainly delegates. After all, John F. Kennedy's *Profiles in Courage* was a very short book. Yet central to the debate of conscience that rages within the more thoughtful public officials is another query: Do citizens have enough information and sense to make rational decisions in their own interest? The best book ever written on the subject was produced by the political scientist V. O. Key Jr. in 1961, *The Responsible Electorate: Rationality in Presidential Voting, 1936–1960*. The final book in Key's seminal career, *The Responsible Electorate* made a painstaking and convincing case for rationality among the electorate. It is not that most voters know the details of policy and politics, but rather that, as a group, they have become skilled at separating wheat from chaff, with both personnel and policies in election campaigns. Since broad-based education has expanded dramatically in the nearly half century since Key's work was written, his conclusions likely have more validity today than then.

Politicians trying to gain power should look to Machiavelli, Plunkitt, and Long. Those trying to use their power well ought to read Madison and Hamilton. Those trying to keep their power by exercising it responsibly should study Key. The here and now of politics is always evolving, but the past is a deep well of refreshment, offering illuminating examples of what works in politics—and also what can get you arrested. In these trying days of Red versus Blue polarization, and indictments galore, it is not obvious which examples will be more useful. Best to be prepared on both counts, whether you are a budding politician or a concerned citizen, and the sources mentioned in this essay are your most reliable guides.

⟡ Machiavelli, *The Prince* (1505)

In *The Prince*, Machiavelli conveys the problems with the ruling class and suggests a series of solutions to bring about the reunification of Italy under the Medici family of Florence. Machiavelli suggests a variety of tactics for the prince to secure his power, and argues that because humans are inherently evil, the ends are able to justify the means. Machiavelli proposes that politics and religion are separate and that future rulers should be concerned with securing power, not adhering to a strict moral code. Above all, Machiavelli was a keen observer of man's political nature, which in many respects is unchanging. Many well-read officeholders through the centuries have studied *The Prince,* including the nation's first elected African American state governor, L. Douglas Wilder, who served in Virginia from 1990 to 1994. Wilder agreed with Machiavelli that, to be successful, "it is better to be feared than loved."

✧ V. O. Key Jr., *The Responsible Electorate: Rationality in Presidential Voting, 1936–1960* (Harvard University Press, 1966)

Through analyzing public opinion data and electoral returns, V. O. Key made the case for rationality in voter choice and suggested that voters choose to reelect incumbents based on their performance in office. Written at a time of much stronger partisan identification than today, Key's book is a tonic for those who wish contemporary political parties were more admired and respected among the electorate. The two major parties may oversimplify the choices voters face, but Key sees them as irreplaceable voting "cues" for busy people who, alas, may not read daily newspapers and study the issues thoroughly.

✧ Robert Penn Warren, *All the King's Men* (Harvest, 1996)

A work of fiction that closely mirrors the political life of Governor Huey Long of Louisiana, the novel tells the story of the rise and fall of southern governor Willie Stark. The story is narrated by Jack Burden, Stark's political right hand, who is able to maintain his integrity while watching Stark rise to political power through dirty politics and back-room deals. In the end, Stark pays a high price for his path to power. This cautionary tale brings to mind many modern political figures, not least a half dozen recent state governors indicted for selling favors and the like. Willie Stark will always be with us, and this volume helps to prepare us, the electorate, for his frequent resurrections.

✧ Alexander Hamilton, James Madison, and John Jay, *The Federalist Papers* (1787 and 1788)

Written during the years 1787 and 1788, *The Federalist Papers* eloquently argue for the ratification of the United States Constitution and explain why this new form of government was the best choice for America. Through eighty-five essays, Hamilton, Madison, and Jay explain how the government would function and explain the theory of democracy. While the papers were originally published in several New York newspapers to persuade New York citizens to ratify the Constitution, the papers remain perhaps the best documentation of the thinking of our Founding Fathers regarding the birth of American democracy. So many of these essays are thoroughly relevant today, such as Federalist

Number 10, which encourages the "flourishing of interests" in order to prevent the overconcentration of power in one or a few groups. Of course, interest groups are less a problem than the lobbyists, such as the notorious Jack Abramoff, who are hired to promote the groups' needs. In the Founders' simpler, happier time, the country's Abramoffs had not yet thought to gather in the lobby to ply their questionable trade.

↪ William L. Riordan, *Plunkitt of Tammany Hall* (Signet Classic, 1996)

This book provides a look into the world of big city "machine" politics from the first person perspective. The journalist William L. Riordan published this series of interviews with George Washington Plunkitt, New York state senator and Tammany Hall ward boss. This remarkable little volume is filled with the timeless wit and wisdom of a hardened "pol," whose views are still common among elected officials today but whose on-the-record frankness has all but vanished. "I seen my opportunities and I took 'em," explained Plunkitt. The reader will delight in his clever distinctions between "honest graft" and "dishonest graft." He took only the former kind, naturally.

The author wishes to thank Cullen Sinclair for his help with research for this essay.

"Politics is a good thing!" is the slogan of LARRY SABATO, Center for Politics founder and Robert Kent Gooch Professor of Politics. He is the author of over twenty books on the American political process and is best known for *Feeding Frenzy: How Attack Journalism Has Transformed American Politics* (Lanahan, 2000). Sabato's latest book, *Divided States of America: The Slash and Burn Politics of the 2004 Presidential Election* (Longman, 2005), breaks down the 2004 races and provides a jumping-off point for the 2006 and 2008 contests.

PAUL FREEDMAN

Media and Politics: Media Effects? Media Bias?

The problem with teaching courses on media and politics is that everybody is an expert. Everyone from your uncle to your coworker to your member of Congress knows what's wrong with the media and how to fix it. Everyone has an opinion, and usually those opinions are unencumbered by empirical evidence and untethered from any kind of scholarly analysis. Moreover, when people do read books about the media, they are apt to choose authors with whom they already agree. What follows are five books chosen to provide a fresh perspective.

In a democracy, the media play a critical linking function, connecting citizens with their elected representatives, as well as with each other. As Tocqueville put it after his famous visit to an earlier America, "The effect of a newspaper is not only to suggest the same purpose to a great number of persons, but to furnish means for executing in common the designs which they may have singly conceived." Newspapers, in other words, made collective action possible, and brought citizens "every day, in the midst of their own minor concerns, some intelligence of the state of their public weal."

More than a century and a half later, the connective function of newspapers has been augmented (and increasingly, many worry, replaced) by radio, television, and the blogosphere. Today, many observers fret that these new forms of media conspire to unravel rather than to reinforce the social fabric that binds us to our nation and our neighbors.

Such concerns reflect a conventional wisdom that usually centers around two assumptions. First, that the mass media have substantial, potentially massive, persuasive effects; that they can shape minds and mold opinions in ways that we need to be vigilant against. Second, that media are rampant with bias, that our sources of news and information are inevitably distorted by political agendas from the left or right that prevent us from a having clear view of the truth.

Both assumptions are at best incomplete. What scholars have learned from a half century of exhaustive study is that the media do have important effects, but that the kind of massive persuasion that early researchers hypothesized and that many contemporary critics assume is actually rare. Instead, the media serve to shape the agenda, influencing what issues or problems citizens consider important. In one famous formulation, the media don't tell us what to think, but they do affect what we think *about*. They also help structure opinion, influencing the standards by which citizens evaluate leaders, policies, and candidates for office.

When it comes to media bias, where you stand depends to a great extent on where you sit. According to a 2002 Pew Center for the People and the Press survey, 69 percent of Republicans but only 57 percent of Democrats considered the media, as a whole, to be "biased." In the aggregate, only about a quarter of Americans said that the media were "not biased." Similarly, during the 2004 presidential election, 52 percent of Republicans but only 23 percent of Democrats said the media were unfair to the Bush campaign. (Interestingly, Republicans were also slightly more likely than Democrats to see the press as unfair to the Kerry campaign, but the numbers here were far lower: 30 and 26 percent, respectively.) For those on the right, liberal bias in the media (and especially at CBS, CNN, and NPR) is self-evident.

For those on the left, concerns about corporate ownership are summed up by two words that tell us all we need to know about media bias: Fox News.

What is the basis for widespread assumptions of media bias? In general, claims about bias take two forms, which I call "inferential" and "observational." Inferential claims are indirect. They usually begin with some oft-quoted statistic about voting behavior ("Ninety percent of journalists voted for Bill Clinton!") or public opinion ("Members of the media are almost universally pro-choice!") or demographics ("Newsrooms are disproportionately populated by white males!") and infer bias as a result.

But does voting or having an opinion (or a gender) render objectivity or neutrality impossible? Certainly many journalists would reject the notion that they cannot do their jobs competently by virtue of having their own political views. In contrast to inferential arguments, observational claims of media bias look to the content of media coverage directly for the specific frames of reference, word and image choices, and other attributes that serve to color, shape, or indeed bias the presentation of news and information. The best studies of media bias take precisely this content-analytic approach.

For anyone with an interest in the questions of media effects and media bias, these five books constitute essential reading.

⤷ Michael Schudson, *Discovering the News: A Social History of American Newspapers* (Basic Books, 1980)

> What does it mean to be "objective"? Schudson's history of the American newspaper is really the story of the emergence of the idea of objectivity in American journalism. Schudson begins with a discussion of the "ideal of objectivity," which he describes as a "peculiar demand" to make of institutions that are fundamentally political and economic in nature. Schudson goes on to describe the rise of the "penny press," rooted in the technological innovations and the social, political, and economic transformations of the nineteenth century, from which the modern notion of "objectivity" first emerged. Penny papers (which, appropriately, cost only a penny) "expressed and built the culture of a democratic market society." This book is essential reading for understanding the roots of contemporary media and contemporary media criticism.

⤷ Thomas E. Patterson, *Out of Order* (Vintage, 1994)

> Patterson's account of media coverage of the 1992 presidential election is a classic but still-relevant study. Through painstaking content analysis, Patterson shows that, over the course of three decades, media coverage of elections has changed in fundamental ways, almost all of them bad. In contrast to an earlier era (which may or may not have ever existed, but Patterson makes a good case), by the early 1990s

media coverage had become more negative, more analytical (as opposed to descriptive), more strategically oriented with a focus on the game of politics and an obsession with the horse race. It also provided fewer opportunities for viewers to watch and listen to the candidates themselves in their own uninterrupted, uninterpreted words. The average candidate sound bite on the evening news has declined from a whopping forty-two seconds in 1968 to less than eight seconds in 2004. "News coverage," Patterson concludes, "has become a barrier between the candidates and the voters rather than a bridge connecting them."

↭ Shanto Iyengar and Donald R. Kinder, *News That Matters: Television and American Opinion* (University of Chicago Press, 1987)

I first read this book as an undergraduate, when it was hot off the presses. I was captivated by the methodological elegance of the research design, the clarity and sophistication of the data analysis, and the importance of the substantive findings. Through a series of deceptively straightforward experimental manipulations, Iyengar and Kinder show that the power of television news lies not in its ability to persuade, but in its capacity to shape what citizens consider to be important (the agenda-setting effect) and to influence the criteria by which candidates, officials, and policies are evaluated (the priming effect). In graduate school I reread the book for several courses, including a research methods seminar with Kinder in which I was taken to task for being insufficiently critical of the work. What can I say? This is a book with few flaws; it is a model of social science written for a general audience, and I assign it regularly in my own classes.

↭ John Zaller, *The Nature and Origins of Mass Opinion* (Cambridge University Press, 1992)

More than a classic, this book is a touchstone in the study of public opinion and provides the essential theoretical framework for understanding the nature of media effects—and the impact of elite political discourse more generally—on how citizens understand and what they know about the political world. Zaller's insights, grounded in past work in public opinion and political psychology, have transformed how scholars study political communication. Zaller's model of the survey response rejects the notion that most of us carry around in our heads fully formed attitudes, ready to offer up to anyone who asks. Instead, we construct our responses out of a store of considerations, which are themselves products of information encountered through the media. Written primarily for an academic audience, Zaller's book can be challenging at times, but the rewards are great.

↬ Bernard Goldberg, *Bias: A CBS Insider Exposes How the Media Distort the News* (Harper Paperbacks, 2003)

In 1996, the CBS News correspondent Bernard Goldberg caused something of a media firestorm when he published a piece in the *Wall Street Journal* asserting what conservative media critics had been saying for years: The mainstream media are controlled by a bunch of liberal elites. "The old argument that the networks and other 'media elites' have a liberal bias is so blatantly true that it's hardly worth discussing anymore," Goldberg wrote. In Goldberg's view, the media are rife with underexamined liberal biases that undermine the objectivity of the news product. Much of Goldberg's book is predicated on the kind of inferential argument described above, and Goldberg is so wrong about so much that it's frustrating. What's more frustrating, though, is what he gets right. Goldberg at his best does provide observational evidence of bias (selectively chosen, of course), and this book (along with rejoinders such as Eric Alterman's *What Liberal Media?*) provides a good glimpse into a heated debate.

PAUL FREEDMAN, Associate Professor of Politics, teaches courses in media and politics, public opinion, political communication, and research methods. He is coauthor of *Campaign Advertising and American Democracy* (Temple University Press, 2007). Since 2000, Freedman has been an election analyst for ABC News in New York.

BRIAN PUSSER

Academic Capitalism: The Political Economy of Higher Education

One of the enduring questions in modern social thought concerns the degree to which public purposes can be achieved by private enterprise. The question of the appropriate role of competition and market forces in the provision of such essential services as health care, national defense, and education has moved to the fore of contemporary public policy debates and into every corner of the global political economy. Higher education is an arena in which this question is particularly salient on a number of levels, yet despite the diversity of disciplines and critical standpoints found in the academy, the question of markets and higher education has largely been addressed through the lens of economics, and an acutely rational economics at that. As the implications of market-driven restructuring of public enterprises have become increasingly clear, new perspectives have emerged, drawing on a variety of disciplines while incorporating both new and time-honored traditions. The books represented here provide critical, historical, and fictional approaches to understanding the role—and limitations—of markets in contemporary society.

At the beginning of the twenty-first century, public and private colleges and universities find themselves facing revenue constraints and an array of contradictory demands. These postsecondary institutions are expected to stand as beacons of opportunity and egalitarianism and to compete for high-achieving students, outstanding faculty, and elite rankings. Public colleges and universities are expected to balance increasing enrollment demand with limited state funding while preserving a historical commitment to low tuition. The faculty and administrative staff of colleges and universities are increasingly expected to be "student-centered" and "consumer-focused" while honoring professional standards of leadership and autonomy. In nearly every dimension of postsecondary activity—knowledge production, teaching, service, student development, economic production, and more—colleges and universities in the United States have been criticized for not being more effective, more efficient, and more accountable. This critique has deepened over the past two decades, despite exemplary contemporary global rankings and a long legacy of excellence.

Among the emerging prescriptions for university reform, none is more prominent today than the demand for greater market competition in higher education. Market advocates in statehouses and in Congress, with the support of lobbying efforts by for-profit colleges and universities, have begun to actively reshape the landscape of regulations and subsidies that have defined the American postsecondary system. While the current sets of demands for change are ubiquitous, they are not by any means new. Over two hundred years ago, Adam Smith contemplated whether efficiencies might be generated through linking faculty salaries to productivity, yet over the ensuing centuries the United States has built a vast system of higher education degree–granting that is overwhelmingly nonprofit, predominantly public, and nonmarket. In an environment where markets are everywhere ascendant, it is imperative that we revisit the historical, theoretical, and institutional dynamics of American higher education, a system that has been at once remarkably successful and uniquely resistant to market control.

The books presented here portray systems in turmoil, beset by contests between ideologies, values, structures, and processes: New Deal and neoliberal, nonprofit and for-profit, elite and mass, equity and excellence, art and commerce. Taken together, these works offer critical reflection that can be equally usefully applied to understanding the role of markets in modern society and in colleges and universities. Their most valuable contribution may be that they present a clash of cultures in a world in which efficiency, franchising, and private gain challenge individual development, professional autonomy, and service to the public good.

↪ Simon Marginson, *Markets in Education* (Allen and Unwin, 1997)

This book is a brilliant work and a seminal effort to apply political and economic philosophy to the study of markets and education. The author offers a powerful challenge to the utility of markets for producing public goods, suggesting that markets in education lead to greater stratification, atomization, and the constraint of innovation. Marginson also quite usefully reminds us that predictions for market behavior are constructs, and as such are quite often driven by both research and ideology. As it turns its focus to such issues as the commercialization of education, the role of neoliberal government policies in shaping higher education systems, and the role of education in social advantage and positional competition, *Markets in Education* sets the stage for the other works profiled below.

↪ Sheila Slaughter and Gary Rhoades, *Academic Capitalism and the New Economy: Markets, State, and Higher Education* (Johns Hopkins University Press, 2004)

Sheila Slaughter and Gary Rhoades have long been two of the most innovative and creative scholars in the field of higher education. Here they present rich data on the expansion of what they define as academic capitalism, the efforts of colleges and universities to generate revenue from entrepreneurial linkages to the burgeoning global economy. The book extends Slaughter's earlier work on the emergence of academic capitalism with examples ranging from new patent and licensing strategies for biotechnology to the outsourcing of campus food services. The research presented here suggests that in a global, information-driven economy, universities increasingly treat knowledge as "raw material" that can be converted to capital and exchanged for equity stakes in for-profit ventures. The authors conclude that academic capitalism presents unprecedented challenges to postsecondary institutional autonomy, faculty work, and the public good.

↪ Eric Schlosser, *Fast Food Nation: The Dark Side of the All-American Meal* (Harper Perennial, 2005)

Market ideology has been so central to global political and economic shifts over the past three decades that it has been virtually beyond reproach. *Fast Food Nation* offers one of the most comprehensive studies of contemporary market activity, and it makes a convincing case that the contemporary fast food industry in America is the most effective market ever implemented. Schlosser covers a vast and complex terrain, from the immense potato fields of Idaho that are the wellspring of McDonald's french fries to the vast Nebraskan meat-packing plants where enormous pools of capital, technology, and immigrant labor combine in what are arguably the most efficient assembly lines yet created. The work is particularly useful where it examines the tension between market competition and public policy in such areas as product regulation and standards, workplace conditions, and public subsidies. While the scope and precision of the fast food market inspire awe, Schlosser here portrays the industry as both a commercial triumph and a challenge to global sustainability. While readers may disagree over the impact of the fast food industry on contemporary society, all who read this book will come away with a more informed perspective on globalization, commerce, and the public good.

↩ Roger L. Geiger, *Knowledge and Money: Research Universities and the Paradox of the Marketplace* (Stanford University Press, 2004)

Knowledge and Money, Geiger's third major volume on the history of higher education in the United States, is an invaluable resource for those attempting to understand the rapid changes over the past three decades in university organization, student quality, institutional selectivity, research productivity, and institutional wealth. In one of his most important contributions, Geiger documents the growing wealth gap between private and public universities and the competitive advantages that predict further stratification in the decades to come. The author also conceptualizes the higher education arena as a market environment, one in which universities are both driven and constrained by competition in ways that are often problematic. He argues that while contemporary commercial activities in higher education have generated significant and useful advances, market competition significantly challenges such essential postsecondary missions as access, equity, and the preservation of diverse bases of knowledge.

↩ B. Traven, *The Night Visitor and Other Stories* (Dee, 1993)

B. Traven is the pseudonym of a writer, perhaps born in Germany or the United States, who lived as a reclusive expatriate in Mexico during the first quarter of the twentieth century. He stands as an unlikely chronicler of market efficiency and its impact on community. Yet in this collection of his early short works he explores the tension between individual desires for social mobility and the benefits of collective, public action in light of the coming of global commerce to an impoverished nation.

Traven most skillfully portrays the contrast between art, community, and commerce in "Assembly Line," his tale of an American businessman's efforts to bring the techniques of mass production to an indigenous artist who creates woven and painted baskets made of plaited grass. Near the end of the story, as the stymied businessman retreats, the artist explains why—no matter the individual benefits— he simply cannot move to mass production. "I've got to make these canastitas my own way and with my own song in them," he explains, "and with bits of my soul woven into them. If I were to make them in great numbers there would no longer be my soul in each, or my songs." In the spirit of Traven's recalcitrant artist, the works presented here raise essential questions about market economies and the human condition. *The Night Visitor,* like other books on my list, demands that we establish a common ground where the hegemony of commerce can be leavened by the spirit of community and the power of creativity in the service of knowledge production and the preservation of essential public goods.

BRIAN PUSSER is Associate Professor in the Curry School of Education. His research focuses on the politics of higher education, the organization and governance of postsecondary institutions, and the role of international, national, and state policies in shaping the postsecondary arena.

PHILIPPE ROGER

Tintin and the American Menace: French (Mis)representations of the United States

One need hardly emphasize the extent of French-American rifts over foreign policy in recent years. However, it is important to distinguish between rationally based, logically articulated differences, on the one hand, and accumulated prejudices and misrepresentations, on the other. In my view, "anti-Americanism" belongs in the second category.

French anti-Americanism is a tradition that has been shaped and groomed by the French intelligentsia. This is especially true of the different strains of anti-Americanism developed in the twentieth century. Its core constituency shifted from Catholic, conservative, and far-right thinkers in the 1920s and 1930s to leftist militants, writers, and philosophers during the Cold War and after. But anti-Americanism's center of gravity never ceased to be where the *intellectuals* were. "Popular" anti-Americanism came late and still lags behind. Polls show that the more educated you are and the more money you make in France, the more likely you also are to profess anti-American opinions. Hence the interest of diving into the seminal ocean of French anti-American literature.

From Baudelaire, who coined the French word *"américanisation"* in the 1850s, to Jean Baudrillard, who in 1986 described America as a non-entity, French poets, novelists, and writers played a decisive part in the elaboration and diffusion of anti-American stereotypes. It is hard to select only five of those numerous texts that contributed to framing a negative and sometimes offensive image of the United States, though my options have been limited, in several cases, by the (understandable) lack of an English translation.

My selection is based on both the literary quality of the texts and their lasting impact on French representations. To provide context and accommodate readers interested in a more historical viewpoint on French anti-Americanism, I have listed some of the most accessible books on the topic written by historians or specialists in the field of cultural studies. In an act of what could be perceived as typically Gallic arrogance, I have included among those references my own book *The American Enemy*. To date, it is the only book that delves into the long history of French anti-Americanism over more than two centuries; let that be my excuse . . .

↩ Georges Duhamel, *America the Menace: Scenes from the Life of the Future,* trans. Charles Miner Thompson (Houghton Mifflin, 1931)

This book will not be easy to find outside of libraries. However, it is such a milestone of French cultural anti-Americanism that I could not possibly leave it off my short list. It was published in French in 1930 by Georges Duhamel, a best-selling novelist and the author of a family saga entitled *The Pasquiers' Chronicle,* as well as a reputed essayist and a brilliant lecturer. His book about America, written after a trip through the Northeast, Chicago, and the Deep South, was an immediate and lasting success. Elegantly written, filled with lively anecdotes, tales, and transcripts of conversations, Duhamel's book is also a compendium of anti-American scenes and *tableaux vivants*. It includes all the new ingredients of Americanophobia in the 1930s: lurid descriptions of the American cosmopolitan metropolis; a spectacular visit to the Chicago slaughterhouses; misogynist remarks on American women enslaving American males; more than ambiguous notes on the conditions of the black population; a hellish depiction of a New York movie theater as half factory, half whorehouse; and much, much more.

Hergé, *Tintin in America,* trans. Leslie Lonsdale-Cooper and Michael Turner (Little, Brown, 1979)

Tintin en Amérique, one of the most famous volumes drawn by the most famous European comic book author, was originally published in 1931. It may not look like serious academic reading material, but it is: the amount of scholarly literature on Hergé is, indeed, quite impressive. *Tintin in America,* drawn in the extremely thin and schematic "clear line" typical of Hergé's style, is the perfect companion book to Duhamel's *America the Menace.* Based not on direct observation (Hergé had never been to America at the time), but on articles serialized in the right-wing magazine *Le Crapouillot* (The Trench Mortar) in 1930, the vision of the United States offered to Belgian and French youngsters is appalling. Gangsters are everywhere: brutal and well-connected, they rule the country through violence and corruption. Most of the action takes place in Chicago, while a long, digressive episode takes the reader to the Wild West to expose the unfairness of the United States toward the Indians. Constantly reprinted since 1931, *Tintin in America* has been a major purveyor of stereotypes of a Kafkaesque America.

Louis-Ferdinand Céline, *Journey to the End of the Night,* trans. Ralph Manheim (New Directions, 2006)

This novel is not only about America. It is about Africa, America, and France—a triangulation that in itself is quite revealing about a declining but still imperial France full of resentment toward the looming domination of an undeclared American Empire after the First World War. When it appeared in 1932, Céline's first and probably best novel was praised by the left as an inspired, dramatic, and at times highly poetic vindication of the poor and the wretched against all forms of social alienation. Only later would Céline turn to vociferous anti-Semitism and twisted collaborationism. Céline's bravura is at its best in the second part, when his hero, Bardamu, reaches the waters of New York harbor, where he is lucky to get a job as a "flea-accountant." Céline's striking depictions of New York and Detroit (where, as a physician, he had spent some time studying the Ford health-care system) are not caricatures like Duhamel's vignettes: rather, they evoke the strong colors and violent brushstrokes of expressionist painters like Grosz. American life here is not derided with intellectual aloofness: it is made part of a tricontinental experience of sorrow, deprivation, and misery. To that extent, Céline's America is more humane than that of Duhamel, the patent humanist.

↶ Jean-Paul Sartre, "American Cities," in *Literary and Philosophical Essays,* trans. Annette Michelson (1955; Collier, 1967) and "New York: Colonial City," in *Modern Times: Selected Non-Fiction,* trans. Robin Buss, ed. Geoffrey Wall (Penguin, 2000)

Sartre's ambivalence about America can be perceived almost physically in his descriptions of American cities, written before he became a stern political opponent of U.S. policies in the world, at the time of his own discovery of America. Responding to an invitation made by the War Information Office to witness the U.S. war effort, Sartre toured the country with a half dozen compatriots. He reported regularly about his trip to the two newspapers that had made him a correspondent for the occasion: the left-wing daily *Combat* and the more conservative *Figaro.* Later on, Sartre selected some of those articles for republication in *Situations III.* "American Cities" and "New York: Colonial City" present us with a creative rewriting of Duhamel, Céline, and other prewar travelers with a new twist: the American metropolis is deemed unlivable not only because of its anonymity and gigantism, but also because of its precariousness: cities in America are always on the verge of being swallowed by an overwhelming, omnipresent Nature.

↶ Jean Baudrillard, *America,* trans. Chris Turner (Verso, 1989)

Years before his infamous piece about the destruction of the World Trade Center, the French philosopher and essayist Jean Baudrillard had written a short book entitled *America,* in part descriptive, in part analytical, always very personal and subjective. Originally published in 1986, *America* reflects the new focus of French traveler-writers on California: the West Coast is the new scene of our future. In Baudrillard's book, California becomes an apt metaphor for America in general and, potentially, the whole world as virtual reality. In Baudrillard's writing, echoes can be found of earlier depictions (like Luc Durtain's in the 1920s), but his insistence on the unreality of America is more systematically suggested than it ever was, in smart prose that associates observation and aphorism. *America* can thus be read as the postmodern version of the perennial French intellectual cynicism about America and American "civilization."

For further reading:

Simone de Beauvoir, *America Day by Day,* trans. Carol Cosman (University of California Press, 2000).

Antonello Gerbi, *The Dispute of the New World: The History of a Polemic, 1750–1900,* trans. Jeremy Moyle (University of Pittsburgh Press, 1973).

Jean-Philippe Mathy, *Extrême-Occident: French Intellectuals and America* (University of Chicago Press, 1993).

Jacques Portes, *Fascination and Misgivings: The United States in French Opinion, 1870–1914,* trans. Elborg Forster (Cambridge University Press, 2006).

Philippe Roger, *The American Enemy: A History of French Anti-American-ism,* trans. Sharon Bowman (University of Chicago Press, 2005).

PHILIPPE ROGER is Professor of French Language and Literature at the University of Virginia and at L'École des hautes études en sciences sociales in Paris. He has written extensively on eighteenth-century literature and other topics, including the works of Roland Barthes (*Roland Barthes, roman* [Grasset, 1986]). His *The American Enemy,* which appeared in French in 2002, has been published in English, Chinese, and Arabic and is currently being translated into Italian and Japanese.

DAPHNE SPAIN

Catastrophes and Commemorations: Shaping Nineteenth-Century Chicago

Nineteenth-century Chicago was a place to behold. Incorporated in 1837, burned to the ground in 1871, and host to the World's Columbian Exposition in 1893, this was a city that constantly reinvented itself. Chicago's history of disasters and successes makes it an icon for urban sociologists and planners alike. For urban sociologists, the "Chicago school" of human ecology at the University of Chicago would create theories that significantly shaped the discipline for decades. Urban planners identify the city as the site of the turn-of-the-century World's Columbian Exposition and the first City Beautiful plan. The books I've chosen feature people and events that shaped Chicago during its critical years. My special interest is in Jane Addams, a Progressive reformer whose accomplishments would eventually become associated with both sociology and urban planning.

Author of *Twenty Years at Hull-House,* Addams was the most prominent American woman of the Progressive era. Her reputation matched that of Thomas Edison and Theodore Roosevelt. Addams founded Chicago's Hull-House settlement in 1889 with Ellen Gates Starr. Addams, Starr, and other settlement house residents lived in the same neighborhoods as immigrants and learned of the deprivations of poverty firsthand. Their daily experiences prompted settlement house residents to lobby for fair labor practices, safe housing, and measures to protect public health. Much of the legislation we take for granted today, like the eight-hour workday and child labor laws, was based on research conducted at Hull-House.

Although we retrospectively celebrate Addams, Starr, and the settlement house residents, the public image of Chicago during the late nineteenth century was far from positive. Chicago gained a national reputation as the symbol of everything wrong about cities. Three disasters put it on the map of people's imaginations as the embodiment of urban fears. The Great Fire killed three hundred people, destroyed two thousand acres, and inflicted $200 million worth of damage to property. The city was in ruins. Almost one-third of the residents lost their homes, and one-third of the downtown buildings were lost. Out of the devastation, though, rose the first skyscrapers in the nation. The Chicago Commercial style of architecture featured steel-framed masonry construction designed by prominent architects like Louis Sullivan and Daniel Burnham.

The Haymarket bombing of 1886 invoked fears of a different order from those associated with the Great Fire. The natural disaster of a fire was easier to understand than the political disorder caused by anarchy. On May 4, a rally of two thousand workers at Haymarket Square, Chicago's wholesale produce district, met to protest the police killings of two workers at the McCormick reaper plant the day before. Its leaders exhorted the group to destroy the legal system that oppressed them. After 10:00 p.m., when the crowd had dwindled to several hundred and the rhetoric had heated up, someone in the group threw a bomb into the line of police assembled to monitor the demonstration. A riot broke out. Seven police officers were killed, and an untold number of civilians killed and injured. Ten of the rally's organizers were arrested, tried, and convicted as anarchists despite a lack of substantial evidence. The authority of the legal system was asserted once again.

The third disaster also involved labor unrest. The railroad magnate George Pullman founded the quintessential "company town," named in his honor, in 1880. Its location on the outskirts of Chicago was chosen to avoid the labor problems epitomized by the Haymarket incident. Pullman was the model of a successful planning endeavor until 1893, when an economic depression hit Chicago especially hard. (The World's Fair was opening its gates just as banks were closing their doors.) Pullman increased the rents on his workers' housing but refused to raise their wages. The resulting labor strike gained notoriety when unions across the country added their support. President Cleveland called out the troops, violence ensued, and the American Railway Union president, Eugene Debs, was imprisoned. Hull-House lost several wealthy patrons when Jane Addams served as an arbitrator in the dispute.

Largely in an effort to polish their bruised civic image, Chicago's business elite lobbied for the privilege of hosting the World's Exposition that would commemorate Columbus's founding of America. Supposedly the nickname "Windy City" was based on the men's incessant campaign to beat New York City in the bidding war. The World's Columbian Exposition of 1893 missed the centennial by one year, but the wait was worth it. Daniel Burnham and the landscape architect Frederick Law Olmsted constructed a temporary miniature city, with grand civic monuments surrounding a central lagoon, where all the latest international cultural and technological achievements were displayed. The fair's design laid the groundwork for the City Beautiful movement that influenced urban planning for several decades.

Chicago ushered in the twentieth century with a nod to the nineteenth when Daniel Burnham designed a City Beautiful plan for downtown. Published in 1909, the Chicago Plan drew inspiration from the World's Fair and set the stage for the city as it is today. It has lived up to Burnham's admonition to "make no little plans, for they have no power to stir men's souls."

⌁ Jane Addams, *Twenty Years at Hull-House, with Autobiographical Notes,* ed. Victoria Bissel Brown (Bedford/St. Martin's, 1999)

Jane Addams and Chicago's Hull-House became the icons of the settlement house movement in America. Brown's abridged version of the original *Twenty Years* is faithful to the original text, with annotations that clarify its meaning for contemporary readers. Originally published in 1910, the book reveals why Jane Addams was such a prominent public intellectual during the Progressive era. She led debates on abstract issues like capitalism, women's suffrage, labor relations, and immigration by drawing on her daily experiences. The appendix includes a weekly schedule of educational, recreational, and social events at Hull-House. Also reprinted is one of Addams's rare satirical articles, "If Men Were Seeking the Franchise" (*Ladies' Home Journal* 1913), in which she speculates on a world in which women, but not men, could vote.

⌁ William Cronon, *Nature's Metropolis: Chicago and the Great West* (Norton, 1992)

This award-winning book has been praised as groundbreaking, intoxicating, and fascinating by some of the nation's most prominent historians. Cronon illustrates the mutual dependence of ecology and economics by identifying Chicago as the nexus of commodity flows and bankruptcy patterns. *Nature's Metropolis* traces the path between the urban market and the natural systems that supply it. Waterways and railroads played a central role in Chicago. Grain was shipped from the western states, or hauled to the city by train, and stored in massive elevator warehouses before being graded for market. The Board of Trade then regulated how it was bought and sold. (Cronon's explanation of the futures markets in wheat and corn clarifies an abstract concept for even those most challenged by economics.) Similar stories of the route from production to commodification are told for lumber and meat. In short, Chicago was essential to the making of the Midwest. Historians, railroad buffs, economists, and environmentalists all have something to learn from this book.

⊷ Maureen A. Flanagan, *Seeing with Their Hearts: Chicago Women and the Vision of the Good City, 1871–1933* (Princeton University Press, 2002)

Was Chicago destined to become Carl Sandburg's "City of Big Shoulders," or might it have developed "from the hearts of women," as an enterprise for human betterment? Men wanted a profitable city while women lobbied endlessly for a livable city during the years between the Great Fire and the Depression. After the fire, the men's Relief and Aid Society gave priority to restoring the lost property of department stores, factories, and banks. Angry women abandoned the men's organization and formed their own society to dispense money directly to residents who had been displaced by the fire. Herein lay the seeds for men's and women's alternate visions of the city. Men won, but not without a fight. Flanagan documents the battle scars incurred by activist women in the long-running conflict over whose vision would prevail. She celebrates their struggles, rather than their losses, during this turning point in Chicago's history.

⊷ Erik Larson, *Devil in the White City: Murder, Magic, and Madness at the Fair That Changed America* (Vintage, 2004)

Larson's best-selling book falls into the genre of "historical novel." Based in fact and embellished with speculation about what people might have said or done, the book is a much better read than most historical monographs. The devil in the story is the serial killer Dr. Henry H. Holmes. Dr. Holmes arrived in Chicago as noted architect Daniel Burnham was constructing the World's Fair, a.k.a. the White City. While Burnham was enhancing his, and the city's, status through the fair, Holmes was using it to lure young women to their deaths. It was easy to do, since so many farm girls sought work at the fair and arrived with little knowledge of the city and even less supervision of their actions. The story documents the parallel pursuits of Burnham and Holmes that would establish such different reputations for each. There is enough accurate information here to satisfy historians, and enough grisly detail to delight murder mystery fans.

⊷ Carl Smith, *Urban Disorder and the Shape of Belief: The Great Chicago Fire, the Haymarket Bomb, and the Model Town of Pullman* (1995; University of Chicago Press, 2007)

The catastrophes that struck Chicago in the latter half of the nineteenth century influenced Americans' perceptions of *all* cities, according to Carl Smith. The Great Fire, the Haymarket anarchists, and the Pullman labor strike became symbols of the disorder that seemed inherent in urban life. These events took on imaginative dimensions shaped by lurid newspaper reports and melodramatic magazine illustrations. The book explores how urban residents responded to disasters that threatened social order and authority. The loss of life and property seem minor, now, compared with contemporary disasters, yet the search for scapegoats, the political turmoil, and the fearmongering that followed these crises are enduring themes recognizable today. Smith's account clarifies why Chicago's businessmen, especially George Pullman, were so anxious to stage the World's Fair. The White City held out the promise of a better century.

DAPHNE SPAIN is James M. Page Professor and Chair of the Department of Urban and Environmental Planning in the School of Architecture. Her scholarship combines a demographer's perspective on gender with a planner's analysis of spatial issues. Spain's most recent book, *How Women Saved the City* (University of Minnesota Press, 2001), explores the importance of redemptive places built by women volunteers at the turn of the twentieth century. Chicago is one of the featured cities.

DELL UPTON

Urban Plans and Urban Realities: Understanding Cities

If cities have attracted little attention in recent decades, Hurricane Katrina changed that for many of us. The appalling destruction of New Orleans, the city's desperate struggle to recover, and the grand, often contradictory plans for reconstruction raise a host of questions about cities generally. What is the relationship between a city's physical form and its social, cultural, economic, or political life? Why do some cities grow and others decline? To what extent is it possible to "plan" a city, that is, to determine its shape or function in advance? Why are cities so fragile? Can a city be successfully reshaped in the wake of human-made or natural disasters?

As an architectural and urban historian, I want to understand the physical qualities of cities, and I find considering these kinds of questions, which I share with geographers, historians, and even archaeologists, to be helpful ways to do so. This has not always been the case in my discipline. In the past, most of my colleagues would have been more interested in the aesthetic qualities of formal urban plans, such as those devised for Washington, D.C., in the 1790s or for Reston, Virginia, in the 1960s, while giving little attention to the relationship between these plans and the cities that they produced. Indeed, some of the most famous and closely studied urban plans, such as Christopher Wren's seventeenth-century scheme for London or Burnham and Bennett's early twentieth-century plan for Chicago, were never built.

While contemporary scholars are still interested in urban design, we are more likely to understand aesthetic planning as only one, and not necessarily the most important, of the factors that shape living cities such as New Orleans, Paris, or Shanghai. We see cities as artifacts, useful and sometimes beautiful objects imagined and made by human beings, like buildings or chairs. However, unlike most buildings or chairs, which tend to be fashioned fairly quickly by one or a few hands and minds, cities tend to be made over long periods of time by many people with varying, sometimes conflicting, ideas about the proper ways to live, the most advantageous ways to make a living, or the precepts of experts, rulers, or deities. Consequently, we understand that the urban artifact is a product of extraordinarily complex intersections of topography, economy, society, and ideas.

The peculiar balance of these and other factors gives each city its unique character, but this also means that there are some patterns shared by large numbers of cities. These range from choice of location—many large cities are sited at points of transition from one mode of transportation to another, for example—to culturally determined habits of spatial organization. Are places of work close to or separated from residences? Are residential districts sorted by ethnicity, class, or other indicators of social standing? Are the largest houses in the center of the city or at its edge? These patterns supplement and sometimes override formal plans, so that a preplanned city such as eighteenth-century Philadelphia and a city without a preset plan, such as eighteenth-century Boston, might resemble one another very closely. The goal of contemporary urban studies, then, is to understand the relationship between intangible structures and practices and the physical character of cities.

Earlier in my career much of my work was devoted to the careful physical examination of individual buildings, as a way to understand the histories of their construction, the ways they were used, and the alterations they might have undergone over the years. My mentor, James Deetz, called this process "above-ground archaeology." No digging was required (except perhaps through layers of grime), but the process of assessing physical evidence and reasoning about its significance was the same one archaeologists use. I have found that a city-artifact can be studied in much the same way. Although a complete analysis requires consideration of the intangible factors mentioned above, an observer who knows something about typical urban physical patterns and has the ability to judge the relative age of individual buildings can develop a serviceable understanding of the history of a city from a map and a walk. Experience will teach a careful observer where she can probably find the central business district, the railroad station (if there still is one), or the fanciest or poorest residential neighborhoods even in an unfamiliar city.

The books that I have chosen range from overviews of world urban history to case studies of individual cities, and an introduction to informed looking by the reader. They differ in their methods and in their emphases, but they share the ability to look at urban artifacts in penetrating ways that show even the most familiar cities in a new light.

⊷ Spiro Kostof, *The City Shaped: Urban Patterns and Meanings through History* (1991; Thames and Hudson, 1999)

⊷ *The City Assembled: The Elements of Urban Form through History* (1992; Thames and Hudson, 2005)

> In these elegantly written and beautifully illustrated volumes, Kostof, one of our great architectural and urban historians, inspects the city-builders' toolbox and demonstrates the varied ways that it has been used during thousands of years of human history. Kostof emphasizes aesthetic ideas and formal elements, but is also sensitive to their social and cultural contexts.

⊷ Mark Girouard, *Cities and People: A Social and Architectural History* (Yale University Press, 1987)

> Girouard is an architectural journalist who followed up a brilliant analysis of the social life of English country houses with a study of world cities in the centuries since the Western Middle Ages. He has a

knack for spotting the telling detail on a street corner or in an urban view that reveals the mundane realities that shaped cities now often treated as charming tourist destinations.

ↄ Peirce F. Lewis, *New Orleans: The Making of an Urban Landscape,* 2nd ed. (Center for American Places and University of Virginia Press, 2003)

This is a classic of urban geography. Lewis shows us the ways that New Orleans's peculiar topography, French and American planning customs, and America's racial history combined to create a beloved city, but one in constant danger. The final chapters, on the catastrophe that the right (or wrong) hurricane could create, is remarkably prescient.

ↄ David Harvey, *Paris, Capital of Modernity* (Routledge, 2005)

Where Lewis stresses topography, David Harvey emphasizes social history and political economy in his exploration of nineteenth-century Paris. Harvey is especially adept at showing us how both the abstract forces of politics and the economy shaped Parisian life and the meanings that the city's residents attached to their city.

ↄ Grady Clay, *Close-Up: How to Read the American City* (1973; University of Chicago Press, 1980)

Finally, Grady Clay's short, sprightly handbook shows how such prosaic elements as highway strips, discontinuous street grids, and the clustering of businesses offer clues to the history of your own city or town.

DELL UPTON was, until 2007, Eleanor Shea Professor of Art History and Chair of the Department of Architectural History. He teaches a lecture course called "Cities in History." Upton is the author of *Architecture in the United States* in the Oxford History of Art series and of *Another City: Urban Life and Urban Spaces in the Early American Republic* (Yale University Press, 2008).

KRISHAN KUMAR

Nations and Nationalism

Most nineteenth-century thinkers assumed that nationalism was a powerful but passing phenomenon. It was, they thought, a necessary but transitional phase on the way to a cosmopolitan world—whether one made by world socialism or the benign operation of international free trade. But nationalism has surprised all of them. At the beginning of the twenty-first century, it remains, it seems, as powerful as ever before and even seems to have intensified in strength.

The revival of nationalism in the last third of the twentieth century is largely responsible for the remarkable renaissance of studies in nationalism, for a time almost abandoned to specialists in "Third World" politics and development. Starting with a sparkling account by the sociologist and philosopher Ernest Gellner, the field very soon attracted an array of distinguished talents from a wide range of disciplines. There was Benedict Anderson, a specialist in Southeast Asia, who used his expertise to produce an unusual and highly original study of how and why nationalism arose. To Gellner's sociological explanation he added a strongly cultural component, pointing out that a modern nation is and must be a largely imagined entity since most members never encounter each other while nevertheless believing and feeling that they belong to the same political community.

Both Gellner and Anderson argue that nationalism is essentially a modern phenomenon associated particularly with the late eighteenth-century "era of revolutions." It was then, they say, that the nation was equated with "the people" and the demand was raised that rulers and ruled should share the same common culture. The nationalist formula is "one state, one (and only one) nation," and even though few states realize this ideal in practice, it is generally held to be the basis of legitimacy in most modern states. Where states are based on many nations, as in the old European empires or the more modern Soviet empire, the nationalist principle seems to point to their more or less inevitable dissolution, as indeed seems to have been the case. Additionally, argued Gellner, no modern industrial economy, with its complex division of labor, could function at all effectively unless the vast majority of its members shared the same culture so that they were, in principle, virtually interchangeable with each other.

Gellner's and Anderson's accounts were powerfully augmented by two further contributions, those by the historians John Breuilly and Eric Hobsbawm. Breuilly showed that the novelty of nations lies in the fact that, unlike ethnic groups, they aim to form their own state. This leads to the political fragmentation of larger political entities, such as the dynastic empires of the Habsburgs or the Romanovs, or the colonial empires of the British and French. Hobsbawm, in a masterly overview of the development of European nationalism, also traced its rise to the era of the French Revolution and the doctrine of popular sovereignty. But he also showed how initially nationalism was not seen as a divisive and competitive principle, but one which, once the nations of the world had found their "natural" political forms, would lead to a worldwide community of the "brotherhood of nations." Only in the later nineteenth century did this liberal belief give way to the realization that nationalism might take aggressive and fanatical forms—a development that seemed to reach its conclusion in the genocidal nationalism of German Nazism.

Gellner, Anderson, Breuilly, and Hobsbawm are all thinkers that Anthony Smith describes as "modernists." They believe that nations and nationalism cannot be found—with the odd exception—before the modern era. Smith by contrast wishes to stress the significant premodern elements that are the necessary foundation of modern nationalism. He draws attention to the fact that all nations are founded on "core" ethnic groups—the English, the French, the Germans—with myths and memories that stretch back into the distant past. Without these ethnic resources, which provide the sense of kinship, nations would be empty shells. Thus while nations might be modern creations, and nationalism a modern ideology, there are many examples in earlier times of communities that display some key characteristics of nationhood—the Jews of biblical times, for instance. While nations may not be "primordial" or "perennial" as some theorists claim, neither are they simply modern. Their long-standing existence is one reason why we should not expect them to disappear anytime soon.

↬ Ernest Gellner, *Nations and Nationalism* (1983; Blackwell, 2006)

In this classic, perhaps *the* classic, contribution to the revival of studies in nationalism, Gellner places nationalism squarely in an account of the rise of modern industrial society. He argues that industrial societies require a sense of shared nationhood—understood as a shared common culture—in order to function effectively. This witty and provocative account draws equally on social philosophy and sociology. We may or may not like nationalism, argues Gellner, but so long as we have industrial societies we are likely to have to live with it. For Gellner, multiculturalism, strictly speaking, is impossible in modern societies; all individuals in a given society must share basic elements of the culture—a function usually performed by the educational system.

↬ Benedict Anderson, *Imagined Communities: Reflections on the Origin and Spread of Nationalism,* rev. ed. (Verso, 2006)

In one of the most influential of recent studies, Anderson emphasizes the cultural dimension of nationalism. Nationalism is associated with the rise of vernacular languages, and with the "imagined community" created by "print capitalism"—the spread, through such agencies as newspapers and novels, of a sense of belonging to a community of members most of whom will never meet face to face. A particularly unusual and attractive feature of this book is the account of "New World"—North and South American—nationalism, and of the way non-European societies transform the basic model of nationalism that they take over from the West. The second edition introduces some interesting new material on the role of maps, museums, and censuses in the formation of nationalist ideologies. It also shows Anderson warming toward nationalism—especially in his specialist area of Southeast Asia (Anderson was an advisor to the East Timor nationalists).

↩ Eric Hobsbawm, *Nations and Nationalism since 1780: Programme, Myth, Reality,* 2nd ed. (Cambridge University Press, 1992)

This is a penetrating account by a leading historian of the origins and spread of nationalism in Europe and the non-European world. Hobsbawm is particularly strong on nationalist ideas and on the shifting meanings of nationalism over the past two centuries. He emphasizes the extent to which most nations invent their past and their supposedly age-old national traditions. As a historian influenced by Marxism, Hobsbawm is skeptical of the claims made by nationalists but appreciates their appeal to their populations and accepts the liberating potential of nationalism in certain conditions (e.g., in the colonial empires). He—unlike most of the authors in this list—nevertheless feels that the globalizing forces of today have made nationalism antiquated, and what we see in contemporary nationalism is very different—more shadow than substance—from the classic forms of the nineteenth and first half of the twentieth centuries.

↩ Anthony D. Smith, *The Ethnic Origins of Nations* (Blackwell, 1988)

This is the principle contribution by one of the most prolific and influential theorists of nationalism. Against those who argue that nations are recent inventions, Smith stresses the extent to which nations depend upon long-lived ethnic communities, with their deeply felt myths and traditions, for their formation. Nations cannot just be "invented"; they depend for their substance on preexisting resources. Smith shows, with a wealth of examples from past and present societies, how ethnicity is formed, and how powerful a force it is in solidifying groups. While not wishing to align himself with those who believe that nations are "natural," quasi-biological, entities, Smith argues vigorously against the modernists, such as Gellner, who assert that nations can be more or less invented by ingenious scholars and statesmen when the need and opportunity arise.

↤ John Breuilly, *Nationalism and the State,* 2nd ed. (University of Chicago Press, 1994)

> Breuilly offers a pioneering study, the most wide-ranging and compelling account of nationalism as a political phenomenon and of its power in modern times. Breuilly stresses the difference between ethnicity and nationalism, and the connection between nationalism and distinctively modern ideas of democracy and popular sovereignty. Nationalism for Breuilly is primarily an oppositional movement, one that mobilizes excluded or aspiring groups, or advances the interests of particular elites in the competition for power. This study is particularly strong on nationalism in Africa, Asia, and the Middle East. Though a historian, Breuilly draws liberally and effectively on work in social and political theory. In the radically revised second edition, Breuilly discusses the work of theorists such as Gellner and Anderson, and answers the criticism that he does not sufficiently allow for the power of nationalist ideologies. He also deals with nationalism in postcommunist central and eastern Europe.

KRISHAN KUMAR is William R. Kenan, Jr., Professor of Sociology. He was previously Professor of Social and Political Thought at the University of Kent at Canterbury, England. Among his publications are *Utopia and Anti-Utopia in Modern Times* (Blackwell, 1987), *From Post-Industrial to Post-Modern Society,* 2nd ed. (Blackwell, 2005), *1989: Revolutionary Ideas and Ideals* (University of Minnesota Press, 2001), and *The Making of English National Identity* (Cambridge University Press, 2003). He is currently working on projects on nations and empires, and the types of identities produced in these two entities.

2

Mathematics

Science

Technology

DENNIS PROFFITT

Light and Life: The Evolution of Visual Perception

"Light, Life, and Vision" was the title of a delightful undergraduate seminar that I cotaught recently with Lars Strother. The books listed below were part of the course's reading list. As its title suggests, the seminar related visual perception both to its informational source in light, and to its role in supporting organisms' ways of life.

Visual perception is a biological adaptation that relates the ways of life of organisms to those pragmatically important aspects of the environment that can be extracted from optical information. Frogs, for example, are hunters; they detect moving insects with vision and attempt to catch them with their tongues. If an insect does not move, a frog will not see it. This system works just fine for frogs. A more elaborate visual system would require more neural machinery, which in turn would require more food to sustain it. The extra brain matter is not worth the price. This example highlights a central theme of the course. Visual systems are shaped by the pragmatic circumstances of their use, and in this regard, vision is no better than it needs to be. This is true not only for frogs, but also for people. There is far more information in light than frogs or we imagine.

The history of light begins with the Big Bang, which occurred about 10 to 20 billion years ago. After about 300,000 years, the initial plasma cooled enough for light to be freed. This light contained not only *energy* but also *information.* Today, this light fills the universe as a cosmic background radiation. To look more closely at this radiation, scientists have built optical devices, which have been sent into space or taken to high mountaintops. These specialized telescopes have allowed scientists to view the cosmic background radiation with sufficient resolution to see some of the structure that was inherent in the universe 300,000 years after its inception. The optical devices that were built mimic in many respects the design of the compound eye, which was the first sort of eye to emerge via biological evolution. This parallel in artificial and evolved optical design is, to me, a wonderful occurrence.

Our planet Earth was born about 4.6 billion years ago, and roughly 1 billion years later, life emerged. The initial life forms were bacteria that used light for energy and archaea that took their energy from volcanic eruptions deep in the ocean's floor. Eventually, strains of bacteria, which used chlorophyll to extract energy from light, came to be ingested by other bacteria; however, the ingested bacteria remained alive and intact. The resulting union gave birth to the complex cells that exist today in plants. In addition to taking energy from light, plants also make use of some of the information inherent in ambient illumination. Some plants will grow or turn their leaves toward light, and thereby act as if they "know" from where light is coming. This sensitivity to where light is located is the key to obtaining the information that light carries. The next step in harvesting light's information came with the evolution of eyes.

The basic problem shaping the anatomy for all animal eyes is the need to detect "how much light is located where." Light surrounds every point of view, with locations differing in intensity and wavelength. The problem for the animal eye and brain is to detect some of these differences and interpret what they imply about the environment. Eyes first appeared at the advent of the Cambrian period, which occurred between 540 and 530 million years ago and marked an explosion in biological diversity and complexity. Eyes profoundly changed the ecological niches of organisms existing at that time and thereafter. Predation suddenly became a much more sophisticated affair as predators and prey came under pressure to detect each other from afar. Eyes evolved independently over and over again, taking two basic forms. Compound eyes evolved first in arthropods, and later, the simple chambered eye came onto the scene. We possess eyes of the latter sort, as do spiders, scallops, and squid.

It is not enough to have eyes; the pattern of light intensities and wavelengths that they detect must be interpreted. This requires neural machinery and its associated costs. Brains are one of the most expensive organs in the body, consuming disproportionate amounts of energy. Brains derive their value through their effective use of sensory information in organizing and guiding behaviors. Visual systems—eyes and brains—evolved to relate light to life!

In the "Light, Life, and Vision" seminar, the following books were read in the order in which they are here presented.

◆ Michael Gross, *Light and Life* (Oxford University Press, 2002)

This highly accessible book addresses many of the topics covered in the "Light, Life, and Vision" seminar. It begins with the Big Bang, describes how cyanobacteria changed the world, and explores how light is used as energy and information by the diverse life forms that inhabit our planet. One of the best chapters is on bioluminescence, "Creatures That Glow in the Dark." The production of light by living things is amazingly pervasive, especially in organisms living in the deep oceans where little or no sunlight can penetrate. One way to make a bioluminescent "flashlight" is to capture luminescent bacteria and to provide them with shelter, food, and oxygen. A number of different species of fish do just this, holding the luminescent bacteria within pouches that can be shuttered when predators are present.

◆ Lynn Margulis, *Symbiotic Planet: A New Look at Evolution* (Basic, 2000)

This little book changed the way that I look at life—biological life in general as well as my own. More than anyone else, Margulis is responsible for the theory that the complex cells of plants and animals arose through symbiosis. Rather than simply evolving independently through mutation and natural selection, bacteria interpenetrated each other and evolved into the organelles of complex cells. The mitochondria in plants and animals, and the chloroplasts in plants, are the remains of what were once independently existing bacteria. Such notions were not taught when I took biology in college, and news of this theoretical development in biology passed me by until I began to prepare for the seminar. In addition to laying out the argument for symbiosis at scales ranging from cellular structure to the oxygen levels of our atmosphere, Margulis purposefully champions a women's perspective on science that I found challenging and engaging. This is a wonderful book.

◆ Russell G. Foster and Leon Kreitzman, *Rhythms of Life: The Biological Clocks That Control the Daily Lives of Every Living Thing* (Yale University Press, 2005)

As the subtitle of this book makes clear, every living thing has a biological clock. These clocks are set by the day-night cycle of our solar day, but they are also capable of running on their own. Why do they exist? They make sure that we do not try to do everything at once. Our daily rhythms proscribe the optimal times to sleep, wake, eat, poop, engage in strenuous activity, and think deep thoughts. Our clocks are synchronized to the day-night cycle by specialized light-sensitive cells in our eyes that project to a master clock in our brains. As a serious science book that does not shy away from explanations framed within molecular biology, the book succeeds in providing detail and depth without losing the interest of the nonspecialist reader. The book includes interesting discussions of seasonal affective disorders, what time of day is best to take medicines, and how to cope with jet lag.

↪ Michael F. Land and Dan-Eric Nilsson, *Animal Eyes* (Oxford University Press, 2002)

Since Darwin, people have wondered how the eye could have evolved. Of what use would a half-formed eye be? And yet, if we look at the variety of eyes that currently exist, then we can see instances of the evolutionary stages through which sophisticated eyes must have passed. Did you know that clams have eyes? They do. They consist of small concavities around the shell's mantel. These concavities possess photoreceptors that detect when a shadow passes over the clam. In response to this decrease in light, the clam will close its shell. *Animal Eyes* beautifully shows how each animal's eye is optimally structured to support its ways of life. For example, predatory birds have two areas of sharply detailed vision, one to guide navigation and one to look for prey on the ground. Nocturnal animals, like opossums, have mirrors on the backs of their eyes to give their photoreceptors a second chance to catch scarce light.

↪ Melvyn A. Goodale and A. David Milner, *Sight Unseen: An Exploration of Conscious and Unconscious Vision* (Oxford University Press, 2005)

Vision uses the information available in light for different purposes. These different functions are sometimes localized in different areas of our brains. Studying patients with brain damage, Goodale and Milner have made astonishing discoveries. The book describes one woman who cannot visually recognize anything; her visual world consists of amorphous blobs. Yet, this woman has little trouble walking about and can pick up objects without difficulty. Her conscious visual experience is impaired, but her visual guidance of actions is intact. Other patients exist who have the opposite set of symptoms; they can visually identify objects but have considerable trouble picking them up. *Sight Unseen* is a short, beautifully written book. It describes how such clinical case studies—combined with neuro-imaging and animal research—support a theory of two streams of processing in the human brain. The book also provides personal backgrounds for the patients, making their stories real and compelling.

DENNIS PROFFITT is Commonwealth Professor of Psychology and the Founding Director of the Cognitive Science Degree Program. He has authored over one hundred research publications, mostly in the area of visual perception. Proffitt was awarded the University of Virginia Outstanding Teaching Award, 1996–97, and the Cavalier Distinguished Teaching Professorship, 1999–2002. He believes that we live in a world of wonders and enjoys sharing with students the joys of discovery.

EDMUND RUSSELL

Everyday Evolution

Many of us think of evolution as something that happened eons ago, but evolution continues today all around us. We tend to think of evolution as speciation, which it is. But evolution also encompasses smaller changes. In some cases those small changes add up over time to create separate species. But most evolutionary change takes place short of speciation and consists of minor adaptations to local conditions. Though we think of evolution as something nature accomplished, people also shape the evolution of other species. Sometimes we do so intentionally, as when we breed plants and animals. In other cases, we do so by accident.

Here's one example of the latter that costs Americans $30 billion per year in extra medical expenses. How? Three processes play roles.

1. Variation. Americans take billions of dollars worth of antibiotics each year to kill pathogenic bacteria. For the most part, those drugs work. But individual bacteria, like individual people, are not identical. By chance, a small number happen to carry genes that allow them to "resist" an antibiotic—that is, to survive treatment.

2. Selection. In environments (human bodies) flooded with an antibiotic, resistant bacteria survive to reproduce while their susceptible neighbors die off.

3. Inheritance. Resistant bacteria pass along genes for resistance to their descendents. In each generation exposed to the antibiotic, the proportion of resistant individuals rises until the antibiotic "loses" its potency and no longer cures a disease. In fact, the antibiotic has not changed (nor has the patient); the target pathogen has.

Doctors faced with failing antibiotics turn to second-choice drugs, which often cost more than the first. Adding up the difference between the cost of the first- and second- (and third-, and fourth-) choice drugs for patients across the country comes to $30 billion.

Money is bad enough, but how about lives? In 1995, about 65,000 Americans died from infections acquired in hospitals. Those unlucky patients entered the hospital for one problem and picked up a fatal infection for another. A large percentage of those deaths resulted from resistant pathogens. Ironically, hospitals harbor some of the least treatable pathogens because the environment—hundreds of sick patients on antibiotics in close quarters—is tailor-made to foster resistance. Worse, having lots of patients taking a variety of antibiotics encourages single strains of pathogens to resist multiple drugs, which is why hospital-acquired infections can be fatal even when treated.

Similar problems occur in farm fields. The combination of variation, selection, and inheritance creates insects, fungi, and weeds that resist pesticides. By 1986, 450 species of insects and mites, 100 species of plant pathogens, and 48 species of weeds resisted one or more pesticides. Applying extra pesticide to affected crops cost farmers—thus consumers—$1.6 billion per year.

The small changes people wring out of other species are not all bad. For the past 10,000 years, humans have been changing plants and animals in ways that have enabled us to feed many more people than we could if we were hunter-gatherers. The ancestral species of domestic crops often are little to look at and even less to taste. By some combination of accident and intention, we have reshaped them to produce more, better-tasting food. The result has been the ability for a few members of society to raise food for many more, freeing the latter to do things like create writing and machinery, run governments, and supply armies. In other words, our society would be impossible without evolutionary changes humans have wrought in other species.

The books in this list describe how and why humans shape the evolution of other species. Together, these books take evolution out of the dusty museum cabinets of dinosaur bones and into our daily lives. They help us predict evolution in our kitchens (where antibacterial soap selects for resistant bacteria) to hospitals to biotechnology labs. The central ideas about evolution are not hard to grasp, but the implications are staggering for our economy and health.

✧ Charles Darwin, *On the Origin of Species by Means of Natural Selection* (1859)

> The inclusion of this book in my list might sound surprising, since we associate Darwin with figuring out how species evolved *in the wild* after voyaging to the Galapagos on the *Beagle*. So he did. But once you read the first chapter, you will be in on one of the great secrets of the history of science: Darwin's journeys helped focus his interest on evolution as a problem, but he figured out how evolution worked by observing how people changed domestic plants and animals in the barnyards of England. (In fact, he collected his evidence for the arguments in *Origin* in a two-volume work titled *Variation in Animals and Plants under Domestication*.) Darwin used the term "natural selection" because breeders of his day called what they did "selection." Don't be intimidated—the book is surprisingly readable.

✧ Jared Diamond, *Guns, Germs, and Steel: The Fates of Human Societies* (Norton, 1999)

> Although Diamond does not hit the reader over the head with the term "evolution," that is what this book is about. Diamond argues that the domestication of plants and animals was the seminal event in human history, and that the process took place because humans unconsciously selected for domestic traits in wild species. Eventually they started breeding with intent. The basic differences among societies, Diamond argues, arose because some had more domesticable species than others. That is, some were more amenable to evolution under human hands than others, and that made all the difference in human history.

✧ Stephen Palumbi, *The Evolution Explosion: How Humans Drive Rapid Evolutionary Change* (Norton, 2002)

> Where Diamond focuses on evolution in the distant past, Palumbi brings the topic right up to date. He stresses that humans have gotten good at changing species very fast, and that these changes will not necessarily serve us in good stead. Genetic engineering, a brute force form of shaping evolution, has now enabled us to move genes across types of organisms that would have been unbridgeable with traditional breeding. That ability is not necessarily bad, but it does mean we are bringing about rapid change with little understanding of the long-term consequences.

↬ Michael Pollan, *The Botany of Desire: A Plant's-Eye View of the World* (Random House, 2002)

In this elegant work, Pollan follows several familiar species of plants, such as potatoes, apples, and marijuana, as they change in response to human desires. He also poses a challenging idea. What makes us so sure we are the ones in control? What if potatoes, apples, and marijuana domesticated us? Pollan came to this idea while watching a bee gathering nectar in his garden. The bee, Pollan assumed, "thought" the flowers were there to serve the bee. But could not the flowers just as logically "think" that the bee was there to serve them? For that matter, could not garden plants "think" that Pollan was there to serve them by planting, watering, fertilizing, and otherwise making life wonderful?

↬ Stephen Budiansky, *The Covenant of the Wild: Why Animals Chose Domestication* (Yale University Press, 1999)

Budiansky makes an argument similar to Pollan's, but in his case about animals. Rather than looking at domestic animals as unfortunates under the thumb of human demigods, might they not have "convinced" us to pour enormous effort into creating good lives for them? That argument might seem far-fetched, but remember it next time you head out the door to earn money to pay for food for the dog that lies home all day in front of the fire.

EDMUND RUSSELL is an Associate Professor with joint appointments in the Department of Science, Technology, and Society and the Department of History. His first book, *War and Nature: Fighting Humans and Insects with Chemicals from World War I to "Silent Spring"* (Cambridge University Press, 2001), won the Edelstein Prize of the Society for the History of Technology. He is now researching the impact of humans on the evolution of other species.

REGINALD H. GARRETT

An Appreciation of Reality: Society and Science

It is folly that, in the twenty-first century, in our highly technological society so reliant on the biology of DNA, the chemistry of petroleum, and the physics of electronic devices, a mind-set has emerged that allows opinion to subvert fact. The loudest voices overwhelm the clearest, and the uncritical follow. We watch placidly as unfettered arrogance dismisses the real problem of global climate change or spawns pseudoscientific conjectures about life's origins through intelligent design. Fantasy supersedes reality, not only in the many modes of escapist entertainment, but also in political theater and decision-making processes. Such apathy to reality is a catastrophic attitude that should concern us all.

A *USA Today*/Gallup poll conducted June 1–3, 2007, found that only 18 percent of Americans definitely believe that humans evolved from less complex forms of life via a process extending over billions of years. On the other hand, 39 percent of Americans accept as definitely true the notion that humans were created by God within the past ten thousand years. Such scientific indifference is stunning, given that the science supporting the theory of evolution is far more robust and extensive than our understanding of gravity. We can describe the structure and behavior of genes, the units of evolution, in exquisite detail, but the particle conveying gravity remains to be deduced and verified by experiment. Yet who doubts the existence of gravity?

Perhaps the reluctance of otherwise intelligent people to embrace evolution stems in part from the role played by chance in change, inheritance, and survival. Life is a roll of the dice, and people crave security. In everyday life, gravity is infallible and thus reassuring. Also, while we are easy with the means to keep accounts and track huge numbers of things, such as billions of dollars, who can grasp the immensity of time represented by several billion years? But we need not, for today we can observe and document evolution over far shorter time intervals than the human lifespan. Humans are still evolving, and cultural behavior can drive the evolution of human traits through selection for particular genetic variants. For example, lactose tolerance among northern Europeans with a cultural history of dairy consumption is a trait quite restricted to few population groups; the default human condition is lactose intolerance.

Unfortunately, the notion that culture can influence natural selection, and thus, evolution, has not penetrated far into sociological thought. In a nation boasting the world's finest institutions of higher learning, the failure to accept evolution is a serious educational liability and an intellectual shortcoming. Evolution is a reality, and as such it is a cornerstone of biology. As sentient beings, we should appreciate our nature and our origins; we are all by our essence biologists. Thus, curiosity must compel us, scientists and nonscientists alike, toward some basic understanding of our biology.

Many readable texts establish evolution as sound science, beginning with Charles Darwin's *The Origin of Species* in 1859 and running through *Before the Dawn: Recovering the Lost History of Our Ancestors*, Nicholas Wade's recently published, highly acclaimed chronicle of human evolution. The books recommended here move beyond evolution per se and are meant to bring readers to the broad interface between biology and contemporary society. The selections are eclectic, collectively musing on knowledge, nature, and the nature of man. They cohere through a common thread of natural history, a mostly descriptive genre of science distinct from analytic studies of nature—the mode of inquiry dominant today. Each makes its own nexus with science—historical, gastronomical, biographical, philosophical, or theological. And each informs society about science through insights into modern biology, a science exhilarating in the scope of its new discoveries about age-old questions.

✎ Jared Diamond, *Guns, Germs, and Steel: The Fates of Human Societies* (Norton, 1999)

Diamond, Professor of Geography at the University of California, Los Angeles, addresses in this Pulitzer Prize–winning volume the conspicuous differences in history between the peoples of the several continents. To encapsulate the issue, one could ask, and he does: "Why didn't the Incas cross the Atlantic and conquer Spain?" Diamond finds the answer to such questions in an unexpected place—the biology of indigenous plants and animals of Eurasia versus Africa or the Americas. Plant and animal domestication proceeded more favorably in the Fertile Crescent and spread westward through Europe, delivering food surpluses that in turn permitted social hierarchies and technological achievement to flourish. Thus, vagaries in the geographical distribution of amenable organisms determined the fate of peoples, not any inferred intellectual or physiological advantages that one group might have had over the others. Diamond's book is a needed admonition against hubris.

✎ Michael Pollan, *The Omnivore's Dilemma: A Natural History of Four Meals* (Penguin, 2007)

"What's for dinner?" This quotidian conundrum sends us to the supermarket to survey the possibilities, each presented in a tasteful manner revealing little of its history. Seldom does our curiosity extend to the origins of the food we eat or the journey by which it reached our plates. Pollan, Director of the Knight Program in Science and Environmental Journalism at the University of California, Berkeley, addresses this incongruity, peeling back the façade of the food industry to expose the flaws of corn-based industrial agriculture and the squalor of the confined animal-feeding operations it fuels. His revelations not only kill the appetite, they appall sensibilities. Fortunately, after defining the problem, Pollan introduces us to one healthful, environmentally sound solution, the Polyface Farm operation and meat-producing system of Joel Salatin, based on grass-fed animals. The point here is that, as always, it is better to know and decide, than to default to what's at hand—food for thought.

↪ Matt Ridley, *Francis Crick, Discoverer of the Genetic Code* (HarperCollins, 2006)

The dispassionate objectivity sought by science can mask the fundamentally human nature of those who pursue it. Personality and individual peculiarities riddle the endeavor. Ridley shows this human side of science by illustrating how historical accidents, proclivities, and preconceptions influence the emergence of ideas. Crick (1916–2004), along with his brash and brilliant young partner James Watson, elucidated the double helical structure of DNA, a signal achievement for which they shared a Nobel Prize. Of greater heuristic consequence is the fact that Crick, more than any other scientist, was the founder of molecular biology. Crick's prescient insights pioneered our understanding of the mechanisms by which biological information encoded in DNA is expressed through the synthesis of proteins. Molecular biology transformed the gene from a conceptual construct into a physical reality. Ridley's book follows Crick from the "middle-class mediocrity" of his early years through his emergence as the epitome of the very British manner of discovery—scientific revelation through relentless conversation with informed colleagues. Ridley brings the science of Crick's years within grasp of the lay reader's acumen and renders a fair portrait of a complex, thoroughly human genius. At the end, you realize that Crick resides in the pantheon with Galileo, Newton, Darwin, and Einstein.

↪ Edward O. Wilson, *Consilience: The Unity of Knowledge* (Vintage, 1999)

Wilson is Pellegrino University Professor Emeritus and Honorary Curator in Entomology at Harvard University, winner of the National Medal of Science, and twice winner of the Pulitzer Prize in general nonfiction. In *Consilience* he writes, "When we have unified enough certain knowledge, we will understand who we are and why we are here." His quest, to fuse the sciences and the humanities into a single coherent philosophy, is about as grand an intellectual endeavor as could be imagined. Wilson strives here to marry the sciences and the arts through the vows of logical induction, a daunting task since each is skeptical of the other's worldview. With his impeccable scientific credentials, Wilson might seem a biased broker. However, Wilson writes exemplary prose and gracefully displays deep literary scholarship. He foresees that, when consilience has been achieved and all knowledge is unified, the hard edges of the physical sciences will have melded with the soft convolutions of the creative arts. It is a hopeful premise.

↪ Richard Dawkins, *The God Delusion* (Mariner, 2008)

Dawkins is the Charles Simonyi Professor of the Public Understanding of Science at Oxford University. Setting aside the irrational, often virulent invective of the fanatics, one finds a rather calm accommodation between science and religion. Many people have a place for both. Stephen Jay Gould, a prominent essayist and evolutionary biologist, often found himself the spokesperson for science in the evolution–creation science debates. He coined the term "nonoverlapping magisteria" to paraphrase the principle that religion and science are not in conflict because their teachings occupy distinctly different realms of conviction—faith and reason.

The increasingly religious basis for violence has no doubt served as a significant prompt for thoughtful atheists to challenge the sensibility of religion; *The God Delusion* is one of those books. Two salient arguments come forth. First, religion does not have a monopoly on morality. Rational bases exist for morality as an evolutionary advantage, independently of religious belief. Second, and perhaps more importantly, serious thinkers, such as Dawkins, establish that science can justifiably ask questions about the human predisposition toward religion and whether or not it conveyed benefits leading to evolutionary success. This being so, Gould was wrong. The magisteria indeed overlap, and scientific inquiry into the role of religion in the natural history of humans is appropriate.

REGINALD H. GARRETT is Professor of Biology and has taught biochemistry at the University of Virginia since 1968. He is coauthor of a leading textbook in biochemistry. His research interests address the biochemistry of nitrogen metabolism and systems approaches to the metabolic basis of nutrition-related diseases. He was a Fulbright Senior Lecturer in Austria, Thomas Jefferson Fellow at the University of Cambridge, and Professeur Invité, Université de Toulouse III, France.

HERMAN H. SHUGART

Starship Earth User's Manual 2.0: Revising the Balance of Nature

The phrase "balance of nature" is lettered on interpretive signs along park trails, celebrated in prose and poetry about nature, and printed in the picture captions of beautiful coffee-table books. It also appears in educational books, for example, *The Hutchinson Encyclopedia 2002*, which serves the United Kingdom's National Curriculum, the body of knowledge mandated by the Education Reform Act of 1988 for children five to fifteen years of age. It defines "balance of nature" as follows: "In ecology, the idea that there is an inherent equilibrium in most ecosystems, with plants and animals interacting so as to produce a stable, continuing system of life on Earth. The activities of human beings can, and frequently do, disrupt the balance of nature." An American text, *The New Dictionary of Cultural Literacy*, 3rd ed., edited by E. D. Hirsch Jr., J. F. Kett, and J. Trefil, and published at the same time with a similar objective of providing young people with what they need to know, defines and then dismisses "balance of nature" in this way: "A concept in ecology that describes natural systems as being in a state of equilibrium, in which disturbing one element disturbs the entire system. The inference is usually drawn that the natural state of any system is the preferred state and that it is best to leave it undisturbed. Modern ecologists no longer believe that a balance of nature exists." So which is it? Is the balance of nature something that people are prone to mess up (for a British fifteen-year-old) or a complicated concept describing something nonexistent (for an American teen)?

It is clear why educators would want young people to understand the balance-of-nature concept, even if they are ambivalent as to what it means. It is part of the rationale for designating parks and nature preserves; for protecting vanishing species; for managing our planet. When one looks from an airplane window, one sees altered landscapes. One samples the atmosphere and documents planet-scale changes arising from industrial technology. One records the species of plants and animals in a region and infers abnormally high rates of extinction from our activities. If human hands are on the tiller of Starship Earth, the Version 1.0 User's Manual is abridged as the balance-of-nature concept. The challenge is to obtain the Version 2.0 Manual—to understand the stewardship of our planet without using the balance of nature as a basis. Ecologists and earth scientists have made remarkable progress in this direction in the past several decades.

The transition from a balance-of-nature, equilibrium-seeking understanding of the working planet to a more dynamic, changing worldview does not imply an abandonment of an environmental ethic. It implies a more informed care of the planet. That landscapes are dynamic does not mean that we do not need parks and reserves to protect an unchanging wilderness. We should have more and larger parks to nurture the components of the ecosystems in the face of change. Knowing that plants and animals naturally go extinct does not mean that we should lose our concern for endangered species. Rather, it means that we should try to remedy a dynamic rate of extinction in a human-managed planet that is thousands of times higher than that before our inheritance of the earth. Aldo Leopold drafted the first lines in the Starship Earth User's Manual Version 2.0 with, "If the biota, in the course of aeons, has built something we like but do not understand, then who but a fool would discard seemingly useless parts? To keep every cog and wheel is the first precaution of intelligent tinkering" (*Round River*, 1993).

The books that follow represent other parts of User's Manual Version 2.0. In the order they are listed, they treat the ethics of understanding and conserving our planet's biota, ecological change through the spread of invasive species (from Europe) over the past millennia, environmental change from interaction between the surface of the planet and the atmosphere under human modification, past outcomes of human societies dealing with environmental change, and our own society in a world of potential global climate change. They deal with the wonderful complexity of the ecosystems of our planet, including considerations for both the aesthetic and the practical reasons for understanding the dynamics of an unbalanced, ever-changing world.

Not included in the list but significant initial background readings on the topic of change in nature are: *The Sea Around Us*, by Rachel Carson (Oxford University Press, 1951), and *A Sand County Almanac with Essays on Conservation from Round River*, by Aldo Leopold (Ballantine Books, 1986). Both are eloquent essays on the connectedness and changedness of the lands and waters of our planet.

↩ E. O. Wilson, *Biophilia* (Harvard University Press, 1986)

Written by a Pulitzer Prize–winning evolutionary biologist, this highly personalized account examines the fundamental appeal of the understanding of living systems. *Biophilia* is rich in insights and narratives about people and places, particularly of the wonderfully complex and diverse wet tropical ecosystems of Surinam, the Amazon, New Guinea, and elsewhere. The nine essays that comprise the text conglomerate a marvelous mélange of images, facts, and ideas. For example, a chapter elucidating the intricately coevolved system of fungus-farming leafcutter ants in Brazil transitions to a chapter on time-scale. Here, Wilson illustrates Einstein's concept of thought-experiments with a historical conversation among America's leading scientists just as Darwin's ideas have reached Harvard in May 1859. Importantly, Wilson engages both the scientific and the aesthetic aspects of the conservation ethic. Conservation of biotic diversity arises as the consequence of the intrinsic appeal of life and things living to our species.

↫ Alfred W. Crosby, *Ecological Imperialism: The Biological Expansion of Europe, 900–1900*, 2nd ed. (Cambridge University Press, 2004)

Europeans have conquered and colonized the modern world, even in the face of seemingly insurmountable odds. The successes of the conquistadors (Cortez against the Aztecs; Pizarro against the Incas) seem unlikely given their numerical disadvantages as conquerors, but the patterns of their domination of a numerically stronger foe are part of a repeating overall pattern. Certainly, the superior weapons were important, but so were allies in the form of European diseases. Novel diseases along with invasive animals and plants, pests, and weeds have attended the spread of Europeans across the planet during the last millennia. Crosby's book illustrates feedback between humans and the environment as they reciprocally alter one another. The continued evolution of weeds and diseases in the face of anthropogenic environmental change is but one of the consequences of human/environment feedback.

↫ William F. Ruddiman, *Plows, Plagues, and Petroleum: How Humans Took Control of Climate* (Princeton University Press, 2007)

This book begins with the premise that humans have altered the earth's environment since about eight thousand years ago, when they discovered and then expanded agriculture. Ruddiman postulates that the long run-up of environmental change over these eight millennia has been less obvious but no less significant than the abrupt alteration of the planet's environment associated with the rise of technology and the Industrial Revolution of the 1800s. From Aesop's fable, the preindustrial change wrought by humans is the "tortoise" to the "hare" of the rapid change in the environment from industrial-human activities. To defend this controversial hypothesis, the author explains the long-term variations in climate and the increasing degree of human control of climate over prehistory and history. The long-term workings of the atmosphere and the possible directions of future changes are presented in a clear narrative voice.

↫ Jared Diamond, *Collapse: How Societies Choose to Fail or Succeed* (Penguin, 2005)

Written by another Pulitzer Prize winner, *Collapse* provides case studies of civilizations dealing with environmental change both from natural causes and from human alterations. Some societies, for example the pre-Columbian Viking colony in Greenland, seem incapable of restructuring to respond to devastating environmental change. Others, such as the Easter Islanders clearing their forest or the Maya overextending their intensification of land use, persist in following disastrous practices until their societies collapse. Modern examples, including the horrific genocide in Rwanda, frame the question of how a society avoids the pitfalls of failing in the face of environmental change.

↩ Elizabeth Kolbert, *Field Notes from a Catastrophe: Man, Nature, and Climate Change* (Bloomsbury, 2006)

This book is an expansion of three essays in the *New Yorker* that earned Kolbert a writing award from the American Association for the Advancement of Science. *Field Notes* introduces current issues in global climate change by giving voice through interviews to the scientists involved with predicting climate change, measuring the thawing ice in the Arctic, or interpreting past climate change. This generates a factually rich and extremely readable account of global climate change issues that avoids the alarmist tone of many of the other recent books on "greenhouse warming." For our society and its political/governmental systems, Kolbert clearly presents the thought-provoking challenge of steering Starship Earth.

HERMAN H. SHUGART is W. W. Corcoran Professor of Environmental Sciences and has been at the University of Virginia since 1984. He is the author or editor of more than three hundred scientific publications, including twelve books. His most recent book, *How the Earthquake Bird Got Its Name and Other Tales of an Unbalanced Nature* (Yale University Press, 2004), treats unbalanced nature and planetary stewardship by using scientific parables about animals.

ROBERT E. DAVIS

Perspectives on Global Warming Science

The possibility that humans are altering earth's climate is among the most important environmental issues of our lifetime. A careful reading of the related popular literature indicates that the impact of global warming falls somewhere between the devastation of life as we know it and a largely beneficial effect that merits little scientific concern or discussion. Although the truth certainly lies somewhere in the murky middle of these extremes, our present science doesn't give us enough good information to know what to expect with a level of precision that is useful.

The pabulum "global warming is a complex issue" has become a modern-day truism. In fact, global warming is not nearly as complex as, say, theoretical astrophysics or biogenetics. Conceptually, the basic principles of the greenhouse effect can be understood by a reasonably intelligent high school student. The real difficulty lies in the fundamentally interdisciplinary nature of global-warming science. To fully appreciate the interrelatedness of earth's climate system, a knowledgeable person needs to understand the principles of climatology and meteorology, as well as those of oceanography, geography, geophysics, environmental chemistry, biology, and ecology. Few individuals have the scientific breadth to speak knowledgeably on all of these topics, so it is not surprising that most research on climate change involves multiple-authored studies and often large, interdisciplinary teams.

As with most scientific issues, the devil really is in the details. For example, we frequently hear that the earth has warmed about 1°C in the twentieth century. But what does that really mean? Rarely do media accounts discuss the number of thermometers in the network, how they are distributed over the earth's surface, the impacts of urbanization and "urban heat islands," the influence of instrument changes, the impacts of changes in observation times, or biases that arise from thermometers being placed where people live (cities develop along rivers and larger water bodies, which have a localized climatic influence). Yet the simple matter of reporting how much the planet has warmed requires the adjustment for, or at least the careful consideration of, all of these factors, about which hundreds of scientific papers have been written. That's a lot of territory to cover in three column inches in your local daily.

Many informed people who lack the background or interest to read about science have the option to ignore much of it. In reality, you can survive quite nicely without fully grasping current theories on the origins of the universe, for example. But politics has thrust the global warming issue upon us. Global citizens are being asked to make personal lifestyle and political decisions based upon their individual understanding of global warming.

Unfortunately, when politics and science interact at this level, what arises from the mire is not pretty. Many of my fellow climatologists believe that global warming has moved beyond the realm of scientific discussion; some feel that the science has become irrelevant. Everyone who writes on this issue has an agenda—governments, which wish to promulgate policies; the energy industry, which is trying to move product; environmental organizations promoting lifestyle changes; the media hyping the issue to sell advertising; and yes, even scientists with their individual angles to publicize and promote. This view, which some might call cynical but I call realistic, is based on over two decades of research on climate change starting with its public nascence as a global issue in the mid-1980s.

My agenda in providing this short list of books is to provide some varied perspectives on global warming that I hope will prove both informative and entertaining. All of these books are readily accessible to the nonscientist, and they should all be read with a healthy dose of skepticism or, if you already have a firm opinion, with an open mind. These volumes will not provide a complete understanding of global climate change, but they will offer readers some sense of the range of opinion that exists within my field of study. I encourage readers who are interested in reading the complete list to read the books in the order listed below. Those who choose to read only one book will be left with a much different impression than will those who take time to read the entire list. Therefore, I have tried to select readable entries of modest length to encourage readers to delve into the topic.

✑ Spencer R. Weart, *The Discovery of Global Warming* (Harvard University Press, 2004)

> The problem with any book on climate change is that it is out of date before it gets published. But Weart's overview, which takes his readers back to the nineteenth-century experiments of Tyndall and Arrhenius on the absorption spectra of atmospheric gases, is the most comprehensive and readable history of an issue whose story is far from complete. Weart hits all of the highlights, from mankind's revelation that humans really *can* influence climate on a global scale, to the obsession with global cooling in the 1970s, to James Hansen's congressional proclamation during the hot, dry summer of 1988 that global warming is already here. In several instances, Weart dramatizes fairly minor events (for example, it was well known long before the early 1990s that greenhouse gases other than carbon dioxide had important climatic impacts), but this history is a very good narrative as told from the viewpoint of a science journalist.

✑ Mark Maslin, *Global Warming: A Very Short Introduction* (Oxford University Press, 2004)

> Mark Maslin is a British paleoclimatologist and academician who views global warming as one of humankind's most significant threats. His abstracted but very readable overview touches on many of the existing data sets that provide evidence for global warming. He succinctly summarizes the basic physics of Earth's climate system and talks about climate change's impact on society and politics. Maslin puts a bit too much emphasis on the importance of long-term climate reconstructions,

but this should not be surprising given his research expertise. In my view, his most interesting contribution is the discussion of how people with differing personal philosophies (individuals are categorized as "fatalists," "hierarchists," "individuals," or "egalitarians") might differently interpret trends in climate data (or, more broadly, the impact of humanity on nature). Although I have scientific disagreements with some of what Maslin writes, I give him kudos for honesty. He writes that "What I hope to do . . . is try to shift your belief from [fatalist/individualist] to [hierarchist/egalitarian], or, if you are already [the latter], show you why your instinctive view of nature may well be correct."

⇔ Patrick J. Michaels, *Meltdown: The Predictable Distortion of Global Warming by Scientists, Politicians, and the Media* (Cato Institute, 2005)

Pat Michaels is a well-known global warming skeptic who has quite a respectable publication record emphasizing climate change in the recent observational record (twentieth century). In this volume, Michaels fires a verbal broadside on the media, certain climate scientists, environmental journalists, and politicians, all of whom he claims are exaggerating the danger or likely impacts of global warming for personal gain. There is a method to this approach that is vaguely reminiscent of Stephan Jay Gould's *The Mismeasure of Man*—at the end of the book, Michaels lays out his thesis, harking back to the seminar work of Thomas Kuhn, that distortion is an inevitable by-product of the politicization of global warming science, so that everyone is acting in their best self-interest. But on the journey, Michaels takes us on a winding trail of melting icecaps, hurricanes, butterflies, droughts, floods, cherry blossoms, and more with a style that is simultaneously funny, quirky, confusing, and outrageous.

⇔ Michael Crichton, *State of Fear* (Avon, 2005)

Why is a fiction book written by one of today's most popular authors on a science reading list? Because this book is not purely fiction. Yes, it is a typical Crichton adventure that teeters somewhere along the edge of science and science fiction, but global warming is the thread that binds together this global adventure. Though the basic plot elements are fiction, Crichton cleverly uses the numerous opportunities when the characters are traveling between sites to educate the readers about global warming. Crichton uses real data, actual references from the scientific literature, and published theories to advance his plot. In a clever construct, the character of Peter Evans, a nonscientist global warming believer (presumably like most readers), transforms into a skeptic over the course of several hundred pages.

ROBERT E. DAVIS's research focuses on large-scale climate impacts and climate variability. He is Professor of Climatology in the Department of Environmental Sciences. Davis has received numerous awards for his research, teaching, and scientific editing work, and he is currently editor of the journal *Climate Research*. He has served as chair of both the American Meteorological Society's Committee on Biometeorology and Aerobiology and the Climate Specialty Group of the Association of American Geographers.

JONATHAN CANNON

The Environmental Other: Finding and Losing Ourselves in Nature

This is a remarkable world in which we find ourselves. It is beautiful, nurturing, serene, harsh, tumultuous, death-dealing. It is the ground of our being. We are here in the form we are because the world has shaped us through evolutionary time to survive and flourish in it. Everything we see, touch, feel, eat, and use comes from this world. Yet we take it for granted. Or we struggle to free ourselves completely, to create a separate world on our own terms, entirely to our liking. This effort, while perhaps entirely "natural" for our species, is ultimately futile, as the gathering calamity of global climate change may serve to remind us. And in the end, the struggle to separate, carried out with the relentless single-mindedness that seems to characterize the current global economic expansion, reduces rather than enlarges our humanity. We forget where we come from and who we are.

In each of the readings I have selected, the author attempts to see the world and our place in it anew. Although some of these readings give attention to policy issues of the day, none of them is fundamentally about programs to protect the environment or preserve natural resources. Instead, from diverse perspectives, these readings portray individuals coming to terms with the natural world, which is paradoxically alien to us, yet our home—and in the process, coming to terms with themselves. Their focus is the intellectual, emotional, and spiritual dimensions of human engagement with that world.

For two of our authors, coming to terms with the environmental other is about coming to terms with God, although not in a conventionally religious sense. If you have experienced awe or joy in natural settings that you associate with religious experience, these writers may appeal to you. John Muir's *The Mountains of California* is a masterful recording of the geological, biological, and aesthetic wonders of the Sierra Nevada Mountains, but it is even more a hymn of joy to the divine energy that Muir sensed everywhere in this wild landscape, watered and blessed by "God's messenger," the rain. Annie Dillard's *Pilgrim at Tinker Creek* is a more self-conscious, less certain, but thoroughly engaging quest for God in the workings of nature. Rather than feeling Muir's exuberant joy, she experiences a deep ambivalence—vacillating between "tranquility and trembling." A God is there somewhere, but it is not a knowable God and not necessarily a benign one.

If you have a strong affinity for wild nature but are reluctant to interpret those feelings within a religious framework, the outlaw of environmental literature, Edward Abbey, may be your choice. In his classic *Desert Solitaire*, Abbey strikes a pose of indifference both to God and other humans. "God," he thinks, contemplating the beautiful emptiness of the Utah desert, "who the hell is He?" He has even less use for the tourists who clutter and defile the desert landscape that he loves.

If you are interested in readings that are more hospitable to humans and their place in nature, John McPhee's *Encounters with the Archdruid* or Vladimir Nabokov's *Speak, Memory* may appeal. McPhee's book records encounters he witnessed between environmental activist David Brower, the "archdruid," and the advocates for development whom Brower opposed. While addressing environmental issues, McPhee's narrative comes to be mainly about the human antagonists in the environmental wars, depicted in all their quirks and contradictions. While *Archdruid* considers fully formed adult characters, *Speak, Memory* explores the formative power of nature in human lives. Nabokov's account of his childhood in Russia, including days spent in the rich forests of his family's estates, is not typically considered an environmental work. But it offers an exquisite rendering of the relationship between an individual's emotional development and experience of the natural world, which in Nabokov's case bred a love for that world that would be important to him for the rest of his life.

These works do not solve the paradox of the environmental other— how human beings feel themselves to be both inside and outside of nature. What they offer are expressions of the richness and power of that paradox in human experience and its importance to our deepest understanding of ourselves.

↩ John Muir, *The Mountains of California* (Sierra Club Books, 1989)

An explorer, naturalist, and writer, John Muir was also the first president of the Sierra Club and championed the creation of Yosemite Park in his beloved Sierra Nevada Mountains. His first book, *The Mountains of California*, was published in 1894 when he was in his mid-fifties. Although it is a naturalist's account of the High Sierras, it is suffused with Muir's spontaneous, extravagant delight in the mountain landscape. Muir interpreted this joy in religious terms—it made plain to him that God was in the mountains. In one of the book's most celebrated passages, Muir climbs a hundred feet to the top of a spruce to enjoy a mountain windstorm, clinging exuberantly to the tree "like a bobolink on a reed." Descending after his exhilarating ride, Muir beholds nature radiant with divine presence: "forests hushed and tranquil [tower] above one another on the slopes of hills like a devout audience," and the setting sun delivers a benediction. This is Muir's nature—luminous, harmonious, holy.

✎ Annie Dillard, *Pilgrim at Tinker Creek* (Harper Perennial Modern Classics, 2007)

Annie Dillard published *Pilgrim at Tinker Creek* in 1974, while she was still in her twenties. The book records her encounters with nature during a year's stay in a cabin on a creek in rural Virginia. The writing is meditative but also urgent and questioning. She stalks nature in her quest to see it clear, and she stalks God, "calling like a child beating on a door: Come on out! . . . I know you're there." What she sees in nature is both beautiful and terrifying, and although she experiences a kind of grace, it is "grace mingled in a rapture with violence." She does not see God, at least not directly, although she senses God everywhere—"a power that is unfathomably secret, and holy, and fleet." And she comes away from her experience with the dedication to live fully and fearlessly even in the face of the death and decay around her.

✎ Edward Abbey, *Desert Solitaire* (Ballantine Books, 1985)

Edward Abbey is the bad boy of environmental writers—profane, irreverent, and misanthropic, particularly when bearing witness to human destruction of wild nature. In addition to his literary achievements, he is celebrated as the patron saint of eco-saboteurs. *Desert Solitaire* records Abbey's season as a park ranger in the remote desert near Moab, Utah, for Abbey "the most beautiful place on earth." Although the book is a celebration of this landscape—"[t]he red dust and the burnt cliffs and the lonely sky"—it is also celebration of all wilderness, "the natural paradise that lies around us all." For Abbey, original sin is not disobedience to God's command, but the ruination of this earthly paradise by our species. Abbey can be harsh in judgment of his fellow humans: "I'm a humanist," he jokes darkly. "I'd rather kill a *man* than a snake" (emphasis in original). But his writing brims with deep feeling for the people and the landscapes he cares about.

⊸ John McPhee, *Encounters with the Archdruid* (Farrar, Straus and Giroux, 1977)

The "archdruid" of the title is David Brower, who led the Sierra Club for seventeen years at the height of the environmental movement and then founded Friends of the Earth. The descriptor captures not only the religious fervor of Brower's environmental crusades, in which he was likened by a colleague to the abolitionist John Brown, but also the mystery of the man himself, who could be obscure and unpredictable. McPhee presents Brower in conversation (or, more often, argument) with proponents of development—a copper mine in the wilderness of the Cascade Mountains, the Glen Canyon Dam on the Colorado River, and houses and golf courses on primitive Hilton Head Island, South Carolina. Each encounter is a little drama, played out on the landscape where the development is proposed or, in the case of the Glen Canyon Dam, has already occurred. This form invites the reader to assess for herself not only the relative merit of the competing views but also the character and motivations of the antagonists.

⊸ Vladimir Nabokov, *Speak, Memory* (Vintage International, 1989)

This luminous autobiography by Nabokov covers the years from his birth in St. Petersburg, Russia, to his exile in Germany and France following the Russian Revolution (1899–1940). It begins with a map of "the Nabokov Lands" outside of St. Petersburg, country estates that the Soviet state appropriated after the 1917 Revolution. On these ancestral lands, "the legendary Russia of my boyhood," young Nabokov spent bucolic summers developing the observational, imaginative, and emotional capacities that would later make him one of the great writers of the twentieth century. There he discovered his lifelong passion for butterfly hunting, wrote his first poetry, and experienced his first love. In a fierce aside rebuking the "idiot" who believes that his quarrel with the Soviets is about money and land, Nabokov writes: "The nostalgia I have been cherishing all these years is a hypertrophied sense of lost childhood. . . . I reserve for myself the right to yearn after an ecological niche."

Jonathan Cannon is Professor and Director of the Land Use and Environmental Law Program at the University of Virginia Law School. Among his recent articles are "Presidential Greenspeak: How Presidents Talk about the Environment and What It Means" and "Environmentalism and the Supreme Court: A Cultural Analysis." He has served in several senior positions in the Environmental Protection Agency, including General Counsel from 1995 to 1998.

TRINH XUAN THUAN

The Epic of the Cosmos: Space, Time, and the Universe

Our universe has a history, and that history concerns us to the highest degree since it leads to us. The epic of the cosmos is also ours. The scientific advances of the last century have radically changed the way we perceive our origins. We now have at our disposal a great historical fresco, always magnificent, and never less than enthralling. Never has this history of our origins spanned such a large time frame and encompassed such a large expanse of space. Never has it been so true because all the sciences, from astrophysics to neurobiology, from physics to chemistry, from anthropology to geology, contribute ceaselessly to refine and precise it. The Aristotelian concept of an eternal and immutable universe—a universe without history—is truly dead. We now think that the universe was created some 14 billion years ago in a "Big Bang," when an unimaginably small, dense, and hot concentration of energy exploded, in the process also creating space and time. This enormous energy drove the universe to a staggering increase of its volume in practically no time at all, a process astrophysicists call "inflation." Since then, space has never ceased to expand. As the universe expanded, it also grew much cooler. Right after the Big Bang, the universe was hotter than Dante's Inferno. As the universe cooled, energy began to be converted to matter and matter could start to organize itself.

The history of the universe is a long ascension toward complexity. Elementary particles that rose out of the primordial vacuum came together to form atoms, then molecules, and finally stars. Those stars assembled together to create galaxies, each containing hundreds of billions of stars, and the hundred of billions of galaxies in the observable universe formed an immense tapestry covering the cosmos. In at least one of these galaxies, the Milky Way, near a star called the sun, on the planet Earth, molecules composed of chemical elements made in the heart of stars locked together to form long chains of DNA, which created life, then consciousness, and finally people capable of asking questions about the world around them and the universe that had caused them to exist. A nice account of this fabulous epic is given by journalist Timothy Ferris in *The Whole Shebang*.

In less than fifty years, the Big Bang theory has become the new paradigm of modern cosmology because it is the only one on the market that is able to explain observations apparently as disparate as the expansion of space, the existence of a cosmic background radiation that bathes the whole universe, and the chemical composition of stars and galaxies. If the universe went through a very hot and condensed state, the primordial radiation from the "fire of creation" should still be reaching us. It was discovered in 1965, cooled down to the frigorific temperature of −270°C because of the energy lost during the 14 billion years of the universe's expansion. As for the chemical composition, stars and galaxies are different from humans. Made of stardust, our bodies contain heavy elements (such as carbon or oxygen) manufactured by the nuclear alchemy of stars. However, that represents a tiny fraction, only 2 percent, of the mass of the chemical elements in the universe. The remaining 98 percent are composed of two light elements, hydrogen and helium, made in the Big Bang. Theory predicts that, about three minutes after the initial explosion, about one-quarter of the mass of ordinary matter in the universe was in the form of helium, and the remaining three-quarters were in hydrogen. That is precisely the proportions observed in stars and galaxies. Steven Weinberg explains how this came about in *The First Three Minutes.*

Science does not yet allow us to go back all the way to the moment of creation. In the universe's story, the infinitely small has spawned the infinitely large. At the moment, we don't know how to unify the twentieth century's two great physical theories, quantum mechanics—the physics of the infinitely small that accounts for the behavior of atoms and light when gravity isn't dominant—and relativity, the physics of the infinitely large, where gravity plays the leading role and the two nuclear and electromagnetic forces are not predominant. And that's the snag: the four fundamental forces were on equal footing at the birth of the universe, and to understand these very first moments we need to unify the two theories in a quantum gravity theory. String theory is such an attempt. It considers elementary particles no longer as points but as caused by vibrations of tiny "strings" of energy existing in ten- or eleven-dimensional space. String theory, the quantum vacuum, the inflationary phase, and the nature of space and time are discussed by physicist Brian Greene in *The Fabric of the Cosmos.* Other researchers, like physicist Stephen Hawking in *A Brief History of Time,* even speculate that space and time may not have a beginning at all. Finally, there is a puzzle to consider. The way our universe evolved depends on its "initial conditions" and on about fifteen numbers called "physical constants" such as the speed of light or the mass of the elementary particles. Physicists have discovered that if these constants and initial conditions were just slightly different, we wouldn't be here, able to talk about them. The universe, right from the start, appears to be have been fine-tuned to an extreme degree for the emergence of consciousness and of an observer. Does this fine-tuning arise by chance or by necessity? This is examined by astrophysicist Martin Rees in *Just Six Numbers.*

All the following books were written for the general public, without scientific jargon and mathematical equations.

Timothy Ferris, *The Whole Shebang: A State-of-the Universe(s) Report* (Simon and Schuster, 1998)

Written in graceful prose by a journalist who has often contributed to the *New Yorker*, this is an easy-to-read and wide-ranging book that puts the cosmological discoveries in a historical perspective, with many anecdotes on the key players.

Brian Greene, *The Fabric of the Cosmos: Space, Time, and the Texture of Reality* (Vintage, 2005)

String theorist Greene explains clearly, patiently, and engagingly the concepts of space and time in the context of the two physical theories of the twentieth century—quantum mechanics and relativity—and why they are incompatible. He suggests that string theory may be a way to reconcile them. There are entertaining discussions on the flow and the direction of time, quantum teleportation, and time travel.

Stephen Hawking, *A Brief History of Time: From the Big Bang to Black Holes* (1988; Bantam, 1998)

Although this book has sold millions of copies worldwide, I suspect it did so because the public was fascinated with a mind having overcome a crippling disease (Hawking has Lou Gehrig's disease and cannot walk, speak, or write) to become the superstar of physics. Discussing the physics of the early universe and of black holes, the book can sometimes be hard going for those without a background in physics. However, it is interesting to have a glimpse of how Hawking's mind works—for example, when he found out that black holes aren't so black after all, and that they can radiate.

Martin Rees, *Just Six Numbers: The Deep Forces That Shape the Universe* (Basic, 2001)

Sir Martin Rees, Britain's Astronomer Royal, explains in simple terms and without mathematics how just six numbers, imprinted in the Big Bang, can determine the essential features of the physical universe. These numbers are, for example, the amount of matter (both luminous and dark) in the universe, the amount of the anti-gravity responsible for the acceleration of the universe, or the number of spatial dimensions in our cosmos (three). Rees shows that these numbers are tuned to an extreme degree to allow the emergence of life and consciousness in the universe: change these numbers ever so slightly, and we wouldn't be here talking about them. This extraordinary fine-tuning can be interpreted in two ways: it can be the result of either chance or necessity. In the chance hypothesis, our universe is one among an infinite number of other parallel universes (a "multiverse") with all possible values of these numbers. But ours was the only one born with just the right numbers to have evolved to create life. All the others were losers and devoid of observers. But if we reject the multiverse idea (it cannot be checked experimentally), then our universe is unique, and to explain the fine-tuning of the numbers, we need to invoke some sort of principle of creation.

✎ Steven Weinberg, *The First Three Minutes: A Modern View of the Origin of the Universe* (1977; Basic, 1993)

Nobel Prize–winning physicist Weinberg describes in an engagingly written book how astrophysicists have managed to unravel the fundamental processes that occurred in the early universe: how the light elements we see today in stars and galaxies were created in the first few minutes of the universe's existence, and how radiation cooled from the time of the Big Bang to leave its imprint on the sky we observe today. There have been many advances in cosmology since the publication of the book in 1977, but the basic features of the universe's story as related by Weinberg remain unchanged.

Trinh Xuan Thuan is Professor of Astronomy; he has also taught at the University of Paris. His main research interests concern the formation and the evolution of dwarf galaxies and the synthesis of light elements in the Big Bang. He has also written several best-selling books, including *The Secret Melody* (Oxford University Press, 1995; Templeton Foundation Press, 2005), *Chaos and Harmony* (Oxford University Press, 2001; Templeton Foundation Press, 2006), and, with Matthieu Ricard, *The Quantum and the Lotus* (Three Rivers Press, 2001).

PAUL FENDLEY

Doing Science: Physics, Genius, and Creativity

Always beware of books that capitalize the word "nature," as in "Scientists are awed by the mysteries of Nature." Scientists (or, for that matter, all who occasionally look up from their daily routines) should indeed be awed by nature's mysteries, but capitalizing the word implies a connection with, well, that Guy who may or may not have created all this in His own image etc. Part of the reason the Scopes trial has been rerun in the twenty-first century is the confusion among many about what science really is.

Very thoughtful people have written books about what science is, but none of these are on this reading list. The reason is that, as virtually any scientist will tell you, the best way to learn something is to work out a bunch of examples. This list is comprised of a novel set in World War II and the present, an exhaustive history of the atomic bomb, a biography of one of the best (and best-known) scientists of the last half century, a collection of his lectures, and a book about important equations.

These examples of science in action, I hope, illustrate not only some part of what we scientists do, but also how we do it and what its consequences are. Having stated that science and religion are not the same thing (shocking!), I'll make the less obvious point that humans doing science behave in the same way as humans doing anything requiring creativity and talent.

To this end, a good way of starting is to look closely at an exceptionally creative and talented scientist. Richard Feynman was a theoretical physicist like I am (the resemblance pretty much stops there). He did his most important work in the decades after World War II; among other things, he invented/discovered several radically new ways of studying physics at very small distances and at high energies. The words "Feynman diagram" are heard daily in any halfway decent physics department. Toward the end of his life (he died in 1988) he became a semi-celebrity, authoring a best-selling book of amusing anecdotes that, oddly enough, made him mostly come across as a brilliant but arrogant jerk.

One of his anecdotes was about how people often seemed to think that by examining nature closely, scientists were destroying its beauty and mystery. They would ask questions along the lines of "Can't you just admire the beauty of a flower without wondering what's inside? Can't you just enjoy a beautiful sunset without wondering why the sun is redder than it is during the day?" His reply was general befuddlement as to how understanding something in more depth could destroy beauty. To Feynman and most scientists, understanding how things work and what they're made of not only enhances their beauty, but is a new form of beauty in itself.

It's obligatory to mention Einstein in any communication of twentieth-century physics to a popular audience (someday I will write a book entitled "Einstein in the Title"), so I figured I would mention that relativity ($E = mc^2$ and the loss of simultaneity and all that) is not really so radical a departure from the physics that came before. In fact, it's little known even among physicists that $E = mc^2$ can be derived without relativity at all. Relativity has some shockingly counterintuitive consequences, but once you accept that anyone traveling at any speed will measure the speed of light to be the same thing, everything else follows inevitably in the way that physics always follows from some profound basic principles. The much more radical revolution of twentieth-century physics came with the discovery of quantum mechanics, which requires accepting the bizarre notion that in many situations it is simply never possible to predict whether or not something will happen, but only the probability of various outcomes. The brilliance of many physicists was required to understand this, and the books on this list convey various bits of the story.

↬ James Gleick, *Genius: The Life and Science of Richard Feynman* (Vintage, 1993)

> This biography of Feynman is much more substantial than his anecdotal memoirs (if not quite as funny). Feynman certainly was an interesting character; the anecdotes he liked to circulate concerned strip joints, bongos, and safe-cracking as well as science. Gleick recounts the more telling (and reliable) of these, but the central theme of the book is much more interesting, asking the question: What is genius? Gleick uses a terrific quote from the mathematician Mark Kac, who explains that there are two kinds of geniuses, the first type being those who are like us, but much cleverer and quicker. The thought processes of these "ordinary geniuses" are no mystery to us: once we see what they've done, we feel we too could have done it. With the "magicians" like Feynman, even once we have seen what they have done, we simply have no idea how they did it. This book is a fascinating illustration of how a genius really can transform a field of science, and since Feynman was so centrally involved in the major developments of post–World War II physics, an excellent history of that era as well.

↬ Richard Feynman, *Six Easy Pieces* (Basic, 2005)

> But there's no better way to appreciate the genius (or is it Genius?) of Feynman than to read the man's lectures. In the early 1960s, after he had already achieved legendary status, he was persuaded to teach the freshman physics sequence at Caltech. The lectures he gave can be found in three volumes (a recent fourth contains a few "lost" lectures). *Six Easy Pieces* collects six lectures comprehensible to a general audience. The material Feynman discusses should be understood by every educated human being.
>
> Feynman's lectures have developed a reputation among the physics community as being incomprehensible for beginning students and appropriate only for more advanced scientists. This is more a commentary on the physics community than on the students. The reason that the lectures are difficult (but miles from incomprehensible) for

beginning students is that Feynman rethought basic physics, and teaches it in a way that hasn't been assimilated by the community nearly a half century later. As I said, the way people do science isn't so different from the way they do everything else, and one common human characteristic is to believe that the way you were taught something is the most natural way of understanding it. It takes a Genius like Feynman to break through tradition and figure out the way things ought to be taught.

↩ Richard Rhodes, *The Making of the Atomic Bomb* (Simon and Schuster, 1995)

When discussing the atomic bomb, people focus on $E = mc^2$ (important), the consequences for humanity (important), and the personalities and struggles of the people who made it (less important, but very interesting). *The Making of the Atomic Bomb* covers all of these in great and interesting detail, but gives as much time to all the experimental and theoretical physics of the first half of the twentieth century that allowed the bomb to be made. That physics is mostly quantum mechanics, and since most of the scientists who first explained this to the world were also the scientists who built the bomb, Rhodes's book doubles as a history of this as well. The making of the atomic bomb truly was a watershed in ways that no work of fiction could plausibly invent. The fact that Rhodes manages to do justice to the many story lines involved, and get the science right to boot, is a spectacular achievement of literature. As a bonus, he conveys how exciting it must have been to be doing science that truly does change both the intellectual and the political world.

↩ Neal Stephenson, *Cryptonomicon* (Avon, 2002)

Cryptonomicon is a novel that conveys the same kind of excitement. It mixes the scientific and military triumph of breaking the German and Japanese codes in World War II with a story of contemporary capitalism, all surrounded by rollicking adventure. You'll often find Stephenson's books in science-fiction sections of bookstores because he did write several novels set in the future. But *Cryptonomicon* is not that kind of science fiction—it is a work of fiction deeply concerned with science. Reading this gives you not only the sense of how people do science, but why they do it, and why it matters.

↩ Sander Bais, *The Equations: Icons of Knowledge* (Harvard University Press, 2005)

The language physicists use to describe nature precisely is called mathematics, and the way we use it is what separates physics from other kinds of science. This is the point of *The Equations.* There's a reason why blackboards in physics buildings are covered with symbols obscure to most of humanity—it's the best way to explain what we mean. Science books for a general audience are usually the equivalent of using a thousand words to paint a picture, but *The Equations* takes the novel tack of putting the equations front and center. Bais shows some of the most important equations in science in all their mathematical glory, and then explains what all these symbols have to do with nature. Just what we physicists do to make a living.

By the way, the sun at sunset is redder because the scattering of light within the atmosphere is enhanced at higher frequencies of light. At sunset, the sun's light has to travel through the most atmosphere to get to you, so the effect of the scattering is the most pronounced. Red light has the lowest frequency, so it's scattered the least, and the sun looks red. Exercise for the reader: figure out how these facts explain why the sky is blue as well . . .

PAUL FENDLEY researches and teaches physics. He has received continuing funding from the National Science Foundation, an Outstanding Junior Investigator Award from the Department of Energy, and fellowships from the Sloan Foundation and the Research Corporation. He saw too many movies when he was young, and a few years ago played bass for a rock'n'roll band. He claims that he will write a book about physics titled *Up Against the Infinite.*

CASSANDRA L. FRASER

Designing Matter: Molecules, Materials, and Their Importance to Society

Often we think that science is just for scientists, but if science is about wonder—curiosity about the natural world and how it works—it is for everyone. These days there is growing uneasiness about leaving chemistry to the chemists and biology to the biologists, and misunderstandings can sometimes arise. Scientific and technological advances call for the involvement of persons from diverse backgrounds and the investment of different sectors of society. While it is neither realistic nor practical to expect everyone to become expert molecular designers or makers of materials, we are all beneficiaries of this knowledge and craft that continue to shape our culture and imagination in countless ways. It is worthwhile, then, for poets, politicians, and polymer scientists alike to develop an appreciation for the stuff of which we and our world are comprised. And with these excellent books as guides, it is entirely possible to attain it.

The molecular sciences reach well beyond the bounds of chemistry to biology, medicine, and engineering, to the study of energy, materials, and the environment, and to many other enterprises too, as these selections nicely illustrate. In the past century much has been learned about atoms and molecules and their likely interactions. For synthetic chemists, those who study and exploit such interactions, selectivity has long been the holy grail. Traditionally, single products, not mixtures, are targeted by rational design processes and separation procedures, and one by one, pure compounds are tested for activity in a given application. Once isolated and understood, these substances can then be recombined in controlled ways for more predictable outcomes, although it is important to note that impurities have led to important new discoveries too. These days, however, the field of chemistry is changing. Entire libraries of compounds can be generated by combinatorial methods and screened at once in genetic testing or in searching for promising new drugs and materials.

Scientists are thinking about aggregates in other respects too. Factors that govern molecular assembly and lead to materials that are organized across different length scales [e.g., nano- (10^{-9}), micro- (10^{-6}), and milli- (10^{-3}) meter] and ways that nested, hierarchical structures correlate with properties are related areas of intense research. Here, natural materials are an abundant source of inspiration for both design and method. Nature's mastery of energy-efficient hierarchical assembly leading to functional structures of breathtaking complexity—ones that can respond and adapt to their environment—remains unmatched by human art. But because so much of life depends upon it—from the resources we use to feed, clothe, shelter, and entertain ourselves, to the fuel used to warm, cool, and propel us, and the molecules, cells, tissues, and organs that comprise us and heal us—we have no choice but to fashion matter, as best we can, to interface with ourselves and our world. All of us, not just chemists and materials scientists, make decisions about matter both naturally and synthetically derived. And when we look at matter across the length scales and other bounds, we quickly discover that it is far less contained than we might think. This too presents both possibilities and responsibilities.

The readings below are about designing matter, how this takes place on molecular and larger scales, and why it matters for science and global society, historically, now, and for future generations. *Stories of the Invisible* provides a good introduction to molecular design and synthesis, placing them in the various contexts in which they occur. *Made to Measure* describes what we know and where we are headed with respect to state-of-the-art materials. *Napoleon's Buttons* looks to the past to tell us why molecules matter, while *Cradle to Cradle* imagines and strives to bring about a better future. *The Periodic Table* tells us something about what it means to be a chemist—one who is engaged in understanding and shaping matter with attention to nature's tiniest of building blocks, as best they are understood at the time—and what it means to be human, over the years and under circumstances both ordinary and incomprehensible. Additional readings provide further examples of molecules in our experience (*Molecules*), describe ways that matter has been used to produce color in art (*Bright Earth*), and point to further information about major advances in the molecular sciences and persons responsible for discoveries deemed worthy of the Nobel Prize.

↔ Philip Ball, *Stories of the Invisible: A Guided Tour of Molecules* (Oxford University Press, 2002)

A part of the Oxford University Press "Very Short Introductions" series, this readable book is an excellent place to begin learning about the molecular sciences. Chapter themes include synthetic chemistry or the making of molecules, the molecules of life, materials, and energy, as well as molecular motors, communication, and information. The volume nicely mingles current topics and historically important advances. Philip Ball, an Oxford- and Bristol-educated chemist, is a celebrated freelance science writer and consulting editor for the prestigious journal *Nature*. His many books for the lay reader are also much appreciated by experts in the field.

↔ Penny Le Couteur and Jay Burreson, *Napoleon's Buttons: 17 Molecules That Changed History* (Jeremy P. Tarcher/Penguin, 2004)

Both natural and synthetic molecules that have shaped culture in significant ways are featured in this book: spices, drugs, dyes, polymers, explosives, and many more. This offering does an excellent job of making connections between molecules and historical events, political movements, economic drivers, and ethical debates. Though the focus of *Napoleon's Buttons* is cultural history, the visual language of molecular design is also introduced for those who are interested.

↔ Philip Ball, *Made to Measure: New Materials for the 21st Century* (Princeton University Press, 1999)

This book explores advanced materials in a way that is helpful to experts and those who are new to the field. Cutting-edge themes such as photonic materials for information storage, biomaterials for drug delivery and tissue engineering, and cleaner energy via more efficient batteries and solar cells are treated. Ball does an excellent job of explaining existing and imagined future uses of advanced materials, important technological advances and challenges, and the basic scientific concepts necessary to understand materials synthesis, properties, and fabrication.

⊷ William McDonough and Michael Braungart, *Cradle to Cradle: Remaking the Way We Make Things* (North Point Press, 2002)

This inspiring book challenges us to consider the "matter lifecycle"— where resources come from, what we do with them, and where things end up when they are no longer useful to us. McDonough and Braungart treat economy and profit, effects on human health and the environment, and social and global equity as essential design criteria. Environmental policies, they explain, often try to make damaging "cradle to grave" processes "less bad" with increased monitoring and regulation. Arguing that we should instead undertake creative "cradle to cradle" redesign to make things good from start to finish, they offer examples of what this new approach might look like. *Cradle to Cradle* is not a "how to" book with specific instructions and answers for all of life's material situations, nor is it the first and only book about sustainable design. Its real strength, right down to its recyclable, waterproof plastic materiality, is its ability to capture the attention and imagination of the reader. It challenges us to think about our relationships, as individuals and societies, to the material world around us, and to take responsibility for the choices that we make. The hard work of what to do with this vision is up to us.

⊷ Primo Levi, *The Periodic Table,* trans. Raymond Rosenthal (Schocken, 1995)

This modern classic by the acclaimed Italian writer and Auschwitz survivor describes his life as a chemist and so much more in twenty-one chapters, stories really, both factual and fictional, each of which bears the name of a different element. *The Periodic Table* begins with argon, the inert metaphor for Levi's ancestors, and ends with the story of a carbon atom, the element of life that "says everything to everyone." In Levi's words, "This is not a chemical treatise. . . . Nor is it an autobiography, save in the partial and symbolic limits in which every piece of writing is autobiographical, indeed every human work; but it is in some fashion a history. It is—or would have liked to be—a microhistory, the history of a trade and its defeats, victories, and miseries, such as everyone wants to tell when he feels close to concluding the arc of his career, and art ceases to be long." This is a powerful, timeless "must-read" book for persons of all backgrounds.

For further reading:

Peter Atkins, *Molecules* (Freeman, 1991)
   (The first edition is preferred for its presentation of chemical structures. The more easily obtainable *Atkin's Molecules,* 2nd ed. [Cambridge University Press, 2003] is good too.)
Philip Ball, *Bright Earth: Art and the Invention of Color* (Farrar, Straus and Giroux, 2001)
Nobel Prize in Chemistry Web site: http://nobelprize.org/nobel_prizes/chemistry/

CASSANDRA L. FRASER, Professor of Chemistry and 2004–6 Cavalier Distinguished Teaching Professor, focuses on bio-inspired design, materials for biomedicine, and green chemistry themes in her scientific research involving the synthesis, responsive properties, and nanoscale assembly of polymeric metal complexes. She has led numerous interdisciplinary initiatives at the University of Virginia: Science, Careers and Society Forum; Color: Across the Spectrum; Biomaterials Workshop; and Designing Matter Common Course. She has also revamped Honors Organic Chemistry II.

DAVID EVANS

How Computing Changes Thinking

> *In their capacity as a tool, computers will be but a ripple on the surface of our culture. In their capacity as intellectual challenge, they are without precedent in the cultural history of mankind.*
> —Edsger Dijkstra, 1972 Turing Award Lecture

Computing has changed the human condition more than any other technology invented in the past hundred years. Without computing, the Allies may not have won World War II, humans would not have walked on the moon, and Wal-Mart would be a small store in Arkansas. The commoditization of computing, along with the global communications it enabled, has empowered ordinary people to do things the richest, most powerful dictators could not have even dreamed of doing twenty years ago.

But the impact of computing goes beyond the geopolitical shifts and everyday conveniences it enabled, to profound revolutions in the way humans understand the world, as well as our own minds and thoughts. Whereas traditional mathematics explores declarative knowledge (what is), computer science concerns imperative knowledge (how to). Computer scientists

study how to describe, understand, and implement information processes. The basic tool is the *procedure,* a precisely defined sequence of steps.

The three most fundamental questions in computing are: (1) *What can
be computed?* (2) *What can be computed in a reasonable amount of time?*
and (3) *Can computers think?*

The first question emerged from Alonzo Church and Stephen Kleene's
work on lambda calculus in the 1930s, and was answered formally by
Alan Turing in 1936. Turing proved that any computer with some mini-
mal functionality can simulate any other computer, and hence, except for
physical limits like the amount of memory available, all computers are
equally powerful. Not all problems, however, can be solved by computing. For some problems, there is no program that a machine based on
conventional physics can execute that always finishes and produces the
correct answer. In particular, Turing showed that it is impossible to create
a program that will always correctly answer questions about interesting
properties of the information processes described by arbitrary programs
such as *Will this program run ever finish?* and *Is this program a virus?*

The second question is known as *P versus NP.* It was posed precisely by
Stephen Cook in 1971, and remains an open problem today. It asks what
problems can be solved by computers in a reasonable amount of time,
where "reasonable" means that the time required to solve the problem does
not grow exponentially with the size of the input (that is, when the input
size increases by one, the amount of work to solve the problem does not
multiply). Many interesting problems such as finding the shape of a protein,
determining the best schedule for using a resource, finding the minimum
number of colors needed to color a map, and winning the pegboard puzzle game are deeply equivalent—a reasonable-time solution to any one of
these problems can be used to also solve all of the other problems. What is
not known, however, is whether all of the problems can be solved quickly, or
none of them can. The question boils down to determining if an omnipotent machine that can always guess the correct move at every step is able
to solve problems significantly faster than a machine without this magical
power. Although it seems obvious that omnipotence should help, we are
surprisingly far away from being able to answer this question satisfactorily.

The third question concerns whether or not computing machines
can think. It is the fuzziest and most difficult to pose meaningfully. The
first notable attempt was Alan Turing's simulation test, which simplified
the question into whether or not a computer could convince a human it
was thinking. Many others have since attempted to pose or answer the
question differently, but no satisfying definition of "thinking" has yet
emerged. Many of the specific tests, like playing champion-level chess and

understanding language, have been achieved by computers, but by throwing tremendous computing power and resources at the problem, not by anything most humans would consider real thought.

The selected books explore these questions and provide insights into how computing changes thinking, how computing has impacted history, how the state of the world today reflects the early stages of the computing revolution, and how the continuation of that revolution will change human existence in the coming decades. The first two books provide insights into the fundamental questions of computing and how it changes the way we think, and the way we think about thinking; the final three books illustrate how computing impacts the past, present, and future of the world.

✎ Douglas R. Hofstadter, *Gödel, Escher, Bach: An Eternal Golden Braid* (Basic, 1999)

> This is the most challenging, and longest, of the listed books, but I place it first because of the elegance, wit, and insightfulness it brings to the fundamental questions of computing. Hofstadter masterfully connects the big ideas in computing to music, art, and philosophy, illustrating complex ideas with dialogues in the spirit of *Alice in Wonderland,* Escher's artwork, Bach's music, and Hofstadter's own clever and thought-provoking inventions. Much of the book focuses on the mind-bending issues and remarkable expressiveness that can be achieved with recursive definitions (for example, your *descendants* are your children and the descendants of your descendants) and self-reference (statements like "This sentence is meaningless"). This book won the 1980 Pulitzer Prize for nonfiction, and was instrumental in many computer scientists' decision to enter the field (including my own).

✎ Paul Graham, *Hackers and Painters: Big Ideas from the Computer Age* (O'Reilly Media, 2004)

> This is a delightful collection of essays by Paul Graham, cofounder of the first Web application company that became Yahoo! shopping, as well as an accomplished painter. The essays explore fundamental ideas in computing, but from a very different perspective from Hofstadter's. Like Hofstadter, Graham highlights connections between computing and art, but from the viewpoint of a creative pragmatist rather than an academic philosopher. The essays delve into topics ranging from why nerds are not popular in high school, to what make design good, to how to grow a successful company. Each essay is meticulously crafted, lucid, and compelling, and the book is full of radically unconventional and provocative ideas.

↬ Simon Singh, *The Code Book: The Science of Secrecy from Ancient Egypt to Quantum Cryptography* (Anchor, 2000)

The desire to keep and steal secrets has been with humans since before language existed. Singh's book tells an engaging and inspiring tale of the history of cryptography spanning several thousand years. Since the 1940s, that history has been closely entwined with computing. Colossus, arguably the first programmable electronic computer, was built by the British to break Nazi command codes, and Alan Turing was instrumental in breaking the Nazi Enigma code. Increasing computing power, combined with number theory, enabled the development of public-key cryptography. Whereas all previous ciphers required the sender and receiver to establish and maintain a shared secret key used for both encryption and decryption, public-key cryptography allows different keys to be used for encryption and decryption, eliminating the need to keep one of the keys secret. Singh explains the mathematics and technology behind cryptography in a clear and direct way, while conveying the excitement, adventure, and obsessive commitment of human efforts to keep and break secrets.

↬ Thomas L. Friedman, *The World Is Flat: A Brief History of the Twenty-first Century* (Picador, 2007)

The *New York Times* columnist Thomas Friedman's widely heralded book is an entertaining and insightful guide to the flat world that has been created by the rapid advance of computing technology, and the global telecommunications infrastructure it enabled. Over just the past few years, the digitization of everything and essentially free, high-bandwidth worldwide communication have enabled work and ideas to flow freely across borders and oceans, so that the Harvard *Crimson*'s archives can be processed by Cambodian war refugees, McDonald's drive-through orders in Missouri are taken in Colorado Springs, and hundreds of millions of Chinese and Indians have entered the middle class. Friedman's writing is sharp and carries an urgency in conveying both the opportunities and dangers of the new flat world.

↬ Peter J. Denning, ed., *The Invisible Future: The Seamless Integration of Technology into Everyday Life* (McGraw-Hill, 2002)

This book grew out of a visionary conference organized by computing's main professional society in 2001. It contains essays from leading scientists speculating on how future computing technology will impact science, society, and everyday life over the coming decades. My favorite essay is "Science's Endless Golden Age," by astrophysicist Neil DeGrasse Tyson, director of the Hayden Planetarium. It is an optimistic romp on the inexorable advance of human knowledge. Other notable essays include *How Biology Became an Information Science,* by David Baltimore, cancer researcher, president of Caltech, and winner of the Nobel Prize in medicine; and Ray Kurzweil's speculations on future technologies that will mimic and extend human brains.

Davⁱᵈ Evⁱns is Associate Professor of Computer Science in the School of Engineering and Applied Science and Director of the interdisciplinary major in computer science. His research interests include program analysis, using diversity and properties of the physical world for security, and applications of cryptography.

Davⁱᵈ Evⁱns is Associate Professor of Computer Science in the School of Engineering and Applied Science and Director of the interdisciplinary major in computer science. His research interests include program analysis, using diversity and properties of the physical world for security, and applications of cryptography.

BRIAN PARSHALL

Symmetry and Group Theory

As a professional mathematician, I am struck by the fact that the greatest advances sometimes come about by some very simple idea that synthesizes widely known phenomena. This is the case with group theory: a branch of mathematics that deals with symmetry, an often mysterious phenomenon that is nonetheless well-grounded in our everyday experience. In nature, a snowflake admits rotational symmetry about its center. Humans exhibit bilateral symmetry: the generic human face is left-right symmetric; the left eye corresponds nicely to the right eye, and so on. Symmetry occurs frequently in architecture (Christopher Wren's St. Paul's Cathedral in London), in art (Paolo Veronese's *Feast in the House of Levi*), even in *New York Times* crossword puzzles, to mention a few cases.

But how do we understand the many other varieties of symmetry? Take the five regular—or Platonic—solids (cubes, tetrahedrons, octahedrons, icosahedrons, and dodecahedrons), studied as early as the fifth century BC by the Pythagoreans. Unlike a Veronese painting or a Christopher Wren building, Platonic solids admit many symmetries: the icosahedron, for instance, exhibits a total of 120, of which 60 are rotations about its center.

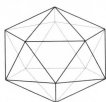

Although Platonic solids have been studied for at least 2,500 years, the problem of organizing them and the many other symmetrical objects in nature under a coherent theory is relatively recent. Not until the early decades of the nineteenth century did mathematicians develop the notion of a "group" to account for symmetries of diverse kinds.

What is a group? Consider the simple example of an equilateral triangle with vertices A, B, C, illustrated below.

The triangle has exactly six symmetries: three rotational symmetries and three reflection symmetries. The three rotational symmetries, s_0, s_{120}, and s_{240}, consist of counterclockwise rotations (about the center P of the triangle and in the plane of the triangle) through the angles of 0, 120, and 240 degrees, respectively. We illustrate s_{120} and s_{240} in the diagrams below. Observe that the counterclockwise rotation s_{240} is the same as the clockwise rotation through an angle of 120 degrees.

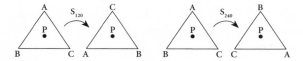

The rotation s_0 is not illustrated; it merely fixes all the points of the triangle, and is known as the *identity* symmetry. The three reflection symmetries each fix one vertex and produce a mirror reflection across that vertex, flipping the position of the other two points of the triangle. These symmetries are named for the vertex that stays fixed, in this case, r_A, r_B, and r_C. These are indicated below.

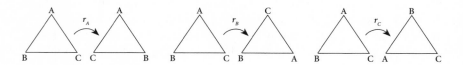

The key idea is that *two symmetries can be composed* (or, in math lingo, *multiplied*) *to get another symmetry.* For example, by first applying the reflection r_A and *then* the reflection r_B to the triangle, we produce the same effect as having rotated the triangle 240 degrees counterclockwise. For this reason, we write $r_B \cdot r_A = s_{120}$.

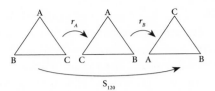

On the other hand, we can change the order of moves: by first applying the reflection r_B and then the reflection r_A, the triangle is rotated counterclockwise through an angle of 240 degrees. Hence, we write $r_A \cdot r_B = s_{240}$.

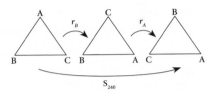

These two sets of symmetries produce different, unequal results, so that

$$r_A \cdot r_B \neq r_B \cdot r_A.$$

That is, this multiplication is *not* generally commutative, in contrast to the familiar multiplication of numbers.

In modern terminology, the symmetries of the equilateral triangle, together with the multiplication we've just defined, provide an example of a mathematical object known as a *group*. A group is a set G (i.e., a collection of objects or *elements*), together with a rule for multiplying any two elements x, y in the group to get a third element xy.

Today, group theory is a huge area of mathematics. Considerable attention focused in the twentieth century on the determination of all "simple" groups—groups that cannot be broken down into smaller constituents in a certain technical sense. The so-called *classification theorem of finite simple groups* is likely the most difficult theorem in the history of mathematics; its proof runs thousands of pages and has involved many mathematicians over decades. Among the simple groups, the famous Monster Simple Group M occupies a special place in the hearts and minds of group theorists. After having been predicted in 1973, its existence was proved in 1980 by Robert Griess at the University of Michigan. Although M has

808017424794512875886459904961710757005754368000000000

elements, it is not the largest simple group with finitely many elements, although it may just be the most interesting, given its amazing connections to other areas of mathematics and physics (e.g., string theory).

It's remarkable that it took thousands of years before the everyday notion of symmetry evolved into the concept of a group. There are hundreds
of books on symmetry and group theory as well as their numerous and
profound applications. Below are four good choices for educated non-
experts, and one just for fun. (For those who want to bite the bullet and
really learn some group theory, two further books of interest are *An Introduction to the Theory of Groups*, by Joseph Rotman, and *The Classification of the Finite Simple Groups*, by Daniel Gorenstein, Richard Lyons, and
Ronald Solomon.)

↬ David Joyner, *Adventures in Group Theory: Rubik's Cube, Merlin's Machine,
and Other Mathematical Toys* (Johns Hopkins University Press, 2002)

Joyner is a professor of mathematics at the U.S. Naval Academy. His
main goal in this entertaining book is to explain how the Rubik's cube
can be solved by pure mathematics. Of course, the mathematics is
group theory, and his book provides an elementary introduction, from
an idiosyncratic point of view, to the group theory necessary to model
Rubik's Cube–type puzzles. Emphasis is placed on examples rather
than on the usual theorem-proof format of mathematics books.

↬ Felix Klein, *Lectures on the Icosahedron and the Solution of Equations of
the Fifth Degree*, trans. George Gavin Morrice (Cosimo Classics, 2007)

Felix Klein (1849–1925) was a great figure in late nineteenth- and early
twentieth-century mathematics. He exerted tremendous influence
on the development of American mathematics through his efforts at
training American students at Göttingen University (see Karen Hun-
ger Parshall and David E. Rowe, *The Emergence of the American Mathematical Research Community, 1876–1900: J. J. Sylvester, Felix Klein, and
E. H. Moore* [American Mathematical Society, 1997]).

Klein formulated the so-called Erlangen Program, equating geometry and group theory. Although his program was not taken too seriously in the nineteenth century, it has proved influential in modern
times, even at the level of middle school mathematics education. The
book above, first published in German in 1884, but still in print, is
difficult for a modern reader, but it contains many observations of
interest to even a modestly sophisticated reader, and it is fun to look
at in any event.

Klein's approach to group theory follows closely his Erlangen
Program. In particular, he focuses his entire book on the rotational
symmetry group of the icosahedron. This group, known to mathematicians simply as A_5, is, in contrast to the monster M, the *smallest* interesting simple group.

✧ Hermann Weyl, *Symmetry* (Princeton University Press, 1983)

Hermann Weyl (1885–1955) came to the United States as a German refugee in the 1930s, and along with Einstein became a professor at the Institute for Advanced Study in Princeton. He made important contributions to group theory, relativity, and quantum mechanics. The book (first published in 1952) presents a survey of symmetry in a wide range of human experiences, from Sumerian art to the Alhambra; from the role of symmetry in biology to the theory of crystals in chemistry. Along the way, the mathematics—group theory—is interwoven in an appealing way. Weyl's point of view is nicely presented by the author himself (145): "Symmetry is a vast subject, significant in art and nature. Mathematics lies at its root, and it would be hard to find a better one in which to demonstrate the working of the mathematical intellect."

✧ Mario Livio, *The Equation That Couldn't Be Solved: How Mathematical Genius Discovered the Language of Symmetry* (Simon and Schuster, 2006)

Livio has written several popular books on mathematical topics. This one, written in a lively style, concentrates largely on the mathematical discoveries of the French mathematician Évariste Galois. Galois first defined the notion of a group in terms recognizable today, and established many of its fundamental properties. In a landmark proof, he showed that there is no formula, like the familiar quadratic formula from high school algebra, for the roots of a polynomial equation of degree at least 5 in an unknown variable. The proof centered on the "symmetries" (in a suitable sense) of the solutions of the equation. Symmetry is discussed in quite a broad context, and this book nicely complements the book by Weyl above.

✧ Tom Petsinis, *The French Mathematician* (Berkley Trade, 2000)

Galois' life story is well known to every mathematician. His ideas were frantically written down (when he was only twenty-one years old) the night before he was mortally wounded in a duel in 1832. Neglected for several decades after his death, his ideas and the notion of a group were well established by the end of the nineteenth century.

Petsinis, a novelist, poet, and playwright who teaches mathematics at Victoria University of Technology in Melbourne, provides a fictional account of the life and times of Galois. Despite his early death, Galois might well be placed on the honor roll of such mathematical greats as Archimedes, Newton, and Gauss. But, in addition to his mathematical talents, Galois was a political radical and general all-around troublemaker whose death by duel may have been a set-up by the police.

Part of this article is based on the twenty-fifth annual William J. Spencer Lecture given by the author at Kansas State University. The author thanks Terrell Hodge and Karen Parshall for insightful comments on a preliminary version of this article.

BRIAN PARSHALL is Gordon T. Whyburn Professor of Mathematics. For over thirty-five years, his research interests have centered on group theory. Presently, he is completing (with several Chinese collaborators) a book on quantum groups that will appear in 2008 in the American Mathematical Society's series Surveys and Monographs in Mathematics. Recently, he helped to initiate a lecture series of mathematical talks of interest to the general university and Charlottesville communities.

JAMES CARGILE

Arguments: Exploring the History of Logic

Logic was developed in ancient times, the first great age of the subject, by philosophers, notably Aristotle and the Stoics. In the Middle Ages, the second great age of the subject, logic remained prominent as a subfield of philosophy. In the third major period, which began around 1900, there was a notable attempt to exhibit mathematics as reducible to logic. It was in this time that leaders in the field came to include both philosophers and mathematicians. This attempt to reduce mathematics to logic was controversial, and some proposed, on the contrary, to reduce logic to mathematics. The connection between logic and mathematics has, in any case, been very fruitful.

One result of the disagreement has been a sharp focus on the question of what, exactly, logic is. The readings below will not answer that, nor are they an efficient introduction to logic as a modern field of research closely related to mathematics. Instead, they are chosen because they are good for browsing (except, perhaps, for Russell, where the order of presentation is more important), or, like the Kneales' great history of the subject, because they offer a more accessible account than a reader might find in the Greek original.

Introductory texts customarily distinguish between "arguments" as something in which humans are unfortunately prone to become involved and the dispassionate "arguments" of logic, the serene and neutral judge. This can be a precarious distinction, often appropriately wide, but subject to collapses into absurdity. The formulation of ground rules for proper argument is often a matter of controversy, and every "law of thought" has been challenged. Nonetheless, even in such debates, a sense can arise again of genuine authority and the possibility of excellence in pure argumentation, guided by principles that resist final codification in writing because they always require fresh formulation to bring them to life in each particular inquiry. This debate influences our ideas about the founding of logic. Some say that logic was founded virtually single-handedly by Aristotle. Though I disagree, this notion fits one view of logic as a foundation for all scientific reasoning. In this view, logic is presented as an indisputable canon that serves as a basis for proper, dispassionate argument and the resolution of disagreements. On the other hand, some will say that Plato also contributed to logic and exhibited its human, dialectical aspect.

One of the simplest logical forms, the syllogism (e.g., All philosophers are human beings; all human beings are mortal; therefore, all philosophers are mortal) can be surprising and forceful despite its simplicity. John Locke said that all syllogistic logic "begs the question," so that its contribution in argument is merely an arid triviality. Some have gone further to say that all valid deductive reasoning is question-begging, since the conclusion is "contained in" the premises. One reply would be to test these challengers at recognizing the *validity* of syllogisms. Even when a syllogism is itself trivial, the ability to recognize the syllogistic pattern behind a less formal argument can be enlightening. For example, someone may offer a syllogism with an unstated premise or conclusion, that is, an enthymeme, such as, "Jones complains that Smith is an unfair editor—Smith must have rejected something from Jones." Validity requires the implausible major premise "All editors who are targets of complaints by Jones are ones who have rejected his submissions," while the plausible major "All rejecting editors are targets of complaints by Jones" makes the inference invalid. Not only may such simple points be of value in real-life conflict, logical verdicts can be profound discoveries.

This may be why logic was highly respected in theology, especially when that subject had its greatest power. The claims logic makes to represent the peak of authority in intellectual matters can also rouse rebels who may confuse logic with the powers who invoke its authority. Marxist hostility to classical logic is just one example. Because logic offers to arbitrate disagreements from a lofty position of neutrality, its practitioners have often been caught up in heated disputes. Mill took part in substantial debates, both academic and political. Bertrand Russell's life was filled with vigorous controversy, especially after he became famous as a reasoner. Critics condemned Antoine Arnauld on various occasions, severely enough to threaten him with imprisonment. Practitioners in any field of study may, of course, become embroiled in harsh controversies. But there is a particular irony in the susceptibility of logicians. Resentment of logic may be fueled in part by its implied claim to stake out the boundaries of the indisputable. Such a claim can be inappropriate and stifling. Spotting the eternal truth is a human activity and thus is itself quite temporal and chancy. But logic can provide glimpses that are compelling and nontrivial, which can be exhilarating. Hopefully, the books below can convey some sense of that.

↬ *Sophismata* found in John Buridan, *Sophisms on Meaning and Truth,* trans. Theodore Kermit Scott (Appleton-Century-Crofts, 1966)

> One of the greatest medieval logicians, also distinguished in general science, Buridan was rector of the University of Paris and often consulted as a mediator in disputes. It was rumored that he had an affair with the queen, for which the king had thugs throw him into the Seine in a sack (this story is cited by François Villon in *Testament*). *Sophismata* are cases in which the standard rules of logic appear to break down or are violated in ways that are difficult to detect. The eleventh sophism is "I speak falsely," which can give the impression of being true if and only if it is false, a verdict forbidden by classical logic. Buridan has ingenious things to say about this and other problem cases. The discussions can be difficult to follow, but they are often interesting, and the text gives a good picture of the style of medieval logic. Chapter 8 of *Sophisms,* on self-reference, can be found in *John Buridan on Self-Reference,* trans. G. E. Hughes (Cambridge University Press, 1982).

↬ Antoine Arnauld and Pierre Nicole, *Logic, or, The Art of Thinking* (Cambridge University Press, 1996)

> A good book to start with. While it does discuss sophisms, it is primarily an exposition of good general rules of logic, illustrated with beautiful examples from literature and elsewhere. For example, these lines from Horace: "How the miser is better than a slave or more free / Stooping at the crossroads to grasp the fastened coin / I do not see: Who covets, fears; / And who lives in fear for me is never free" are exhibited as the syllogism: "He who is in continual fear is not free. All misers are in continual fear. Therefore no miser is free." The quantification in that syllogism is clear, unlike the following: "The Gospel promises salvation to sinners. There are wicked men who are Christians. Therefore, the Gospel promises salvation to wicked men." Arnauld brings out the ambiguities in the latter. This book can be read start to finish or browsed.

↬ John Stuart Mill, *A System of Logic, Ratiocinative and Inductive: Being a Connected View of the Principles of Evidence and the Methods of Scientific Investigation*, 8th ed. (Harper and Brothers, 1874)

> This would be a long reading project, but opening at random, one is likely to be immediately engaged in what is going on. The range of examples is even greater than Arnauld's, and there is similar penetrating wisdom.

↬ Bertrand Russell, *Introduction to Mathematical Philosophy* (Cosimo Classics, 2007)

> This is a good introduction to the modern question of the relation between mathematics and logic, representing the "logicist" side, which holds that mathematics is reducible to logic. The literature on the subject is now vast, and there are many more up-to-date introductory surveys, but Russell's book is highly accessible and discusses topics that are intrinsically interesting. It is brief and best read straight through.

↬ William and Martha Kneale, *The Development of Logic* (Oxford University Press, 1962)

> This is a distinguished history of logic. Its coverage of Aristotle and the Stoics is very good and is more accessible than the originals. It is not a survey of current work in the subject, but it gives the best general picture of logic offered in this list.

JAMES CARGILE has written a book on logical paradoxes, *Paradoxes: A Study in Form and Predication* (Cambridge University Press, 1979), and articles on various logical topics. His primary activity is teaching elementary logic.

3

Literature

STEPHEN CUSHMAN

At the Edge of War: Five from the 1850s

World-shaking writing often follows world-shaking violence. First came World War I, for example, and then the gigantic achievements of modernist writers in Europe and North America. In the case of five books published in the United States in the five-year stretch from March 1850 to July 1855, however, the sequence of violence and writing is reversed. It remains one of the puzzling coincidences—some might say awful ironies—of literary history in the United States that five important works of literature, Nathaniel Hawthorne's *The Scarlet Letter* (1850), Herman Melville's *Moby-Dick* (1851), Harriet Beecher Stowe's *Uncle Tom's Cabin* (1852), Henry David Thoreau's *Walden* (1854), and Walt Whitman's *Leaves of Grass* (1855), significantly advanced the prospects for a national literature just as the nation itself began falling apart.

In 1850, Millard Fillmore became president after Zachary Taylor died, California joined the Union as the thirty-first state, and the population numbered 23,191,876 people. In that year, which also brought the Compromise of 1850 and the Fugitive Slave Law, Hawthorne published his famous tale of love and transgression in seventeenth-century puritan Boston.

Writing against a background of private grief (his mother had died the previous summer) and political troubles linked to his position as surveyor of the Port of Salem, he blended history with romance in giving us one of the great studies of what William Faulkner, whose work owes much to Hawthorne, would later call the human heart in conflict with itself.

What Hawthorne didn't teach Herman Melville, whaling did, and *Moby-Dick* is, among many other things, Melville's attempt to merge a realistic account of the whaling industry with the romance of Ishmael, Ahab, and the White Whale. Having seen more of the world by the age of twenty-five than most of us do in a lifetime, Melville brought to the writing of his ambitious novel a vision more capaciously global than much of what has emerged subsequently under the rubric of literary globalization.

In the case of *Uncle Tom's Cabin,* we have a novel that not only preceded great violence; according to some, it may even have helped cause it. Lincoln is supposed to have said to Stowe something along the lines of, "So you're the little lady who started this big war," and even if he didn't, the reaction in the southern press to Stowe's sentimental, best-selling novel testified to the explosiveness of her initially serialized narrative of Uncle Tom (who has his own entry in many dictionaries), little Eva, Simon Legree, and the rest, a narrative that invites us to consider the role that the social efficacy of literature plays in our valuation of it.

If we take social efficacy as a measure of literary value, few American writers rank higher than Henry David Thoreau, whose writings directly influenced the nonviolent movements for independence and civil rights in India and the United States respectively (both Gandhi and Martin Luther King Jr. cited Thoreau's "Resistance to Civil Government," later known as "Civil Disobedience," as crucial to them) and continue to hover inspirationally over the environmental movement that began in the second half of the twentieth century. But *Walden,* that hybrid of memoir, natural history, philosophy, social criticism, and extended fable, also towers as a lasting monument of figurative imagination, variegated tonality, and resplendent prose, one that exalted creative nonfiction as a genre long before the genre had a name.

Like Thoreau, Walt Whitman never left North America, but like the New England nature lover, the bard of Brooklyn and Manhattan has become an internationally recognized literary icon of this country. Part of Whitman's achievement is that he succeeded in projecting and embodying something he represented as essential Americanism, and although any representation of essential Americanism will make some people uncomfortable, the fact remains that many readers of American literature outside the United States still point to Whitman as a paradigmatic American original. Whitman also changed the landscape of American poetry and made new things possible for subsequent poets that had not seemed possible, or even thinkable, before. Whenever one feels tempted to dismiss Whitman for bombast and boosterism, it may change things to remember that he looked on his book of 1855 as his contribution to holding together a disintegrating country. When a few years later the country broke apart anyway, Whitman gave himself fully to the mission of ministering to the casualties of that breaking, and he lost his own health in the process. Writing and dying before the age of prestigious awards and prizes, Whitman, like the four other writers here, would not become a fixture in the canon of American literature until the following century, and even then it would take more large wars to interest many citizens of the United States in the celebration of that literature.

All these books come in various paperback editions, each of which has its strong points. For reading *Moby-Dick* and *Walden,* editions with footnotes or endnotes will come in especially handy.

↜ Nathaniel Hawthorne, *The Scarlet Letter* (1850)

Hawthorne's carefully crafted, architecturally balanced novel also stages one of the archetypal collisions of American literature, that of individual desire with communal law. In following out the rupture between the one and the many, Hawthorne chose to look back over his shoulder into the puritan past of New England, or into his gothic version of it, but was he also looking forward, consciously or unconsciously, to the rupture to come? *Reading Tip:* Those who falter in the long introductory section, called "The Custom-House," should skip it and come back later.

↜ Herman Melville, *Moby-Dick* (Norton, 2001)

Along with the global sweep of the novel and its cast of singular characters, Melville left us a treasury of language, his own sentences everywhere rippling with the rhythms of the Bible and Shakespeare's tragedies. *Reading Tip:* In the cetology chapters, Melville includes extensive detail about whales and whaling, details gleaned from his experiences aboard the *Acushnet* in 1841 and 1842. To some, these chapters feel like digressions and distractions from the romance of Ahab and the White Whale, but their value depends partly on watching Melville transform the literal details of whales and whaling into figurative images of the same supernaturally charged world that Ahab and the Whale inhabit.

↜ Harriet Beecher Stowe, *Uncle Tom's Cabin* (1852)

Reading Stowe after Hawthorne and Melville raises many provocative questions about the nature of literature and its production. What is literary failure and what is literary success? (*Moby-Dick* flopped during Melville's lifetime, but only the Bible sold more copies in this country than Stowe's novel did during hers.) What is the relation of popular to high-brow literature? How does the international reputation of a book (Stowe was honored by Queen Victoria) affect its national standing? *Reading Tip:* My colleague Stephen Railton has constructed a prize-winning Web site devoted to *Uncle Tom's Cabin* (www.iath.virginia.edu/utc/), and it's well worth a visit before, during, and after reading the novel.

⊷ Henry David Thoreau, *Walden* (1854)

Choosing one book to reread at successive moments in a life may illuminate that life, and *Walden*, which meditates so boldly and bracingly on what living means, would be a strong candidate for that choice. *Reading Tip:* Thoreau's first chapter, "Economy," is also his longest. It introduces several of the principles that informed his two-year experiment at Walden Pond, and many readers consider it the meat of the book. But those who find it dragging can always skip ahead to the shorter second chapter and then return to take "Economy" in smaller chunks.

⊷ Walt Whitman, *Leaves of Grass* (Penguin, 1961)

Once one has read him, it is hard to be indifferent to Whitman. Insufferable egotist or democratic egalitarian, tiresome blabbermouth or lyric innovator, alienated misfit or ecstatic visionary, he shows us in *Leaves of Grass* that these alternatives do not necessarily exclude each other, and in his case often go together. *Reading Tip:* Most readily available volumes of Whitman's poetry follow the so-called Death Bed edition of *Leaves of Grass,* published in 1891–92. Some of these volumes include the 1855 edition of Whitman's most important poem, the originally untitled one that eventually became "Song of Myself." If possible, start with this first version of that poem and with the 1855 prose preface that preceded it.

STEPHEN CUSHMAN is Robert C. Taylor Professor of English. He joined the faculty in 1982 and since then has published both scholarship and poetry. His most recent book of prose is *Bloody Promenade: Reflections on a Civil War Battle* (University of Virginia Press, 1999); and his most recent books of verse are *Cussing Lesson* (Louisiana State University Press, 2002) and *Heart Island* (David Robert Books, 2006).

JAHAN RAMAZANI

Mourning and Modern Poetry

Your mother dies after a long illness. Cancer kills a friend at work. You are plunged into grief by terrorist attacks, whose victims seem like they could have been you or members of your family. Where do you turn, if the banalities of mass-printed sympathy cards, the ritual language of religious institutions, the flat statements in the newspapers, and various other forms of mass-mediated or prepackaged understanding and comfort fail you? Whether grieving over the intimate loss of a loved one or the collective losses of those killed in wars, disasters, and violent conflict, many have turned to poetry. Why? Because poetry is especially rich in feeling and thought, because it is vivid and self-conscious, compressed and idiosyncratically patterned. Poets have been writing about the dead, after all, for thousands of years. When you write or read poems of mourning for the dead, you are participating in the ancient tradition of the elegy.

Some traditional aspects of the elegy may seem insufficiently vexed for our difficult and disturbing times—when it smoothly rounds the bend from loss to recuperation, when the dead quickly ascend to the stars in heaven, when the ending imposes a near-perfect closure or finality, when the dead seem perhaps a little too wonderful to be believed. For just these reasons, modern and contemporary poets, as I have argued at greater length in a book on the twentieth-century elegy, have renewed the genre by vigorously rewriting—sometimes even exploding—its conventions. Their language of mourning is complex and ambivalent; at its best, it refuses to simplify the crooked and even recursive path that grief often takes. Instead of following a set pattern of denial, anger, bargaining, depression, and acceptance, modern and contemporary poets represent mourning as a vastly more irregular and unpredictable experience. In their poems, the wounds of grief heal only to break open again and again, sometimes when least expected. The English poet Thomas Hardy writes elegy after elegy for his dead wife; acknowledging the ambivalences in their relationship, he offers us a portrait not of grief resolved but of an agonized and conflicted mourning that mounts and recedes, only to begin again. In modern and contemporary elegies, affectionate grief for, and bitter quarrels with, the dead are represented as extending beyond the closure of the poem's last line.

Nor are the dead angelic in modern and contemporary elegies. Instead of idealizing the dead, some poets even risk naming the flaws and inadequacies of the people they mourn. When W. B. Yeats commemorates some of the victims of the 1916 insurrection that eventually led to Irish independence, he says he thought one rebel a "drunken, vainglorious lout," and he deems these revolutionaries perhaps too single-minded and stone-hearted in their fanatical pursuit of political change. When the English poet W. H. Auden mourns Yeats in turn, he has learned from the Irishman how to write the ambivalent style of public elegy Yeats fashioned—and so Yeats is remembered as a great poet misled by his reactionary politics and aristocratic pretensions. In the late 1950s and the 1960s, American poets fuse their psychoanalytic self-understanding with the modern, de-idealizing elegy, now recast for mothers and fathers. Robert Lowell, Anne Sexton, John Berryman, Allen Ginsberg, and other poets rage against the dead parent—most famously, Sylvia Plath in her elegies for her father, in which she declares, "Daddy, daddy, you bastard, I'm through."

The contemporary Northern Irish poet Seamus Heaney's moving and graceful elegies for his mother and father restore some of the traditional consolations of the genre, heightening its affectionate intimacy in a heart-breaking sequence of sonnets for his mother. But as a poet from a country torn by sectarian violence, Heaney, like other poets of the twentieth and twenty-first centuries, has had to grapple not only with personal loss but also with the collective deaths resulting from war, terror, and reprisal. He looks back to the example of the English poet Wilfred Owen, perhaps the twentieth century's most famous war poet, who arrived at a kind of war elegy that mourns the dead without making sense of the senseless—the devastation and atrocity that killed many millions in World War I and countless other wars since. Struggling to comprehend the astonishing scale of modern death, poets such as Owen and Heaney have continually warned themselves and others against saccharining the muck and brutality and madness of modern death, against beautifying or redeeming losses by way of ideologies of the nation or the church.

Modern and contemporary poets sternly hold back from recuperating irrecuperable losses, instead mourning death with an intensity, an honesty, and a depth of understanding that send us back to poetry when more simple and consoling kinds of writing fail us. At a time when grief has often been seen as an embarrassment to be hidden or a step-by-step process to be completed, poetry holds open a more subtle and complex understanding of our difficult and protracted dealings with the dead.

↪ Thomas Hardy, "Poems of 1912–13" (1914), in *The Complete Poetical Works of Thomas Hardy*, 5 vols., ed. Samuel Hynes (Oxford University Press, 1982–95)

In this sequence of elegies, Hardy mourns the death of his estranged wife, Emma. After she died in 1912, Hardy discovered a prose text she had written about him that excoriated and denounced him. He also discovered a more tender set of reminiscences of their courtship forty years earlier. On the basis of these and his own reflections on their difficult marriage, he wrote a series of elegies that, nearly a century later, still seem astonishing for the directness with which they explore the contradictions of mourning. These elegies strip bare the psychological process of mourning, acknowledging that not only love but also self-reproach, anger, and skepticism vex secular mourning and the act of writing about it.

⊷ Wilfred Owen, *The Poems of Wilfred Owen,* ed. Jon Stallworthy (Norton, 1986).

(Owen's poems were first published by fellow war poet Siegfried Sassoon in 1920, but Stallworthy's edition provides useful corrections and annotations.)

Although Owen's "Anthem for Doomed Youth" and "Strange Meeting" are widely known, it is worth reading further among the poems of this gifted young poet who died in battle a week before the end of World War I. In his draft preface to his poems, Owen said, "These elegies are to this generation in no sense consolatory." Owen helped fashion a new kind of war elegy that refuses bland pieties or stock compensations, while putting to startling new uses lush sonorities, religious language, and literary allusions. Owen remembers the conventions of pastoral elegy but turns them on their head. He powerfully conveys the terror, pain, and grief of the modern battlefield.

⊷ W. H. Auden, *Selected Poems,* ed. Edward Mendelson (Random House, 2007)

In this collection, you will find the texts of Auden's greatest elegies as they were first published in his books, including "In Memory of W. B. Yeats" and "In Memory of Sigmund Freud." In these and other elegies, Auden brilliantly negotiates the relationship between his own views and the person he mourns. He berates Yeats, for example, for his politics, yet celebrates how the Irish poet found joy in tragedy, "rapture" in "distress." Similarly, he writes a psychoanalytically informed elegy for the father of psychoanalysis. Auden's elegies remain models for how to write elegies for public figures without betraying either the dead or a poet's idiosyncrasies.

⊷ Sylvia Plath, *Collected Poems,* ed. Ted Hughes (Harper Perennial, 1981)

Plath's elegies for her father, who died when she was eight, represent an explosive new kind of poem of mourning, expanding the range of feeling permitted into the genre. Among her most accomplished elegies are "The Colossus," "Little Fugue," and "Daddy," in which she draws on unconscious and taboo feelings, such as hatred, desire, and masochism. Her poems for her father are the first elegies in English to explore such searing grief and rage toward a dead parent. Shattering the emotional boundaries of the elegy, Plath also harnesses the resources of poetry in her brilliant deployment of figurative language, of words both tender and furious, of incantatory rhythms and rhymes, and of such poetic devices as apostrophe, or address, to the dead father.

↪ Seamus Heaney, *Opened Ground: Selected Poems, 1966–1996* (Farrar, Straus and Giroux, 1999)

Heaney is often said to be the most gifted poet writing in English today. Among his most accomplished works are his elegies, including "The Strand at Lough Beg" and "Casualty," mourning victims of both Protestant and Catholic violence in Northern Ireland. In these elegies, Heaney writes in traditional verse forms without pretending to redeem the irredeemable carnage of modern political violence. That is, he commemorates the dead but without prettifying or exploiting them or the motives that led to their deaths. Other elegies he has written are intimate poems mourning the deaths of family members, most notably his sonnet sequence for his mother, "Clearances," in which he remembers the love and laughter, the awkwardness and tenderness shared by a mother and son.

JAHAN RAMAZANI is Edgar F. Shannon Professor and Department Chair of English. His books include *Poetry of Mourning: The Modern Elegy from Hardy to Heaney* (University of Chicago Press, 1994), a finalist for the National Book Critics Circle Award. He is an editor of *The Norton Anthology of Modern and Contemporary Poetry* (2003) and *The Norton Anthology of English Literature* (2006). He is the recipient of a Guggenheim Fellowship, an NEH Fellowship, a Rhodes scholarship, and the William Riley Parker Prize of the MLA.

MARCIA DAY CHILDRESS AND JULIA D. MAHONEY

Doctors, Lawyers, and the Classics: Reading for Ethical Values

Being a doctor or a lawyer has a strong moral component, and moral imagination and self-reflection contribute to a professional's attentiveness, effectiveness, and well-being. But the demands of training can leave na-scent physicians and lawyers too little time to consider just what it means to forge a professional identity and to serve the troubled, sick, and dying among us. Though students of medicine and law can learn basic rules of conduct in the clinic and lecture hall, a more open, conversational forum, like a book discussion, may provide a better venue for developing empa-thy and ethical awareness, along with the sort of measured engagement that protects against burnout.

The two of us teach "The Interprofessional Seminar in Ethical Values and Professional Life," a class that uses literature to spark inquiry into the values, responsibilities, and rewards of life as a doctor or lawyer. Se-nior medical and law students, six each, gather in the home of one of us on five evenings over the school year to discuss texts, including—indeed, especially—ones that have little or no obvious connection to modern medical or legal practice.

The books on our list come from a seminar organized around the theme of tradition, inheritance, and generational change. We chose this theme be-cause medicine and law continually struggle to determine which ideals and practices to retain over time, and which to modify or abandon. Both medi-cine and law are deeply conservative institutions that often resist change, for each assumes its practices represent a distillation of preceding gen-erations' wisdom and so deserve profound respect, if not complete defer-ence. At the same time, these professions must adapt to society's evolving needs. An individual doctor's or lawyer's stance toward her field's received tradition—how should I decide what to keep, and what discard?—is a key component of both her professional and personal identity.

In the class titled "Generation to Generation," we use plays and novels as springboards to discussing the exhilarations and challenges of genera-tional succession. *King Lear* spurs students to examine the institutional structures that promote and frustrate orderly transfers of power, and to consider what it means to be "competent" to make decisions. Reading Sophocles' *Philoctetes*, the class discovers an ancient counterpart in ap-prentice warrior Neoptolemus, who must choose between the wily tactics of his captain, Odysseus, and the ways of a father he scarcely remembers, Achilles. Considering *Howards End*, they ask of our own time and our increasingly diverse society a version of the question that prompted E. M. Forster, in 1910, to write his novel: Who are England's rightful heirs?

For most of our students, this seminar is their first encounter with each other's professional worlds. They explore the assumptions and at-titudes of medicine and law, and share tales of their own experiences, re-vealing to each other how doctors and lawyers are made. Jane Austen's depiction in *Persuasion* of the marriage mart of early nineteenth-century

Britain prompts students to reflect on the highly ritualized processes that match today's law graduates with clerkships and medical students with residencies. Discussing *The Burial at Thebes,* a medical student planning a career in psychiatry recognizes in Antigone's principled defiance glimmers of the psychosis affecting one of her patients—but she sees, too, a new nobility in her patient. *The Burial at Thebes* also calls attention to rites that families customarily accord the bodies of their dead. One medical student complains that liability and ethical concerns now constrain trauma surgery trainees from practicing invasive procedures on the bodies of newly dead patients. Some law students, mindful of the weight the law accords bodily integrity and the rights of surviving relatives over corpses, are aghast: "You wanted to do *what*?" The response of their classmate—who plans a career in emergency medicine—is simple: "How else can I learn to save your life?"

Because we encourage students to connect and contrast the books we are reading, by year's end we share a rich network of plots and protagonists. We invite the students to consider their own lives too in light of the texts, for they themselves are the new generation, apprentices about to inherit systems of health care and the law that they will one day lead, and young adults even now choosing career paths, mates, and lifestyles. As a result, our conversations address lofty themes and classic dilemmas but also have urgent practicality. And the students come to know they are not alone as they commence their life's work, for they have their classmates, to be sure, but also some literary companions.

↩ Sophocles, *Philoctetes,* in *Sophocles,* vol. 2 of *The Complete Greek Tragedies,* ed. David Grene and Richard Lattimore (University of Chicago Press, 1991)

> This play of Sophocles' old age, less well known to modern audiences than *Oedipus Rex* or *Antigone,* is enjoying a resurgence thanks to medical humanities scholars who find compelling authenticity in its portrayal of woundedness, pain, and the "island" exile that is illness. In deciding how to undertake his assigned mission—ensuring that the marooned, embittered Philoctetes returns to fight with the Greeks in the Trojan War, bringing with him the magic bow of Heracles needed for victory—young Neoptolemus wrestles with the morality of methods of persuasion and deception. At the heart of the play, when Neoptolemus attends the suffering Philoctetes, doctors discover a model of fidelity to the patient.

↩ William Shakespeare, *King Lear,* ed. R. A. Foakes (Arden Shakespeare, 1997)

> Shakespeare's towering tragedy has at its heart a struggle over succession and a blind, vengeful abuse of power. Lear's mercurial nature and

peevish insistence on the most superficial forms of fidelity lead him to divide his kingdom between his two elder daughters, disinheriting his beloved Cordelia. This rich play invites readings from many disciplinary perspectives. Medical students consider diagnosing Lear's folly—his mind grown too imperfect to recognize his rightful heirs—as dementia, while law students schooled in institutional analysis ask whether the roots of this tragedy lie in the flawed monarchical system. Students of medicine and law alike hone in on issues of conflict of interest, and how, in using royal authority to elevate two of his heirs at the expense of the third, Lear neglects his social and professional responsibilities to the kingdom.

↪ Jane Austen, *Persuasion*, ed. Gillian Beer (Penguin, 2003)

Like Austen's other novels, *Persuasion* examines inheritance—of values even more than of property—during a time of social transition. When debts force vain, profligate Sir Walter Elliot to rent out his ancestral estate, the aristocratic Elliot family relocates to the spa town of Bath. There, interactions among relative strangers are governed less by knowledge born of long familiarity than by social appearances and conventional courtesies. How should Anne Elliot respond to the "persuasions" of sisters and friends, who question whether self-made Captain Wentworth is a suitable match for a baronet's daughter? Like Anne, students about to become practicing professionals wonder how to "read" character and navigate elaborate social rituals so as to make the best match (of mate or career opportunity) and how to trust their own observations, discernment, and moral compass in their new, adult lives.

↪ E. M. Forster, *Howards End* (Modern Library, 1999)

Forster's inquiry into the fate of Edwardian England seeks a moral, even spiritual, solution to questions of self-fulfillment and inheritance. Property figures centrally in the novel, especially the benefits and burdens conferred by owning material and intellectual goods and the importance of testamentary disposition. Readers can probe the different meanings property holds for various characters, recognizing that, for each, its possession (or lack) is crucial to crafting a life and, for all, the laws of property both further and frustrate personal development and achievement of life goals. Young doctors and lawyers must confront their ability to "only connect," as Henry Wilcox cannot, with others who lack the privileges they themselves enjoy. They must also come to terms with the cruelty, injustice, and even ill health wrought by class divisions and differential codes of conduct.

↶ Seamus Heaney, *The Burial at Thebes: A Version of Sophocles' Antigone*
(Farrar, Straus and Giroux, 2005)

This is the second play by Sophocles that Nobel laureate Heaney has adapted for modern audiences (he earlier remade *Philoctetes* as *The Cure at Troy*). The Irish poet makes fresh the monumental collision of Oedipus's daughter Antigone, who insists on obeying the gods by performing the funeral rites due the body of her slain brother Polynices, and King Creon, who aims to solidify his authority by denying burial to an enemy of the state and by prosecuting Antigone for breaking his law. Young physicians and lawyers engage for themselves the play's sharp clashes between religion and statecraft and between duty to past generations and obligation to generations yet to come. And readers discover in the person of Antigone a striking, even chilling, model of principled autonomous action and a provocative challenge to the cultural pluralism and communal accommodation that prevail today.

MARCIA DAY CHILDRESS is Associate Professor of Medical Education, director of programs in humanities in the University of Virginia School of Medicine's Center for Biomedical Ethics and Humanities, and a scholar of the British writer Virginia Woolf. She teaches and writes about literature, narrative, and medicine, and uses the humanities and arts in preparing physicians for professional life. She also directs the Medical Center Hour, the university's weekly public forum on medicine and society. In 2004–5, she chaired the Faculty Senate.

JULIA D. MAHONEY is Professor of Law and David H. Ibbeken Research Professor at the University of Virginia School of Law, where she teaches courses in property, nonprofit institutions, cultural property, and ethical values. Her articles include "Kelo's Legacy: Eminent Domain and the Future of Property Rights," in the *Supreme Court Review* (2005), and "Perpetual Restrictions on Land and the Problem of the Future," in the *Virginia Law Review*.

STEPHEN ARATA

Marketing Fiction: Victorian Serial Novels

The one thing everyone knows about Victorian novels is that they tend to be long. Very long. Victorian publishers were acutely aware of the need to break up these long prose narratives into manageable, reader-friendly units. Although the Victorian novel is one of the glories of literature, it is fair to say that the dazzling creativity of the novelists themselves had a counterpart in the ingenuity of publishers intent on cultivating the widest possible readership for their wares. The history of the Victorian novel is tightly entwined with the development of various "novel-delivery systems"—that is, with practices of marketing and distribution designed to attract, and to keep, the attention of the novel-reading public.

In his 1846 essay "The Philosophy of Composition," Edgar Allan Poe—never a man to avoid controversy when he could help it—contentiously asserts that when it comes to literature there is no such thing as a long work of art. "There is a distinct limit," Poe writes, "as regards length, to all works of literary art," which is precisely the limit of what can be read in a single sitting. For if even "two sittings are required, the affairs of the world interfere" with the unity and intensity of the artistic impression, and the reader's aesthetic experience is "at once destroyed."

You might suspect that Poe has rather overstated his case, yet he is on to something fundamental about our experiences of art, namely that they are closely bound to our experiences of time. More than that: Poe points us to the fact that all societies develop norms for determining how long an artwork can reasonably make demands on our attention. "A single sitting" is in fact the rough rule for most of the aesthetic encounters that punctuate our lives, from feature films to music concerts to theatrical performances to professional sporting events. While we can all think of exceptions—twelve-hour movies, three-day-long operas (or cricket matches)—few of us would want those to be the norm.

The novel is an obvious exception to the single-sitting rule. A novel of even moderate length is difficult to take in at one go; most novels far exceed the capacities of even the most heroic attention span. If we consult our own reading experiences, we find that as a rule novels try to accommodate our desire for single-sitting portions of text by means of such familiar conventions as, say, chapter breaks. Novels are divided into chapters or sections for many reasons, but one is surely to assist our efforts to regulate the rate of our aesthetic consumption. My students often report feeling exhausted or disoriented by their first experience of reading novels written before division into chapters became the norm, such as Daniel Defoe's *Robinson Crusoe* (1719). The same disorientation can occur with modern or experimental novels that dispense with chapters, such as Virginia Woolf's *Mrs. Dalloway* (1925).

Over the course of the nineteenth century, publishers in Great Britain experimented with numerous different publishing formats designed with the limits of attention span in mind. Today, most readers acquainted with Victorian novels know that many were originally published serially. Fewer are aware of just how many different kinds of serial publication there were. To take only a few of the more common options: Many novels were published in monthly "parts"—24- or 32-page units (roughly the equivalent of three or four chapters) stitched together, usually with an illustrated paper cover. Others were serialized in monthly or bimonthly periodicals. Others still appeared in weekly installments. (Charles Dickens, possessed of a keen entrepreneurial sense, published novels in all the above formats.) Once serial publication was completed, novels were then published in their entirety, usually in three volumes. Until late in the century, relatively few novels appeared first in volume form.

What writers and publishers saw as necessity—making novels marketable to an audience that wanted to read long narratives in short increments over extended periods of time—became in practice a spur to the creativity of Victorian novelists. This was never simply a matter of ending each installment with a cliffhanger. The distinctive virtues of the best Victorian novels are intimately bound up with their mastery of pacing, rhythm, narrative anticipation and retrospection—with temporality in all its many dimensions. That mastery was in many, if not most, cases a product of the demands of writing serially. For twenty-first-century readers, becoming aware of those demands through historical study can help make the reading of nineteenth-century novels an even more pleasurable and rewarding activity.

The books in this list are all engaging and informative studies of Victorian publishing practices. But of course the best way to experience the pleasures of serialized fiction is to read Victorian novels.

✎ J. A. Sutherland, *Victorian Novelists and Publishers* (University of Chicago Press, 1976)

A concise and highly informative account of Victorian publishing between 1830 and 1870. Part 1, "The Novel Publishing World," provides a historical overview of the many factors—economic, cultural, and psychological—that spurred the development of serialized fiction. Part 2, "Novelists, Novels, and Their Publishers," offers case studies of eight novelists ranging from the famous and successful (George Eliot, Anthony Trollope) to what Sutherland calls the not-quite-first-rank (Harrison Ainsworth, Charles Lever). Sutherland is especially interesting on the often complex negotiations between writers and publishers, with each side striving to maximize its profits while (usually, anyway) keeping up the pretense that publishing, being a genteel profession, was above the sordid world of commerce and profits. The temperament of an author was often most visible in interactions with publishers and booksellers, as was the case with two of the century's most popular novelists, Trollope and Dickens. Trollope, ever cautious in money matters, insisted on lump sum payments and never negotiated for profits based on sales, while Dickens, Trollope's opposite temperamentally and utterly secure in his sense of his own genius and ability to give the public what it wanted, went through different publishers at a rapid clip, always convinced that they were out to cheat him.

↪ Linda K. Hughes and Michael Lund, *The Victorian Serial* (University Press of Virginia, 1991)

The best and fullest examination of how the Victorian novel was shaped by the challenges of serial publication. Hughes and Lund show in fascinating detail how different novelists tailored their fictions to suit the needs of serialization. They show too how the practices and expectations of readers changed as a result of part-publication. Today we nearly always read, say, *David Copperfield* in a single-volume paperback edition, a format that gives us complete control over the speed with which we make our way through the novel. By contrast, the first readers of *Copperfield* had to spread their reading over nearly two years, from late 1848 through the middle of 1850, as the novel appeared in monthly installments, a few chapters at a time. Hughes and Lund speculate on how serial reading affected one's sense of time and of history (its pace, its direction, its ends); they also show in persuasive detail the role that serial reading played in the life of families and of other small social groups.

↪ Robert L. Patten, *Charles Dickens and His Publishers* (Oxford University Press, 1978)

A fascinating study of Dickens's relationships—always spirited, often acrimonious—with his publishers, and of the many ways that he sought to increase his readership (and his bank account) through innovative publishing and marketing practices. The unprecedented success of *The Pickwick Papers*, Dickens's first novel, did more than anything else to establish serial publication as the dominant form of novel publication. Dickens experimented with numerous "novel-delivery systems" over the course of his career, from weekly publication to simultaneous publication in different formats to a variety of collected editions of his works aimed at different strata of the reading public. He also made sure that whatever financial risks were involved were shouldered by publishers, who for their part were generally happy to take those risks in return for the potentially lucrative connection to the novelist who called himself "The Inimitable."

↤ Graham Law, *Serializing Fiction in the Victorian Press* (Palgrave, 2000)

A scholarly study that expands our sense of what serial publication included by examining the many popular (and now-forgotten) novels published in newspapers. Especially after 1880, with the rise of syndicates, "newspaper novelist" could be a lucrative profession. Law brings to light novelists whose popularity in their own day is matched by the utter obscurity into which they have fallen.

↤ Richard Altick, *The English Common Reader: A Social History of the Mass Reading Public, 1800–1900* (1957; Ohio State University Press, 1998)

Though not primarily concerned with serial publication, this book remains indispensable reading for anyone interested in nineteenth-century writers and their publics. The publishing explosion of the nineteenth century was triggered by the vast increase in the reading public in the first decades after 1800. That increase was accompanied by widespread changes in attitudes toward novel reading, which had always been considered by the pious as a frivolous and potentially sinful activity. Serial publication helped make the novel respectable by making novel reading an activity that took place within the family circle. Lively, learned, witty, and always illuminating, Altick's book has yet to be superseded in the fifty years since its publication.

STEPHEN ARATA, the Richard A. and Sarah Page Mayo NEH Distinguished Teaching Professor and Associate Professor of English, teaches nineteenth- and twentieth-century British literature. He is the author of *Fictions of Loss in the Victorian Fin de Siècle* (Cambridge University Press, 1996) and the editor of classroom editions of William Morris's *News from Nowhere*, George Gissing's *New Grub Street*, and H. G. Wells's *The Time Machine*.

KAREN CHASE

Love, Guilt, and Reparation: Fiction That Guides Us

American culture treads perilously close to the borders of moral parochialism and the extremes of economic globalism. It is a potent combination, and dangerous because, instead of contradiction, which might provoke a dialectic and propose a synthesis, these two conditions work in silent parallel, each indifferent to the other, forcing an ever-widening gap between what we do and what we believe to be good. The books I choose here do teach, but they do not preach: their greatest contribution is to rouse full personhood, to unsettle complacency, and to give deep not shallow pleasures. They pry us open to acknowledgment of the "uncanny" in Freud's sense of the word: both strange and yet known from long ago.

Charles Dickens and Fyodor Dostoevsky were accused of violating conventions of realism in their portraits of characters and society. Both objected, appealing to a "higher realism" that would expose "the romantic side of familiar things," in short, a realism that excludes nothing in advance, not even fantasy, dream, or whimsy. This provocation troubles the borders we use to distinguish one thing from another, and it demands recognition that just as human bodies bleed, so may the possibilities of literature bleed together. In one of his books, Dickens asks, "What connection can there be?" between a crossing sweeper who brushes mud (and horse excrement) from the road and the highest power and privilege in Britain. Dickens and Dostoevsky disturb the boundaries between peoples and places, thoughts and emotions, the surface and depths of experience. They rely on accident, chance, and coincidence, not only because these things operate apart from our will, but because what we call chance is often only the result of our own determination, slightly disguised or concealed. The last border that they attempt to cross is the one separating literature and life; they insist that reading is no holiday.

I leap more than a hundred years to see how Rohinton Mistry follows the tradition of Dickensian social realism, though in his work naturalism predominates over fancy. Mistry composes long novels, works massive enough to engage the massive problems that concern him: above all, poverty and the poverty of feeling. Much of his India is a nightmare, in which bad grows worse, and worse grows insupportable, but the unsentimental task of his novel is to recover relics of our humanity. Humor is an indispensable resource. Those of his characters who find comedy, "however dark or ironic, brief or laconic," those who manage to meet incident with the ability to affirm life anyway, achieve the dignity reserved for those whom we most admire.

William Trevor's characters are equally precarious, though not nearly so dispossessed through class or caste. Mistry recovers detail within the immensity of Indian social life: his vision is panoramic. Trevor, on the other hand, narrows the scope until the Irish whole is eclipsed by its smaller parts. Trevor's characters are so busy trying to comprehend the warp of their own minds and the shape of their bodies that they can't see their entanglement in the rest of the world. Their only hope resides in striking out, often absurdly or futilely, stumbling in the direction of one another.

Ian McEwan is more insistent, even more brutal, willing to inflict the shock of recognition: we are always involved—if not downright blameworthy, at least significantly entwined—with all events, large and small, visible or concealed. Humiliation, cruelty, rape: we do not desire connections with these terrors; it is simply the condition into which we have been thrown. Even though we can deny or distort our involvement (and we do), we can never extricate ourselves from responsibility. McEwan presses on remorselessly. In the spirit of T. S. Eliot's "Gerontion," he asks, "After such knowledge, what forgiveness?" and asks further, "What will you do now?" and, "What will you ever do?"

These are the questions that act on us most strongly when we forget to ask them. If we fail to pose them, then we act blindly, out of habit rather than deliberation, and often in ways that contradict our avowed beliefs and principles. The books I have chosen heighten our self-consciousness and simultaneously demand that we shed the self in pursuit of others, including that other who lives inside us.

↭ Charles Dickens, *David Copperfield* (1849; Penguin, 2005)

Everyone has heard of it, and many already assume they know characters like Micawber, Uriah Heep, or Mr. Dick. But too few actually read the *ur*-text, which draws on Dickens's own traumatic childhood in order to portray the fullest range of emotions available even to the youngest among us. When David is suffering imprisonment at the hands of his sadistic stepfather, he consoles himself by "reading as if for life." Even in the midst of genial tones and the erupting hilarity, the novel sustains the intensity of that vocation; it means to be read, as if for life. The novel is brisk and biting toward social failure; it engages with the plenitude of an emerging modernity—problems of education, professionalism, class, men, women, marriage; but even its grimmest recognitions are healed by the laughter.

↭ Fyodor Dostoevsky, *The Brothers Karamazov,* trans. Richard Pevear and Larissa Volokhonsky (Farrar, Straus and Giroux, 2002)

More than any other work I know, this novel alters with each rereading. Through investigation of the murder of a repellent but vital old man that instigates the plot, Dostoevsky explores the mental recesses of guilt, the desire for freedom, the necessity for love, spiritual faith, and moral responsibility. Like Dickens, by whom he was influenced, Dostoevsky locates, not innocence, but hope, in children, or in the repossession of a childlike openness and vulnerability on the part of adults. The tormented souls for which he is known all exhibit various forms of that personal and social canker, spite, which explodes when it encounters forms of emotional plenitude. The part of the novel (in)famously detached, entitled "The Grand Inquisitor," puts all of humanity on a rack, and can be read justly only when set against the humble narrative of the "other" father whose death provokes the plot, Father Zossima.

⊷ Rohinton Mistry, *A Fine Balance* (Vintage, 2001)

If Dostoevsky responded to the yearning for a complex portrait of innocence in his reading of Dickens, Mistry responds to Dickensian panorama. Epic in ambition (he has been compared to Tolstoy for his breadth of vision), Mistry asks fiction to encompass the scale of his native India, above all its vast cities that draw the millions of inhabitants who come to find a better life. The rigid class- and caste-divided world that seeks to maintain distinctions constantly erupts into chaos, as the surge from below provokes oppression from above, and desperation becomes general. But what stands out, stands not *a*part but strikingly as *part of* this world, is the resilience of certain characters, and the capacity of realist fiction to embody forms of hope. To see as clearly as this novel does and to notice fine distinctions even within the gloom is itself an act of defiance.

⊷ William Trevor, *Two Lives: "Reading Turgenev" and "My House in Umbria"* (Penguin, 1992)

This is a quiet classic, for Trevor is perhaps the most understated writer of fiction today. The book consists of two novellas, *Reading Turgenev* and *My House in Umbria*. The first of these stories asks, "what happens to the quality of gentleness in an extremity of harshness?" and we are not surprised to discover that madness, or at least mental instability, is the response. The delicacy of Trevor's story resides in his ability to convey madness as something remarkable, if not desirable, a small and heroic instance of resistance against the course of history and the current of modernity. At first glance, the second story relates to the first by way of contrast: it is loud, coarse, and insistent. A bomb explodes on a train, and the survivors in the unlucky carriage are invited by one of them to gather for recuperation at her villa in northern Italy. The owner is a writer of romances, whose mental unsteadiness is continuous with themes in the first story. Gradually we realize that *both* stories are contemporary romances, stories about the kind of love that can persist, even flourish, within the most strange and constrained spaces. This is an aesthetic of fragility, a study of the most breakable beauty.

⊷ Ian McEwan, *Atonement* (Knopf, 2003)

Spanning much of the twentieth century, McEwan's novel takes a Dostoevskian turn. It too puts crime in its center, in this case two crimes, a personal one and the massive transgression of the Second World War, as an audacious way to expose the emotional contours of the modern mind. In this novel, guilt marks the transition from youth to adulthood, and like every book on my list, this one requires universal accountability; it asks us to accept blame for acts committed with our implicit or explicit consent, and responsibility for acts committed with or without our consent. Moreover, as its title suggests, the novel goes further than guilt, blame, and even responsibility. It is a study in reparation, and it understands guilt as the first step in the direction of repairing the wrong. The extent to which a wrong *can* be repaired is profoundly uncertain, and the provisional character of all attempts, "the capacity for actions to be made and remade repeatedly," makes a solution less necessary, less satisfying than the troubled quest.

KAREN CHASE, Professor of English, specializes in nineteenth-century literature and culture. She has written about a wide range of authors, including Charlotte Brontë, Charles Dickens, and George Eliot, as well as an examination of the public life of the Victorian family. Her current project addresses the conditions and experiences of the elderly in the latter half of the nineteenth century.

LISA RUSS SPAAR

Beside Ourselves: Ecstatic Poetry

Ecstasy, associated with frenzy, rapture, drugs, and fervor, derives from the Greek *ekstasis* (*ex* [out of], *histanai* [to stand, to place]) and signifies a motion away from stasis, of being "beside the self." It implies a foray from an ordinary to an extraordinary situation, from a normal or contained to an altered or "other" state, from one condition of feeling or knowledge to another, and though rare, no human experience is beyond its reach. Religion, sex, politics, sports, consumerism, eating and drinking, war, crime, investing, travel, and illness can all involve transformative, transgressive passages into wonder, mystery, and otherness. The banner-waving politico in a thrall of conventioneering mania, the sports fan ranting at his wide-screen television, a raver high on X in the electric pong of the mosh pit, the swaying snake-handler, the "lunatic, the lover, and the poet" can all, in the throes of their various beyondings, appear, as Shakespeare said, "of imagination all compact."

Thinking. Reading. Writing. Even these activities can be ecstatic. Who has not had a sudden discovery or loss of self while daydreaming or reading another's sentences? Most of us have felt at least once the urgent need to embody a private grief, wrong, or yearning in lines of ink or type or the flickering cyberscript of an e-mail message. Whether larger than language or coextensive with it, human consciousness depends upon a rapturous, rupturous struggle with words and their edges and with the charged, paradoxical electricity these f(r)ictions create. Like the dizzying disruptions of erotic attraction or the transport of dervish dancing, language acts remove the thinker/writer/reader from time and place, changing breathing patterns and blood pressure, conjuring ulterior realities, creating truths from fictions, and "outering" inner worlds. Once we move beyond symbiotic infancy, where the mouth reigns as primal mind, and become self-conscious, how better to articulate our postlapsarian longing for what is lost or beyond saying than through poetry?

Little wonder that poetry, the manipulation of language until it is able to articulate the inexpressible, should be a special precinct of ecstasy. But *is* the poetic utterance of every delirious lover or religious zealot an ecstatic poem? The carnal twitch of verses like "There once was a girl from Nantucket" and wooings of the "Roses are red / Violets are blue" ilk cannot compare with the pent erotic lyricism of Emily Dickinson in the *Master Letters:* "No rose, yet felt myself a' bloom, / No bird—yet rode in Ether," or the desire-whetted declarations of the Shulamite in the ancient Song of Songs: "Let me lie among vine blossoms, / in a bed of apricots! / I am in the fever of love." Even the most ardent religious proselytizing pales beside the self-wrung cries of Gerard Manley Hopkins:

> I wake and feel the fell of dark, not day,
> What hours, O what black hours we have spent
> This night! what sights you, heart, saw; ways you went!

Dickinson's "Dare you see a Soul *at the White Heat*?" evokes the attempt of ecstatic poetry to breach the gap between inner and outer, to confront complex questions: What is the self? What is in the heart? What is our connection to an obdurate and infinite universe? Anne Carson argues that it is in engagement with this fissure between our desire and its object, the limitations of words and the inchoate enormity of our feeling, that the project of ecstatic poetry resides: "Literate training encourages a heightened awareness of personal physical boundaries and a sense of those boundaries as the vessel of one's self. . . . The poets record this struggle from within a consciousness—perhaps new in the world—of the body as a unity of limbs, senses, and self, amazed at its own vulnerability." René Char writes, "The poem is the realized love of desire still desiring." To the Sufi poet Rumi, ecstatic love is an ocean and the Milky Way a flake of foam floating in it, suggesting, like Roland Barthes, that "the brio of a text is its will to bliss" (interestingly, Barthes' word "joissance" also connotes orgasm). And when the *bhakti* mendicant Mirabai calls to her Lord, "a vision of you has driven me mad,/separation eats at my limbs," one feels the powerful transgression by which the words of passion are made holy, and vice versa. Across gender, culture, and time, visionary poems attempt to word the unwordable, making out of fervor material evidence of the motions of ecstasy. Reading such poems is itself a profound ecstatic pleasure.

↬ Patricia Hampl, ed., *Burning Bright: An Anthology of Sacred Poetry* (Ballantine, 1995)

> The poet Hampl provides an articulate introduction to this anthology, modeled after medieval books of hours or ancient *silva rerum*, marking through *time* (morning, noon, and night) the sacred poetic utterances of countless poets across generations and culture. The book draws chiefly on poems evoking what Gore Vidal called the "three sky-god religions of the West"—Judaism, Christianity, and Islam. Ecstatic poems by John Clare, Marina Tsvetaeva, Yehudi Amichai, Gerard Manley Hopkins, Paul Celan, John of the Cross, Christopher Smart, and many others are here.

↬ Anne Carson, *Eros the Bittersweet* (1993; Dalkey Archive, 2006)

> Ever intrepid and inventive in her connection making and insights, the classicist, poet, and essayist Anne Carson here offers philosophical, phenomenological, and poetic investigations into what Sappho coined the *glukupikron* (sweet bitter) paradigm of Eros, a triangulation of desirer, desired, and obstacle that speaks directly to the heart of ecstatic poetry. Her prodigious and hungry mind wanders discerningly through topics ranging from mythology to language ("What is erotic about reading [or writing] is the play of imagination called forth in the space between you and your object of knowledge. Poets and novelists, like lovers, touch that space to life with their metaphors and subterfuges," for example). Reading this necessary book must lead the reader to Carson's own provocative ecstatic poems and to her magnificent translation of Sappho, *If Not, Winter: Fragments of Sappho* (Vintage, 2003).

↬ Emily Dickinson, *The Master Letters of Emily Dickinson,* ed. R. W. Franklin (University of Massachusetts Press, 1998)

> "I find ecstasy in living," Dickinson once wrote, but readers who have found her intense poetry impenetrable may find an avenue into it through these three extraordinary draft letters discovered in Dickinson's papers during the week after her death, all addressed to someone she

calls "Master." Though two of the letters, cast in ink, appear ready for mailing, no evidence exists that any of these was ever posted or that they represent part of a larger, reciprocal correspondence. What we find in these vulnerable, passionate human documents is an embodiment of the poetics of desire—the speaker in them is aroused, awakening to her own mastery as a writer. They stand, as Franklin writes, "near the heart of [Dickinson's] mystery." This special edition contains facsimile copies of the letters, which conflate erotic seduction with prayer and supplication ("Let Emily sing for you because she cannot pray").

✎ Sam Hamill ed., *The Erotic Spirit: An Anthology of Poems of Sensuality, Love, and Longing* (Shambhala, 1999)

This beautiful anthology, spanning thirty-five centuries and a rich range of cultures, includes ancient Egyptian love lyrics ("My lover is a lotus blossom / with pomegranate breasts; / her face is a polished wooden snare. // And I am the poor wild bird / seduced / into the teeth of her trap.") as well as contemporary poets like Adrienne Rich and Dorianne Laux. The book is rife with poems that work the ecstatic borders of the beloved and the Beloved, as in "Bamboo Mat" by Yuan Chen (779–831): "I cannot bear to put away / the bamboo sleeping-mat: // that night I brought you home, / I watched you roll it out"). Also included are Catullus, Ovid, Petrarch, Shakespeare, Neruda, Paul Laurence Dunbar, and many, many others.

✎ Ariel Bloch and Chana Bloch, trans., *The Song of Songs: The World's First Great Love Poem* (Modern Library, 2006)

Many memorable translations of this breathtaking ancient poem of yearning exist, among them the King James version. The Bloch version, which follows the oldest extant text of the entire Hebrew Bible (early eleventh century CE), is equally beautiful, and balanced by an introduction providing scholarly, historical, linguistic, and cultural context. The erotic urgency of the poem is undeniable: "My love reached in for the latch / and my heart / beat wild. // I rose to open to my love, / my fingers wet with myrrh, / sweet flowing myrrh / on the doorbolt" (5.4–5). As the introduction states, "The Shulamite, with her veil off, is a figure all of us recognize, and we find the frankness about erotic love more natural than did earlier audiences. . . . 'The Song of Songs' locates that kingdom in human love, in the habitable present, and for the space of our attention, allows us to enter it."

LISA RUSS SPAAR's poetry collections include *Blue Venus* (Persea, 2004), *Glass Town* (Red Hen Press, 1999), and *Satin Cash* (Persea, 2008). She is the editor of

Acquainted with the Night: Insomnia Poems (Columbia University Press, 1999) and *All That Mighty Heart: London Poems* (University of Virginia Press, 2008). Her poems have appeared in *Virginia Quarterly Review, Poetry, Kenyon Review, Ploughshares,* and elsewhere. She has received awards from the Rona Jaffe Foundation and the Academy of American Poets and is Associate Professor of English.

ALISON BOOTH

The Euphoric Suffering of Modern Heroines

There is nothing particularly modern about heroines who suffer or die tragically. Very old traditions give us both the happy endings in which Cinderella marries her prince and the plots that have it in for female characters. The suffering woman may be divinely good, like Alcestis, who, according to ancient Greek mythology and Euripides' play, gave her life to save her husband, Admetis. Or a woman who is "bad"—angry, sexually or politically defiant, wild—must be purged, like Queen Vashti in the biblical Book of Esther, or like the green-skinned Wicked Witch of the West in *The Wizard of Oz*. By the nineteenth century, novelists relied on now-familiar conventions for the destinies of women of different temperaments. While the hero might fulfill his ambitious dreams and get the girl along the way, the heroine either settled down in marriage or perished in an effort to find fulfillment of another sort.

There are several notable patterns in romantic plotting for female characters from about 1840 to 1930. Often the heroine would be contrasted with another woman, her "foil." The fate of such foils served as a warning for women both inside and outside of the fiction. For example, feminist critics have often read *Jane Eyre*'s madwoman in the attic, Bertha Mason, as the double of the heroine, Jane. Bertha is a mad, promiscuous drunkard from a slave colony, a creature combining all that is savage and impure, and it seems good riddance when she dies burning down the house of her husband, Rochester. But this suicidal revenge conveniently punishes Rochester and frees him to marry Jane, thus helping the English middle-class woman to fulfill both her ambition and her romantic plot. Few narratives of the period achieve even this uncomfortable compromise; most heroines have to forfeit learning, career, or power to end in felicity. Many of the finest female characters deserve our pity more than our congratulations.

It is no accident that I began by mentioning a fairy tale, a classical myth, and a sacred book as well as a film and novel with magical effects along a heroine's journey. Often the underlying patterns of character and plot relate to the legendary or supernatural, that is, to ways of explaining what is beyond rational comprehension. Since the early 1800s, however, fiction for serious readers tended to avoid supernatural special effects. Accordingly, I have selected realistic works by well-known English and American women writers. The three novels and two novellas, published during campaigns for women's equality, show the influence of an outgrowth of realism known as naturalism, a movement before and after 1900 to portray the struggle for survival in "low" life with scientific objectivity. At the same time, these works draw upon the power of myth. A woman associated with natural cycles undergoes a trial, a season in the underworld or in exile. Her transformation is not always immediately redemptive, though the suffering may be euphoric, at least for the reader. Whereas these authors achieved mixed triumphs in their careers and personal lives, their heroines were often caught in provincial circumstances and hopeless conflicts. Sad as these works are, they move readers with their exquisite renditions of landscapes, food, colors, everyday sensations as well as extraordinary desires. The structure, imagery, and style of each work seem perfectly designed, and offer unique pleasures for rereading.

The list could be approached chronologically and biographically, both because each author evokes her own memories of an old-fashioned society, and because they appear to be answering the previous works. Like Eliot's and Gaskell's portraits of young women too educated for country living, Chopin's and Wharton's novellas offer pastoral romance, but their heroines are both less knowledgeable and less innocent than Maggie Tulliver or cousin Phillis. By the 1890s, naturalism encouraged representations of adultery and dark outcomes, not to mention contemptible characters. These stories tell not only the suffering of one woman, but the evolution of the society that constrains those around that woman as well. In the embers of old ways of life we see what might have been a phoenix.

Successful women writers rarely allowed their heroines the fulfilled lives they had designed for themselves. Not that these authors' success came without penalty, or that their renown necessarily lasted. Portions of Gaskell's and Wharton's substantial output and almost everything by Chopin and Larsen had fallen out of sight until the rise of feminist and African American literary studies. Such criticism has emphasized the ways that gender roles—along with race, class, and other differences—shape works of literature. Feminist criticism entails a good deal more than reading characterization and plot, or adding up the final scores for women or men in a work. Nevertheless, these narrative conventions provide insights into social codes and traditions that still affect us. A heroine's catastrophe sharply outlines the contours of what is lost: the great potential for women in reality if not in fiction.

↪ George Eliot, *The Mill on the Floss* (1860)

Eliot (Marian Evans) in her second novel re-creates rural middle-class life in the 1820s, testing clever Maggie Tulliver's loyalties to her repressive brother Tom, her good cousin Lucy, and her intellectual companion Philip Wakem against her overwhelming sexual desire for Stephen Guest. Eliot herself made it from the provinces to London intellectual circles, but her union with a married man meant that decent women, including Elizabeth Gaskell, shunned her. Yet everyone admired the all-knowing voice of the always sympathetic narrator. *The Mill on the Floss* is one of the strongest portraits of childhood ever written; old rural English life emerges as both harsh and luscious; and the legends of the river resonate like symphonic music.

↪ Elizabeth Gaskell, *Cousin Phillis* (1863–64), in *Cranford/Cousin Phillis* (Penguin, 1986)

Gaskell provoked controversy not through her personal life but through her defenses of workers and fallen women. One of Gaskell's last publications, *Cousin Phillis* is an exception for its male narrator and pastoral setting; Paul Manning, apprenticed as a railroad engineer, enjoys visiting his cousins' timeless farm. An average guy, he merely observes the ballad of his learned but innocent cousin Phillis's unrequited love for the handsome, cosmopolitan engineer who breaks her heart. This lyrical delight—you can almost smell the orchards and fields—also critiques the old-time ideals of farmer Holman, dissenting minister and amateur scholar, who has reared a learned daughter but has failed to see that she has grown up.

↪ Kate Chopin, *The Awakening* (1899)

Edna Pontellier, at the outset a married mother at the seaside like Mrs. Ramsay (in *To the Lighthouse*), gradually undergoes an education of the senses among the cultivated or physical French Catholics of New Orleans. Chopin's precise yet warm style helps us to feel Edna's growing awareness of music, art, light, desire. This restrained tragedy withholds judgment on the lover who leaves because she is married, the seducer who doesn't care, or Edna, who abandons her family. I like to think of this work not so much as the feminist classic it has become, and certainly not as Chopin's autobiography (she ended her career because of the scandal that followed publication of *The Awakening*, but she was no Edna), but as a harbinger of European impressionism and modernism in Victorian America.

✎ Edith Wharton, *Summer* (1917; Bantam, 1993)

Charity Royall similarly undergoes a sexual awakening through an educated lover, but a depressed New England village provides even fewer outlets than mixed-race Helga Crane finds in *Quicksand*. Wharton herself had escaped a difficult marriage in high society, had a fulfilling affair, and lived in style in France. *Summer* shares the criticism of provincial prudery of Eliot's, Chopin's, and Larsen's works. I find in it several historical and emotional surprises: the varied festivals and customs of New England; the evocations of landscape and architecture; the frank depiction of illegitimacy, incest, and a single woman's pregnancy. Remarkably, this fallen heroine mainly looks out for herself, without any notion of dying for purification like Maggie Tulliver. Melodrama there is, but it's a sustained, powerful stroke of a work.

✎ Virginia Woolf, *To the Lighthouse* (1927; Harvest Books, 1989)

In this novel, as much of a classic as *The Mill on the Floss*, Woolf like Eliot evoked her childhood while also tracing national history and mythic divisions between men and women. The treatment of time and point of view is markedly modern: fragments of multiple characters' thoughts disperse through the three parts, resembling the three flashes of the lighthouse: one evening; a long interval during World War I; and a day ten years later in which the sail to the lighthouse is fulfilled. Woolf partially solves the puzzle of family obligation and artistic vocation—insoluble for Edna Pontellier—by splitting her heroine into Mrs. Ramsay and the younger, unmarried painter, Lily Briscoe.

✎ Nella Larsen, *Quicksand* (1928), in *"Quicksand" and "Passing,"* by Larsen, ed. Deborah E. McDowell (Rutgers University Press, 1986)

Larsen's novella pursues the discouraging arc of rebellion and decline that Wharton sketched for her unpromising village girl. Published during the Harlem Renaissance (one year after *To the Lighthouse*), *Quicksand* is modernist in some aspects, though its technique is closer to Chopin's and Wharton's than to Woolf's. Larsen was hampered as a woman of color; after being accused of plagiarism for a later story, and after a humiliating divorce, she returned to her career as a nurse. Helga Crane, rather like Edna Pontellier, drops out of respectable society (teaching at an African American college, Helga is engaged to a dull fellow). Instead of becoming an artist herself, she is turned by her European admirers into a work of art. Only belatedly does she make a sexual choice, but it is to submit to biological destiny and provincial obscurity. Again, this novella is skillfully shaped and a pleasure to visualize, while it dramatizes a range of social contexts of historical interest.

ALISON BOOTH, Professor of English, has taught at the University of Virginia since 1986. Her books include *Greatness Engendered: George Eliot and Virginia Woolf* (Cornell University Press, 1992) and *How to Make It as a Woman: Collective Biographical History from Victoria to the Present* (University of Chicago Press, 2004). Her current projects include an edition of *Wuthering Heights* and a study of literary tourism. An editor of Norton's *Introduction to Literature,* she enjoys reading and teaching literature of all kinds, and now and then finds time to write poetry, fiction, or memoir.

CAROLINE RODY

Abroad at Home: Contemporary Interethnic Fiction

Studying and teaching ethnic American fiction over the past decade and a half, I have tracked a fascinating shift: what we have long read as "ethnic literature" is becoming "interethnic literature." That is, beginning in the last decades of the twentieth century, amidst the massive migrations, globalized economies, and fluid interactions that have shaped our multidiasporic society, American authors of minority backgrounds have begun to shift focus away from the singularity of any ethnic experience, and toward the experience of being ethnic amidst heterogeneous others. Many readers will expect texts by ethnic minority writers to be rooted in narratives of tradition and memory, and this surely is still true; we may also expect ethnic fiction to focus on an individual's struggle to find his or her place in a complex world, and this, too, remains the case. The difference in texts from recent decades is a growing impulse to explore the imaginative possibilities offered by contemporary multicultural America. What most compels plot and shapes narrative form in the new ethnic American fiction is the encounter with ethnic others and their stories.

To point to the interethnicity of these texts is to follow a general trend in literary and cultural studies toward regarding culture as a dynamic space of intergroup borrowing, imitation, affiliation, and rivalry. That cultures are always the historical products of hybridization is now a truism in many fields; postcolonial studies in particular has contributed richly to our understanding of the processes by which the often unequal and violent encounters of different peoples eventually bring about distinctly new linguistic, cultural, and aesthetic formations. Studies of the expressive culture and arts of the United States now take the long historical relationship between African and European Americans to be an indispensable, shaping force. An African American influence indeed continues to be central to the contemporary ethnic American fiction I describe here, even as writers engage a heterogeneous mix of other cultural elements that are transforming our culture, from the practices of daily life to novelistic experimentation. By reading with attention to this interethnic impulse, we can open up startling new visions of our increasingly hybrid home—national and global. The interethnic imagination of these texts is far more nuanced than the banal celebrations of diversity we see in consumer advertising; it is ambivalent and ironic, characterized at once by deep attraction to the promise of a hybrid culture, fear of otherness, and longing for dialogue to repair the social breach born of racism and injustice.

The texts I recommend demonstrate an interethnic impulse most vividly in their plots and characters. Recent ethnic fictional protagonists do not struggle for a place in the American mainstream, but rather, seek a vital role in an intercultural arena. And beyond the familiar plot of conflict between immigrant parents and American-born children, these young protagonists step outside the family home and into the multicultural streets, where their complex encounters across racial, ethnic, and class lines lead them to puzzle out an Americanness incompatible with binary notions of "us" and "them."

These novels also foreground interethnic encounter by means of their narrative structures—often juxtaposing multiple narrators, points of view, or plotlines; their multilingual textures; and their diverse, sometimes surprising display of cross-ethnic literary influences. In tone and vision, they range from the hopefully and even zanily comic to the anguished and tragic; in their characters, from teenagers to old men; in their landscapes, from the U.S.-Mexico border to post-Soviet Ukraine. Most delve only a few generations back in history so as to privilege the hazards and possibilities of the present, though some depend profoundly on the changes a few decades can bring, and one includes a character who remembers Columbus. Languages encountered in these novels range from English and Spanish to Chinese, Korean, Russian, and Yiddish, and international border crossings are made by plane, boat, train, car, and foot. Somewhere in the narration of each novel, a character makes an error of speech, betraying his or her origins through imperfect command of English, and in most cases, that error is taken up, humorously and affectionately, by someone of another background, as a key to all that is unspeakably different, and yet shared, between them.

The five novels listed below are drawn from recent Asian American and Jewish American literature, two fields in the vanguard of interethnic experimentation. But these are books that take us deep into the realm of cross-ethnic hybridity, perhaps leaving conventional literary categories behind altogether.

✧ Chang-Rae Lee, *Native Speaker* (Riverhead, 1995)

In this ambitious first novel, a young Korean American hero works out his racial alienation and his life's tragedies by becoming a New York City spy, among a bureau of motley multicultural impersonators. A poetic tribute to the heterogeneous mix of the great city, Lee's novel positions its conflicted hero amidst the compulsions and appeals of whiteness, Koreanness, blackness, and the multicultural crowd. A marriage to a white woman and numerous literary connections to African American precursors (Richard Wright, Ralph Ellison) enrich the cross-cultural texture of the novel, but the hero's greatest challenge comes when he is assigned to sabotage a Korean American politician who dreams of uniting the city across all its differences and tongues.

✧ Gish Jen, *Mona in the Promised Land* (Vintage, 1997)

Perhaps no novel has engaged more wittily the meaning of American identity than Jen's tale of a 1970s teenage Chinese American heroine who, confounding her parents and all literary tradition, converts to the Judaism of her suburban New York neighbors, thus bringing about an unexpected Chinese-Jewish-American novelistic hybrid. As it celebrates self-transformation, *Mona* also seriously examines the boundaries of family, friendship, ethnicity, and community, most vividly when Mona and her teenage friends turn a parent-free mansion into a poignantly disastrous experiment in multiethnic communal life.

✧ Karen Tei Yamashita, *Tropic of Orange* (Coffee House Press, 1997)

A Japanese American novelist who lived for a decade in Brazil, Yamashita presents a fabulously imagined vision of the changes now being made by the economic forces drawing Latin American masses north to the United States. Crossing and recrossing the U.S.-Mexico border, this novel's tragicomic, media-saturated vision merges Latin American magic realism and the tradition of Los Angeles disaster fiction to concoct an epic story of cultural collision. A "HyperContexts" chart helps us follow the plots of seven characters of diverse ethnic and national origins who are swept up in the tumult along with a veritable cast of thousands, as the Tropic of Cancer moves magically northward across the U.S. border to Los Angeles, dragging behind it the peoples, the cultures, and the conflicted history of the Southern Hemisphere.

✧ Philip Roth, *The Human Stain* (Vintage, 2001)

To avoid giving away the well-crafted secrets of this powerfully compelling plot, I'll say only that Roth, after more than twenty novels mostly focused on Jewish characters, here departs to imagine, through his familiar narrator Nathan Zuckerman, the lives of different kinds of Americans, and especially the extended concealments they may feel it necessary to take on, so as to live free of others' determining definitions of their possibilities. The perspective of old age and approaching mortality richly informs the book's meditations on the personal choice of radical freedom over the tyranny and hypocrisy of social propriety. Always a master of characterization and voice, Roth here develops several memorable monologists, whose accounts of themselves shift and shimmer in the light of the novelist-narrator's recurrent lament that no one can ever truly know the life of another.

✧ Jonathan Safran Foer, *Everything Is Illuminated* (Harper Perennial, 2005)

This brilliant and ambitious first novel by a very young writer features a semi-autobiographical character by the author's own name, who travels from the United States to Ukraine, attempting to uncover the story of his grandfather and ancestral Jewish village from the time of the Holocaust. But while the quest yields few answers about origins, it does produce ebullient imaginings of the ancestral past, as well as an astonishing encounter with someone in the present: a Ukrainian teenager and family, whom the American Jew had not suspected would share the devastating inheritance of the World War II era. Letters from the luminous Alex, whose English is thesaurus-born, helps make this a poignantly comic and uniquely dialogic Holocaust novel.

CAROLINE RODY is Associate Professor of English and a specialist in ethnic American fiction. Her first book is *The Daughter's Return: African American and Caribbean Women's Fictions of History* (Oxford University Press, 2001), and her current project, developed while teaching courses on Asian American, Jewish American, and contemporary interethnic fiction, is provisionally titled "The Interethnic Imagination: Roots and Passages in Asian American Fiction."

MARÍA-INÉS LAGOS

Women between Cultures: Latina Writers of the United States

"Brilliant," "marvelous," "moving," "lyrical," "tender," "poetic," "remarkable," "exceptional": so critics embraced the Latina coming-of-age narratives that appeared in print in the United States during the 1990s. The books I've chosen from this period present a cross-section of the Hispanic immigrant experience in the United States from the 1940s to the 1960s, told from a girl's perspective. These are stories of doubleness, of growing up between two cultural codes and two languages, within communities that struggle to maintain an identity while adapting to their new surroundings. They also look in two directions in time and space, offering a view of a Latin American diaspora as a consequence of political repression and persecution by dictatorial regimes—the case of Julia Alvarez's *How the García Girls Lost Their Accents* and Cristina García's *Dreaming in Cuban*—and the promise of attractive opportunities in the United States. As we have come to recognize in the American immigrant experience of many groups, it is the children in these coming-of-age narratives who adapt more easily to the new circumstances, while the parents tend to maintain a nostalgic view of the past and dwell on the traditions and customs of their home country, especially if they are political refugees longing to return to their homeland. Perhaps the success of these narratives stems in part from their very familiarity to us; yet, each immigrant group has particular stories to tell.

Although these narratives are based on personal experiences and contain autobiographical elements, only Esmeralda Santiago's *When I Was Puerto Rican* is a memoir. The others are fictional accounts. Centered on female protagonists, all five books I've listed explore, in an ultimately uplifting manner, a woman's struggle to assimilate to U.S. culture.

In many of these narratives, a daughter deviates from her mother's model. Women from the younger generation are more independent, live away from home, and frequently change personal and career paths. Families adapt to unfamiliar concepts of authority. Girls become aware of gender differences and the changing position of women, a trend that encourages them to gain autonomy and independence. Nevertheless, these gains do not come without a price, as Yolanda in *García Girls* reflects when comparing the stable confident attitudes of her cousins in the Dominican Republic and her own life of ups and downs in the States. The protagonists also learn to stand up for their convictions. When she moves from Puerto Rico to New York, Negi, from *When I Was Puerto Rican,* demands to be placed in the grade corresponding to her age and background. She could not have uttered such a request in her more restrictive culture.

These books represent the most important Hispanic groups in the country, both historically and numerically: Mexican Americans (Cisneros), Puerto Ricans (Mohr and Santiago), Cuban Americans (García), and Dominican Americans (Alvarez). To a large extent, people of Latin American descent are considered to be a monolithic group by the outside observer, and these narratives counter such a notion by showing how varied these populations can be and how contact with U.S. culture and values transforms them. It is important to keep in mind that there is no consensus among Hispanics/Latinos in the United States as to how to identify as a group. Scholars and theorists agree that it is difficult to define a population whose national origins and racial, educational, and class differences vary so widely. In the introduction to the Spanish version of her memoir, *When I Was Puerto Rican,* Esmeralda Santiago remarks that in the United States she is considered to be "Latina o Hispana, con letras mayúsculas" ("with capital letters"), but asserts that she does not know the meaning of those terms when she uses them to fill out forms or support the leaders of her people. Recognizing herself as "Puerto Rican," she includes in that category her North American experience, her biculturalism, and her "espanglés" ("Spanglish"). As we meet the characters in these narratives, it becomes clear that people of Latin American descent are heterogeneous. The writers I have chosen show us that class, gender, racial distinctions, and the coexistence of different religious practices and beliefs characterize the Latin America from which their characters have emigrated. But these complexities, bequeathed to the new generations of Latina women in the United States, also give rise to their active creation of their own lives as they alter family traditions without completely forgetting them.

↭ Nicholasa Mohr, *Nilda* (Arte Público Press, 1986)

Told from Nilda's perspective, this novel presents a glimpse into the life of a working-class Puerto Rican family in New York City's barrio in the early 1940s, a time when immigrants from the island started coming in greater numbers to the mainland in search of a better life. Given their lack of skills and education, these U.S. citizens find that the American Dream is not so easily attainable. Nilda, mostly a passive character, witnesses the obstacles her family must overcome to get ahead. Several episodes show interactions between the barrio inhabitants and the authorities. Among Nilda's lasting memories are a happy stay in summer camp, her mother's advice to have a life of her own (by remaining in school and avoiding unwanted pregnancies), and, above all, her day-to-day sharing in family life.

✦ Sandra Cisneros, *The House on Mango Street* (Vintage, 1991)

This book focuses on Esperanza, a Mexican American teenager living in a large U.S. city. Having moved with her family to their own house, she finds that this is not the home she was dreaming about and resolves to move out of this neighborhood. Evoking her life in Mango Street through brief vignettes, she dwells on the details of family life. Everyone in her family has a different type of hair—straight, frizzy, dark, lighter, etc.—thus revealing a shared, heterogeneous background as well as each person's individuality. Esperanza tells how girls learn to be grown-ups by imitating women wearing high heels and moving their hips, and she also addresses damaging events and uncomfortable situations, such as teachers making derogatory remarks, boys and an older man trying to seduce her, and disappointment with her first sexual experience. Several vignettes describe older women spending their lives waiting at home looking through the window, like her grandmother. But as her name suggests, Esperanza (Hope) has her own plans.

✦ Julia Alvarez, *How the García Girls Lost Their Accents* (Plume, 2005)

This novel centers on the four daughters of a well-to-do Dominican family, the Garcías, forced to leave their homeland due to political persecution. In spite of their background—the father was a physician in Santo Domingo and the mother descends from Spanish conquistadors—in New York they are perceived as any Hispanic immigrants by neighbors and people of authority, often having to confront prejudices and stereotyping. Told in reverse order, the story begins when one of the daughters visits the Dominican Republic, after almost thirty years in the United States, toying with the idea of staying there. Having experienced the social transformations of the 1960s involving women's changing roles and increased opportunities, the narrator compares the upheavals of her life to the apparently more stable and secure lives of her female relatives in the Dominican Republic.

✦ Cristina García, *Dreaming in Cuban* (Ballantine, 1993)

Told from different perspectives, this fragmented narrative about the lives of several generations of Cuban women, both on the island and in New York, offers a panorama of the Cuban exodus after Castro took power in 1959. Pilar, a college-aged woman, feels very close to her grandmother, a staunch Castro supporter living in Havana, and dreams of visiting the island. Her mother, a devout American and successful businesswoman antagonistic to the Revolution, sees the world in black and white, while her father has never adapted to the United States. The extended family represents Cuban heterogeneity as it concerns political views, race, class, and generations. Pilar and her mother finally go back to Cuba in 1980, just before the Mariel boatlift. There, Pilar reflects on her conflicted identity, pondering whether she will ever feel that just one place is home.

↩ Esmeralda Santiago, *When I Was Puerto Rican* (Da Capo Press, 2006)

In this memoir, Esmeralda Santiago re-creates the world of her childhood in rural Puerto Rico in the 1950s. Although not married, both parents are devoted to their children and try to provide for them as best they can. But the father has other women, and the mother, tired of his infidelities, decides to move to New York when Negi (Esmeralda) is thirteen years old. Most of the narrative deals with life in Puerto Rico. The family moves frequently, so Esmeralda, a good student, changes schools often and has many responsibilities in taking care of her siblings—especially when her mother is at work, an activity her neighbors do not approve of. Life in New York opens up new opportunities for the girl, whose memoir ends as she applies to enter the Performing Arts School in Manhattan.

For further reading:

Isabel Allende, *Paula,* trans. Margaret Sayers Peden (Harper Perennial, 1996).
Rosario Ferré, *The House on the Lagoon* (Plume, 1996).

María-Inés Lagos, Professor of Spanish, has published extensively on Latin American women writers and teaches courses on contemporary Latin American literature and Latina authors.

Randolph D. Pope

Where Spain Is Real: The Nineteenth-Century Spanish Novel (and Beyond)

Novels should disappear, at least if they are realist, and make us forget we are reading. I like authors who are friends, and not teachers or priests. My favorites have a refined sense of gossip and scandal, compassion, and subtle humor. They get out of the way to draw us into their complex so-cieties, where people are worried about power, sex, money, and religion. They know life is short and some events crucial.

My recommendations start with a playful novel that is almost noth-ing, a tale many times told: Alarcón's *The Three-Cornered Hat*. The book was written late in the nineteenth century, when Spain was just beginning to industrialize and trains did not reach many points of the nation. It is pure nostalgia, set in Andalusia just before the Napoleonic troops come to unsettle the old regime in 1808. Alarcón has a talent for the odd detail. The miller, married to a beauty, is ugly and hunchbacked, but has good teeth. His wife, Frasquita, comes from northern Spain and therefore shows more of her arms than is convenient. They are happy, industrious, and visited often by their friends, priests and the town administrators, among them the mayor, who also is a hunchback. To reveal too much of how the miller comes to see through a keyhole proof of his dishonor, how confusion prevails as in any good slapstick comedy, and how all is resolved would spoil the fun.

Great novels are like arias in grand opera. The pleasure we experience is comparative, since we have heard most plots before and the music is famil-iar, so the novelist and the soprano rise to the challenge of the giants in the field, past and present. Clarín, a young lawyer and critic living in the pro-vincial town of Oviedo, read Flaubert's *Madame Bovary* and in *La Regenta* imagined it occurring in Spain. Infidelity was the nightmare of a proper home everywhere, and women, especially those who read too much, could become bored. Ana Ozores, who is married to a husband whose idea of pas-sion is a chaste kiss on the forehead, lives in Vetusta (the Very Old Town), which is similar to Oviedo and wholly Spanish, dominated by the cathe-dral's spire. Her heart and body, just as Emma Bovary's, long for emotion and adventure. What Clarín brings to the story is a slow and absorbing re-creation of the town. This is a novel that will have you wondering for its first fifty pages if it is going to get started. Suddenly you will realize you know the talented, handsome, ambitious priest, Fermín de Paz, his church, and the neighborhoods he prowls, charming young women into the nun-nery and asking parents to donate to the Church. When you are admitted into Ana Ozores's room as she undresses completely and steps sensually on a tiger's fur, you know by then that you care about these characters.

Galdós was a good friend of Clarín, who sent him his *La Regenta*. Galdós was disturbed and could not sleep for days. He saw the story dif-ferently. Not just one woman, Emma or Ana, being seduced, but two, For-tunata and Jacinta, who love the same man. Since Fortunata is poor and Jacinta rich, Galdós brings in all their friends, family, and neighborhoods. Galdosistas, as scholars who study Galdós's work are known, still visit Ma-drid in pilgrimage as students of Joyce revere Dublin. Galdós had been a journalist and writes a lively prose. One can highlight his deft use of symbols—a wall that rises, hiding the horizon, a water pump, a famous raw egg—or the complexity of his numerous characters, but what makes him a master is that his world rings true to ours, with people trying to get along in a society where truth, heroism, loyalty, and long-lasting love are not to be found, yet are pursued nevertheless, since some moments of muddled illumination make it all worthwhile.

Emilia Pardo Bazán, not surprisingly for nineteenth-century Spain, sees the world as dominated by men who very rarely understand women and their problems. For her, bodies have a violent life of their own, and desire is frustrated in a society that is seldom nurturing. Why read, then, what would appear to be a dismal portrait? I enjoy seeing through her eyes, attuned to elegance and its perversions, as well as visiting her decadent manors and intellectual salons. She is intelligent, unforgiving, and compassionate. What she tells us, we can't forget.

We close the list with Unamuno's story of the priest who has lost his faith yet continues to teach it, *San Manuel Bueno, Martyr,* published in 1930 and a devastating (and funny) dismantling of nineteenth-century realism. Should we care about absolute truth, or is it wiser to believe in what makes you happy? The topic is serious, the voice of the novelist urgent. There is not one line in this novella that does not seem necessary. Spain was now far from what Alarcón had idyllically described. Six years after *San Manuel* was published, the Spanish Civil War began.

☞ Pedro Antonio De Alarcón, *The Three-Cornered Hat,* trans. Peter Bush (Hesperus Press, 2004)

> Originally published in 1974 as *El sombrero de tres picos,* this work has enjoyed notable and lasting success. It became a ballet in 1919 with music by Falla and has been shown with set and costumes by Picasso (1919) and Dali (1949). Alarcón took a popular ribald story and gave it a lighthearted ending. The town mayor, who wears a three-cornered hat as a sign of his authority, attempts to seduce the wife of a miller who, believing his wife has betrayed him, dresses as the mayor and goes in search of the mayor's wife, who, as the miller puts it, is also good-looking.
>
> Alarcón's craft is wonderful; note how he interweaves scenes, how he incorporates mules, grapes, fire, and water into the story, and how a four-cornered handkerchief counters the three-cornered hat at the end.

☞ Leopoldo (Clarín) Alas, *La Regenta,* trans. John Rutherford (Penguin, 1985)

> Both a priest and an aging Don Juan (called here Don Álvaro) try to seduce a young woman who is married to an older and indolent man.

One of them succeeds, but the ending is not happy. The novel, first published in two volumes (1884, 1885), scandalized the Church and was repressed during the years of the Franco dictatorship (1939–75); it is now considered a masterpiece of the nineteenth-century Spanish realist novel. It is hard to resist the impression when finishing this book that you have not read about Vetusta, the city in which the action takes place, but visited it and become forever part of its life.

Clarín can be ruthless in showing the suffocating atmosphere of a small town, but he also lets us see people having fun, loving one another, and reasonably experiencing a sublime thrill when their shoes touch under a table.

↪ Benito Pérez Galdós, *Fortunata and Jacinta: Two Stories of Married Women,* trans. Agnes Moncy Gullón (Penguin, 1989)

Galdós is comparable to Dickens and Balzac. (Usually Spanish authors are mentioned by their first family name, which is the father's, in this case Pérez. But two Spanish authors are known by the mother's family name, Galdós and Lorca—whose whole name was Federico García Lorca. Both Pérez and García are very common names, and these authors are anything but common.) The novel starts with a lengthy description of how the young Juanito Santa Cruz's family became prosperous as merchants in Madrid. A casual encounter of Juanito with the beautiful but lower-class Fortunata starts the conflict of the novel. Both Juanito and Fortunata marry, yet not each other. How Jacinta, Juanito's wife, and Fortunata deal with the wandering and good-for-nothing charmer Juanito is only part of the story, which re-creates Madrid as no one has done before or since.

What does the end mean? Do the upper and lower classes find a common future? Is Fortunata co-opted? Scholars disagree radically, so you are free to make up your own mind, one more way in which this prodigious novel is more real than many cities in which we have lived.

↪ Emilia Pardo Bazán, *The House of Ulloa,* trans. Paul O'Prey and Lucia Graves (Penguin, 1991)

Her novel follows a young priest who goes to the countryside of Galicia to serve in a decadent manor where all the forces of primitive nature are let loose, this novel being Spain's *Wuthering Heights*. The vivid portrayal of the characters is unforgettable: the well-meaning priest, the cunning administrator, and the young bride brought from the city to civilize the house are all presented with psychological insight and caring interest in their passionate lives.

↬ Miguel de Unamuno, *San Manuel Bueno, Martyr,* in *Abel Sánchez and Other Stories,* trans. Anthony Kerrigan (Regnery, 1996)

> This novella appears in all lists, not only because of the extraordinary place its author has in Spanish culture—a philosopher, novelist, poet, and rector of the University of Salamanca, plus being an eloquent polemist—but for its engaging story of a priest who has lost his faith and continues to minister to his parishioners, believing that it is better for them to live happily a lie than face the desolation of a life without the hope of everlasting life. This short novel is widely used in the United States in intermediate Spanish courses, so it is the closest we come to a common text that represents Spanish culture.

RANDOLPH D. POPE is Commonwealth Professor of Spanish and Comparative Literature. He has written more than one hundred essays on the Spanish and Latin American novel, as well as books on Spanish autobiography, the Spanish novel after the Civil War, and Juan Goytisolo. He recently coedited a book of essays on Spanish Generation X writers and rock music.

MICHAEL LEVENSON

Joyce's *Ulysses,* Five Ways

We were invited to name the five works that mattered most to us, and I am happy to disclose the obsessive course of my commitments by choosing all five from within a single book. That book is James Joyce's *Ulysses,* a novel in eighteen episodes, and because I believe that almost all of those episodes can stand alongside any novels in the tradition, I decided to honor this assignment by making difficult choices among the eighteen separate triumphs that for me justify the vocation of literary study.

Ulysses has a legend and an aura draped around it. For so many, it is the novel you meant to read, the one you tried to finish, the book you assume that others only pretend to enjoy. It is true that its difficulties are formidable. But once you make your peace with the many references—political, historical, ethical, theological, etc.—and accept that they offer a liberal education in themselves, then you can encounter the real and breathtaking difficulty, which has little to do with reference or allusion. Joyce called *Ulysses* "the epic of two races (Israel-Ireland) and at the same time the cycle of the human body as well as a little story of a day (life) . . . also a kind of encyclopaedia." The strain of the novel lies in the attempt to live up to such totality, to say everything—or at least as much as possible—about our modernity, the fate of heroism, the prospects of Ireland, the rhythm of cities, the course of desire, the abyss of loneliness, the chances for love.

People who know nothing else about *Ulysses* know that it rewrites the *Odyssey*, but this idea usually leads to the assumption that it will be solemn, lofty, grand. In fact it is wild and unpredictable, as full of broad jokes as visionary prospects. The novel is always (Joyce's word) "jocoserious." It keeps breaking its own molds, changing the style that it perfects. It uses the noble precedent of the *Odyssey*, but just as often abuses it. The Homeric plot of a long return home delayed by many threats and lures, a son's rediscovery of his father, and a husband's reunion with his wife—Joyce saw this as a foundational human narrative. It was also a flexible framework for brazen experiments in form, ethical and political inquiry, wild irony, and emotional revelation.

↪ James Joyce, *Ulysses* (Vintage, 1990)

"Proteus"—Episode 3

"Ineluctable modality of the visible: at least that if no more, thought through my eyes. Signatures of all things I am here to read, seaspawn and seawrack, the nearing tide, that rusty boot"—this is how the episode known as "Proteus" begins, with a lyricism compounded of abstract thought, the music of ideas as much as the color of the physical world. The counterpart in Homer is a scene in book 4 of the *Odyssey*, where Menelaus must wrestle the shape-shifting Father of the Sea, Proteus, in order to learn the secret of his way home. Joyce takes this as a richly generative conceit in order to stage the drama of Stephen Dedalus. Stephen is still the young artist at an impasse, who must wrestle with nothing less than the primal conditions of being: sensory, intellectual, historical, psychological. There on the watery beach, he is caught in the midst of it all, "seaspawn and seawrack," living late in history, revolted by his own pretensions, then revolted by his revulsions. Later he will be compared to Antisthenes, of whom it was said that "none could tell if he were bitterer against others or against himself." Stephen in "Proteus" completes the trajectory that he had launched in *A Portrait of the Artist as a Young Man* and reaches a near-final stage of self-involution, where the will to art confronts all that opposes it, everything within, everything without.

"Calypso"—Episode 4

Even as he brought Stephen Dedalus to an ultimate pitch of self-consciousness, Joyce announced that he had lost interest in this character who had "a shape that can't be changed." The memorable result is the invention of Leopold Bloom, who enters the novel and literary history in this fourth episode; famously, the clock turns back three hours to mark the ceremony of his arrival. Stephen Dedalus, noted Joyce, has no body as *Ulysses* begins: he is all ferocious mind. Bloom, though, is mind-in-body—in Freud's phrase a "bodily ego," one whose thought is never abstracted from his senses and who moves through a world that ceaselessly fascinates him. One of his leading characteristics, established early, is the patient effort to think himself into the experience of the other, even as here the experience of a cat ("Wonder what I look like to her. Height of a tower? No, she can jump me"). Entangled within the failure of his marriage, Bloom is the one who shops and cooks for his wife, Molly, who imagines oranges and melons in Palestine, who brings his wife a letter from her soon-to-be lover, Blazes Boylan, and who closes the episode by enjoying his defecation in the garden outhouse. At the end of "Calypso," Bloom prepares to leave home for his long wandering through the streets of Dublin.

"Cyclops"—Episode 12

The conceit of an epic condensed to a day—heroic episodes recast within the daily round of everyday life—means that each hour in the "dance of hours" brings a different phase of life, a different emotion, a new style, even a different ethics. In the course of Bloom's journey through Dublin, he comes in the late afternoon to a pub, Barney Kiernan's, where he has agreed to meet a few others on a small errand of mercy. Realizing that Blazes Boylan must now be with his wife, he is restless and agitated. Called into the gathering around the bar, he chatters incautiously, challenging the rabid nationalism of the "Citizen," deflating superstitions, standing up for the "natural phenomenon" against political mysticism. Joyce paints Bloom as the sensible and moderate man, but he also insists on moderation as a radical principle, not a weak compromise. As tempers rise, Bloom becomes the target of anti-Semitic abuse, and in the midst of charge and countercharge, the mild man speaks out. It's "no use," he says. "Force, hatred, history, all that. That's not life for men and women, insult and hatred." When pressed to say what life then is, he delivers his awkward, unforgettable answer: "Love, says Bloom. I mean the opposite of hatred." Within the extravagance of this "Cyclops" episode, within its wild rhetoric and long lists stretching down the pages, Bloom finds his way to simple utterance. The ambition of Joyce's epic is to be faithful to life's plenitude, the sheer carnival of contingency, but here, elsewhere, and in its final words, the novel also seeks the improbable simplicity of affirmation.

"Ithaca"—Episode 17

How to bring the epic of the everyday to its end? Joyce, who struggled with the question, decides to end his novel twice. The first time, what he calls the real ending of the novel, is here in "Ithaca," which takes place after the long-delayed meeting of Bloom and Stephen Dedalus in a Dublin brothel and after Bloom has persuaded Stephen to come home with him for food and shelter. They drink, talk, and urinate side by side. The narrative of this episode takes the form of a catechism: an unnamed voice puts questions about the two men—"Were their views on some points divergent?" "Who drank more quickly?"—and the answers are given in an austere formality. "All events are resolved into their cosmic, physical, psychical, etc. equivalents," wrote Joyce, "so that not only will the reader know everything and know it in the baldest coldest way, but Bloom and Stephen thereby become heavenly bodies, wanderers like the stars at which they gaze." Within the Homeric frame, the two characters stand as Odysseus and Telemachus meeting at last, but as "Ithaca" unfolds, their identities are revealed as overlapping, intersecting, and multivalent: beyond father and son, they connect on the shifting ground of science and art, Ireland and Israel, mind and body, resilience and resistance. Having discussed matters high and low, earnest and trivial, and having shared a vision of the night sky as a "heaventree of stars hung with humid nightblue fruit," they separate with a handshake, their future relation unknown, while Bloom crawls back "reverently" into bed with his unfaithful wife, "the bed of conception and of birth, of consummation of marriage and of breach of marriage, of sleep and of death."

"Penelope"—the eighteenth and last episode

Call me sentimental, call me ironic, but I know of nothing—nothing!—that moves and excites, renews and restores me as much as the last episode of *Ulysses*. You may think you know its force because you have read the novel many times, but when the sentences flicker again across your mental screen, the whole brain shudders. We see it now as an audacious and risky move, Joyce's decision to invest his virtuosity in constructing a woman's mind within her fully described, openly desirous body. But for some of us, *Ulysses* is indomitable just because it risks being bad—ethically, politically, aesthetically—in pursuing its version of the good. "Ithaca" imagined human life from the cold distance of the stars, but the last sequence of *Ulysses* begins with Molly Bloom, her husband now returned and asleep beside her, lying awake with thoughts of the day's adulterous lovemaking and with memories of desire for other men (and women). But as she dozes and remembers, her mind keeps turning again to Bloom, because, after all, "I know every turn in him" and "here we are as bad as ever after 16 years." Her reverie reaches its exhilarating crest in its last thousand words when she thinks back to childhood in Gibraltar—"the Spanish girls laughing in their shawls and their tall combs and the auctions in the morning the Greeks and the jews and the Arabs and the devil knows who else from all the ends of Europe"—back to her first kiss, and then again to Bloom's proposal on the hillside among the rhododendrons and her acceptance: "yes." Having been an epic of Ireland and Israel, an epic of the modern city, of modernist style, of the fleshly body within a universe of objects, it ends as an epic of marriage, of love fading and flaring through time.

MICHAEL LEVENSON is William B. Christian Professor of English. The focus of his teaching, research, and writing divides between Victorian and modernist studies. Although his interests range across these two wide areas, he always returns to Joyce and *Ulysses*.

PAUL BAROLSKY

Ovid's *Metamorphoses*

I know of no book more wonderful than Ovid's *Metamorphoses*. Even those who have never read his poem or have read only selections, bits and pieces, are familiar with many of its stories, those of Apollo and Daphne, Narcissus and Echo, Pyramus and Thisbe, Icarus and Daedalus, Orpheus and Eurydice, Venus and Adonis. Ovid's book is about the causes of things, about how birds, beasts, trees, flowers, and rocks came to be, a book about why things are the way they are. His poem is nothing less than a history of the world from its creation out of chaos up to Ovid's own day, the age of Augustus Caesar. *Metamorphoses* has been so influential, if not inspirational, that it is a kind of lens through which we can see the cultural history of the modern world.

Ovid's poem has been read by classicists, philologists, and by scholars studying art history, literature, myth, and religion across various periods of Western culture. Ovid is also read by poets, novelists, painters, sculptors, architects, composers, librettists, playwrights, theater directors, and makers of film. Ovid is read by people who love a good story, a story told well, a story that gives pleasure. In that respect, Ovid belongs to everybody.

In over three and a half decades of university teaching, one of the most gratifying courses I have had the privilege to teach is a seminar that I offer every autumn to twelve students, which is about mythological art in general but is in particular a sustained discussion of Ovid's *Metamorphoses* and how it inspired the art of Botticelli, Michelangelo, Titian, Brueghel, Rembrandt, Rubens, Boucher, Fragonard, Rodin, Picasso, among many others. This seminar is in effect a meditation on the poetic imagination and how, in Shakespeare's Ovidian terms, it "bodies forth the forms of things unknown . . . turns them to shapes, and gives to airy nothing a local habitation and a name."

As the course unfolds, students gradually become intimate with Ovid. They come to know his moods and whims; they delight in the beauty of his descriptions of both art and nature; they appreciate his playfulness, his wit and cunning; they recoil at his accounts of catastrophe (flood, conflagration, famine, plague, and war), which sharpen their awareness that, although Ovid writes of changes, some things never change. For, as Ovid suggests, disaster is a sad constant in human history. My students respond almost viscerally to the poet's tales of cruelty; they take personally his stories about passion, about love, about love lost, about suffering in love. They are moved by his stories of grieving lovers. By the time our seminar has run its course, they realize that in Ovid they have a friend. They come to see that one can live intensely and pleasurably with a single work by a great writer over a period of months and scarcely fathom its depths. Having also discussed Ovid's relations to Dante, Chaucer, Shakespeare, Montaigne, Keats, Kafka, Rilke, T. S. Eliot, W. H. Auden, Calvino, or other writers whom they had previously encountered elsewhere, they now sense that in their own involvement with Ovid they are members of a wide community, a community of art, woven out of Ovidian threads.

And here I come to the heart of the course, where my students join most fully with Ovid. I tell them that in order to be worthy of their friend and mentor Ovid, they must, like him, write artfully. Because they love Ovid, they cannot let him down, and so instead of writing just another "term paper," they must themselves write poetically, beautifully. Some of the most inspired writing I have ever read by university students is the work of these young disciples of Ovid who, having absorbed something of his poetry (even in translation), find through the sweat of many drafts veins of poetry within themselves previously unsuspected and thus untapped. For these students, their Ovidian meditations are a rite of passage, one that gives new meaning to the final words of *Metamorphoses,* when Ovid expresses his fervent hope that he will live through the ages. For he indeed lives on in the incipient poetry of his young readers, whose own words and sentiments resonate with those of a great and enduring storyteller.

The students in our seminar also come to see that Ovid furnishes us with a rich understanding of the mythic origins of the arts; in other words, the poet provides us with a mythological structure for the entire history of the arts, a structure that lies beneath the surface of modern analytic histories of the various arts. Reading *Metamorphoses* intensively, they gradually come to see that the poet, who identifies with all of the artists of whom he writes, is the foundational figure in classical antiquity both for our modern idea of the artist as hero and for the modern notion of art as autobiography. Let us look briefly at five of Ovid's artists in order to see what the students extract from their close reading of his poem, bearing in mind that one could easily write more than a single book of commentary on each of these mythic artists.

"Narcissus"

Ovid endures in modern culture as a paradigmatic artist who is implicitly the subject of his own poem. Painting with words, he pictures the world in all its chromatic beauty, its golds and purples, blues and greens, blacks and whites, reds and yellows, rendered from an extensive and evocative verbal palette. In *Metamorphoses,* he portrays various painters who reflect his own pictorial ambitions, above all, Narcissus, whose reflection in a pool he presents as if it were a self-portrait of the beautiful youth. In the Renaissance, Ovid's Narcissus came to be seen as the first painter, and it was proverbial to say that every painter paints himself—a notion of artistic self-reflexiveness that became a hallmark of modern European culture, from Dante and Michelangelo to Beethoven and Picasso. Every painter, sculptor, architect, craftsman, weaver, musician, poet, storyteller, and rhetorician in his book is a reflection of Ovid. *Metamorphoses* is in various ways a self-portrait of its author.

"Pygmalion"

In the poetry of *Metamorphoses,* Ovid transforms the myth of Narcissus, whose love is unrequited, into that of Pygmalion, whose desire is fulfilled astonishingly when his sculpture of a maiden carved out of ivory comes to life and becomes his bride. Ovid is himself a Pygmalion with words when he describes the sculptor's hands upon the statue, "the ivory softening under his pliable fingers, like wax growing soft in the sunshine." No less than Narcissus, Pygmalion haunts the imagination of modern artists and critics. He epitomizes the aspiration of countless sculptors, painters, poets, and storytellers to bring their subjects alive—from Donatello to George Bernard Shaw.

"Daedalus"

The ancestor of all modern architects from Brunelleschi to Frank Gehry, Daedalus is one of the single greatest artificers whom Ovid brings to life. Ovid celebrates Daedalus's labyrinth in Crete beautifully, if briefly, when he likens it to the river Meander, which plays in the Phrygian fields and, doing so, flows back and forth in its deceptive and ambiguous course. Daedalus is thus the model for Ovid himself, whose *Metamorphoses,* as a work of literary architecture, is labyrinthine in its compelling craft and complexity. Part of our pleasure in reading Ovid is that of losing ourselves in the cunning corridors of his literary labyrinth and then finding our way out again as we follow his clues. Doing so, we come to admire the ingenious structure of his poem, which is worthy of the archetypal ancient architect.

"Orpheus"

If Ovid's poem is architectural, it is also musical. Of all the artists in *Metamorphoses,* Orpheus is unarguably the most haunting, the artist with whom Ovid identifies most fully. The son of Apollo, Orpheus brings together the arts of song, poetry, and storytelling. He is thus the model for Ovid, whose poem mirrors such Orphic artifice. Like Orpheus, Ovid is capable of great pathos, and the poet becomes one with Orpheus when he portrays his great artist hero playing the lyre in grief after the death of Eurydice. The power of Orpheus's music is such that the shades of the underworld weep and, for the first time, even the Furies shed tears. Ovid transforms the pathos of Orpheus's music into his own deeply moving, soulful song.

"Proteus"

In *Metamorphoses,* Ovid not only assumes the personae of Orpheus, Daedalus, Pygmalion, and Narcissus, he also transforms himself into Pan, who invents and plays the pipes; Mercury, who tells a beguiling story of musical origins; Vulcan, who builds the dazzling palace of the Sun God; and Arachne, who weaves a stunningly brilliant tapestry. In this respect, he is like Proteus, whose capacity to transform himself into many forms is itself a form of art. Ovid intensifies his Protean identity by developing an exquisite series of correspondences and analogies linking all of the arts—thus foreshadowing the weaving together of the arts in Wagner, Baudelaire, the Symbolists, and Proust. Two millennia ago Ovid was our first modern artist. The threads of his wonderful web of poetry are woven into the fabric of our cultural heritage.

Ovid, *Metamorphoses,* trans. Rolfe Humphries (Indiana University Press, 1955)

(There are also many other admirable translations available [for example, by Horace Gregory, Allen Mandelbaum, Charles Martin, A. D. Melville, David Raeburn, and David Slavitt], each of which renders different tones from Ovid's lyre.)

This appreciation is dedicated to the alumni of my annual senior seminar on Ovid.

Commonwealth Professor of Art History, PAUL BAROLSKY has written extensively about Ovid, especially in the pages of *Arion: A Journal of the Humanities and the Classics.* He is also the author of various books on art and literature, including the trilogy *Michelangelo's Nose* (1990), *Why Mona Lisa Smiles* (1991), and *Giotto's Father* (1992), published by Pennsylvania State University Press.

CLARE R. KINNEY

Beyond Shakespeare: Some Other High Points of English Renaissance Drama

Early in the movie *Shakespeare in Love,* some actors are auditioning for Will Shakespeare's new play. To the chagrin of its young author, player after player declaims a speech beginning "Was this the face that launched a thousand ships?"—rapturously celebrating Helen of Troy in the words of Christopher Marlowe, Shakespeare's (at the time) much more successful peer. Tom Stoppard's screenplay offers a whimsical glimpse of theater history, but this moment nicely emphasizes the fact that in Elizabethan London, Shakespeare wasn't the only gifted writer in town. (It is indeed Marlowe, not Shakespeare, who is credited with first developing the dramatic possibilities of the blank verse line.)

There was a lively market for plays in the London of the late sixteenth and early seventeenth centuries. The Globe Theatre used by Shakespeare's company could hold three thousand people, and Londoners of all classes were avid playgoers. You need to be literate in order to read a poem; you don't need to be literate in order to enjoy the performance of a play: the works that are now classified as high culture in the English-speaking world were artifacts of popular culture four hundred years ago. The theaters had extremely busy repertories: we know, for example, that in one year the company called The Lord Admiral's Men performed thirty-eight plays, twenty-one of them newly written. Hundreds of these plays have survived; many of them are poetically compelling and dramatically satisfying in their own right. To read "beyond Shakespeare" is to enter exciting literary territory.

Shakespeare's contemporaries were fascinated by the power of language to seduce, to persuade, to remake the very nature of reality. Influential treatises like Machiavelli's *The Prince* and Castiglione's *Book of the Courtier* had suggested the theatricality of power politics and of courtly "impression management." Drama's capacity to set ideas and voices in opposition with one another also spoke directly to the needs of an era in which competing religious, scientific, and political models for representing experience were in circulation. Tragedies of state set in more or less exotic locales could safely glance at debates about the proper powers and responsibilities of monarchs that were taking place at home, especially during the reign of Elizabeth I's successor, King James I. Satiric comedies, whose action was often located in the more familiar space of London, spoke to the anxieties of a community in which old hierarchies had been destabilized, and where social climbers and aspiring power brokers were laying claim to (or performing their way into) new identities.

To read across a wide range of Elizabethan and Jacobean plays—to explore the works of Christopher Marlowe, Ben Jonson, Thomas Middleton, John Webster, Francis Beaumont, John Fletcher, and John Ford—is to discover imaginative spaces that Shakespeare himself did not always enter. Jonson's *The Alchemist* and *Bartholomew Fair* offer us thickly textured and rather darkly colored comedies in a highly particularized London setting; Beaumont's *Knight of the Burning Pestle* hilariously depicts London tradespeople taking charge of a play in performance and inflicting their own taste for melodramatic romance upon its action. Middleton and Webster take revenge tragedies—plays in which a tormented individual tries to enact "a kind of wild justice" in a corrupt world in which all the usual machinery for achieving judicial satisfaction has been undone—into regions even darker than the court of Elsinore in *Hamlet*. And unlike Shakespeare, Middleton and Webster show a good deal of interest in placing female characters at the very center of their tragic action.

In reading Shakespeare's contemporaries, one finds that Shakespeare has no monopoly on astonishing poetry. In his last hour on earth, Marlowe's doomed and damned Dr. Faustus, who had wanted powers that would take him beyond all human limits, begs the God he spurned that some kind of boundary be set on the suffering that awaits him: "Impose some end to my incessant pain, / Let Faustus live in Hell a thousand years, / A hundred thousand and at last be saved!" Webster's Duchess of Malfi faces her murderers with wit and aplomb—when asked whether she is terrified of the cord with which they are to strangle her, she replies, "Not a whit. / What would it pleasure me to have my throat cut / With diamonds . . . or to be shot to death with pearls?" The inventive plotting and poetic panache of the following five works suggest just some of the pleasant surprises awaiting the reader who ventures beyond Shakespeare.

All of these works may be found in the following anthology: David Bevington, Lars Engle, Katharine Eisaman Maus, Eric Rasmussen, eds., *English Renaissance Drama* (Norton, 2002).

⌘ Christopher Marlowe, *Doctor Faustus* (1588–89)

Long before Goethe dramatized the Faust legend, Marlowe offered his account of the scholar who sells his soul for magical powers. What Faustus does with his magic is ultimately less interesting than his fantasies of what he *might* do—Marlowe brilliantly suggests his imperialism of the imagination. Marlowe also gives us a surprisingly sympathetic devil, who warns an oblivious Faustus that hell is not a place but a state of mind ("Why, this is hell, nor am I out of it," says Mephistopheles, looking around Faustus's study). The play's Christian moralizing shows us Faustus succumbing to the sins of pride and despair, ending up screaming, "I'll burn my books!" as hell possesses him. But Marlowe's overreaching hero also speaks the play's most magnificent poetry: it is Faustus wooing a succubus Helen of Troy that the audience remembers, not the pieties of the virtuous characters who try to save his soul.

⌘ Ben Jonson, *Volpone* (1606)

Jonson's dark and ingeniously plotted comedy unfolds in a corrupt Venice where respectable citizens disinherit their sons and prostitute their wives as they seek to bribe their way into the will of the ostensibly dying plutocrat Volpone. In this universe of fools and knaves (which includes two grasping and wonderfully silly English tourists, Sir Politic and Lady Would-be), Volpone and his servant Mosca are the quick-change artists pulling everybody's strings. The brutal satire of the play's two climactic trial scenes suggests that the state's judicial machinery is no match for their powers of invention and improvisation; Mosca and Volpone meet their downfall only when they push their trickery too far, undoing themselves at the moment of their greatest success. Throughout *Volpone*, Jonson's representation of their chicanery as an art form in its own right offers a teasing commentary on the illusions and sleights of hand of theater itself.

↪ Francis Beaumont, *The Knight of the Burning Pestle* (1607)

The prologue of a sentimental comedy, *The London Merchant*, is interrupted when George, a London grocer, climbs onto the stage to deplore the players' unsympathetic treatment of honest citizens. His wife joins in the argument: she wants their stage-struck apprentice Rafe to defend the honor of all grocers by entering the play's action as "The Knight of the Burning Pestle." In the ensuing metatheatrical romp, the actors attempt to perform their own play, George and Nell offer a lively running commentary, and Rafe invades the script at intervals to drag things in the direction of chivalric romance. Things get particularly interesting and hilarious when all these parties collide in the same playing space. Beaumont skewers naïve London theatergoers; he also gets in some very good jabs at the hack dramatists of his day and at his culture's insatiable appetite for rambling tales of knightly adventure.

↪ John Webster, *The Duchess of Malfi* (1613–14)

A beautiful widow is also a head of state. Her powerful brothers want to control her marriage choices and inheritance; defying them, she secretly woos and marries a worthy but lowly gentleman. Webster creates a dark and decadent world. One of the Duchess's brothers is a corrupt cardinal, the other, Ferdinand, is perversely obsessed with his sister's sexuality; together they set the sinister, discontented Bosola to spy on her. When Bosola discovers the Duchess's secret marriage, her kinsmen imprison her and Ferdinand orders his servant to drive her into madness and despair—but Bosola's confrontation with the resolutely unbroken Duchess turns the spy into her would-be revenger in the play's bloody conclusion. As a female tragic protagonist whose greatest transgression is to wish to enjoy private happiness as well as public sway—and as a loving wife whose language sparkles with wit and passion—Webster's heroine is unique in Renaissance English drama.

↪ Thomas Middleton and William Rowley, *The Changeling* (1622)

A willful young lady loathes a sardonic, disfigured servant in her father's household but exploits his desire for her to persuade him to murder her unwanted fiancé—only to find that he is not to be paid off in gold alone. "A woman dipped in blood, and talk of modesty?" mocks the hated de Flores when Beatrice-Joanna tries to defend her virginity. In the play's curious double plot, Beatrice-Joanna's descent into ever deeper acts of vice and deception unfolds in suggestive counterpoint to the story of virtuous Isabella, who must fend off the aggressive attentions of two gentlemen who have feigned lunacy in order to enter her husband's private madhouse. A "changeling" in early modern usage can be a person transformed by disguise or by trauma, a fiend who takes the place of a human being—or a madman. Middleton and Rowley explore all the word's meanings in their disturbing play.

CLARE R. KINNEY, Associate Professor of English, teaches both dramatic and nondramatic Renaissance literature. She is the author of the book *Strategies of Poetic Narrative: Chaucer, Spenser, Milton, Eliot* (Cambridge University Press, 1992), and her many articles include essays on Chaucer, Spenser, Sidney, Shakespeare, Marlowe, and Lady Mary Wroth. She is currently at work on a book exploring sixteenth-century experiments in prose fiction.

JEFFREY A. GROSSMAN

Dangerous Knowledge: Faust, Frankenstein, the Golem, and the Castle

The pursuit of knowledge is an ideal central to Western culture. Or is it? In an earlier time, one could be persecuted—tortured, for instance, or burned at the stake—for asserting such heretical notions as that the earth revolved around the sun, or that, all appearances to the contrary, one was not a witch. The drastic reactions to such claims point to the threat that certain forms of knowledge could pose, especially when that knowledge opposed dominant worldviews and institutions (the church, the monarchy, the medical and legal institutions, etc.). Yet, knowledge, even false knowledge, and power could also interact to create new realities. This helps explain why not a few victims of witch hunts could come to accept the charge or to believe, at least, in their own magical powers, or why some victims of Stalinist purges came to view themselves as traitors to the revolution, or why large parts of a society could believe it right to enslave or segregate its black population or deport its Jewish one to death camps en masse.

One way to approach works of imaginative literature—fiction, drama, or poetry—is to ask how those works relate to the question of knowledge. What kinds of knowledge do they produce? How—if read in certain ways—do they decompose our own assumptions about the world, while composing alternative views in their stead? And what questions might such imaginative works raise about the interaction of knowledge with power? Might they speak a kind of (poetic) truth to power? The works on this reading list—the chapbook commonly known as the *English*

Faust Book or Johann Wolfgang von Goethe's far more complex dramatic work *Faust,* Mary Shelley's gothic, romantic novel *Frankenstein,* H. Leivick's apocalyptic modernist drama *The Golem,* and Franz Kafka's elaborate novel fragment *The Castle*—all illuminate the various ways in which their characters pursue and produce knowledge, often finding themselves blinded no less than enlightened, cut off from insight or understanding into the effects and meanings of those pursuits.

Goethe's Faust, for instance, masters all forms of the human sciences and undertakes numerous political, economic, and social projects, but finds himself ultimately blinded and depleted late in life, having, in part inadvertently, destroyed the lives of a poor elderly couple in the effort to rebuild an empire. The monstrosity of Mary Shelley's *Frankenstein* consists, ultimately, not in Victor Frankenstein's monstrous "creature," but in his efforts to forget that he created him in the first place. Leivick's *Golem* points to the hopes of a Jewish minority to escape persecution, but anxiously creates visions of apocalypse that threaten to overwhelm the more mundane efforts at self-emancipation. And Franz Kafka's *The Castle* presents the unraveling of the individual self that arises when one confronts a modern and authoritarian bureaucracy that calls upon one to carry out a task, but simultaneously inundates one with conflicting messages, meanings, and forms of knowledge, each unmaking the other—and ultimately, all understanding.

All of these disparate works map their characters' struggles with the question of knowledge and its interaction with power. That knowledge may be empowering, but it may also come in the shape of knowledge withheld, knowledge repressed, or knowledge misused across a range of different contexts (historical, cultural) and social positions within those contexts.

Those mappings, in turn, present readers with complex models of human thought and action, pursued under variously imagined conditions. By studying these models, we can better understand our own world—a world in which we are bombarded by complex and often manipulative messages that shape our view of things and even the things themselves.

↬ Anonymous, *The History of the Damnable Life and Deserved Death of Doctor John Faustus* (1592); better known as *The English Faust Book* (Cambridge University Press, 1994)

This translation, completed by an unknown author using the pseudonym P. F. Gent, introduced English readers to the German Reformation text published five years earlier, in 1587. The story tells of a scholar (Faustus) who sells his soul to the devil in exchange for unlimited knowledge and powers in what has become known as the "Faustian pact." Faustus masters necromancy, travels the earth and heavens, conjures up Helen of Troy, punches out the pope, and outwits the Great Turk to seduce his harem, all while defying the norms of the Protestant Reformation. Central to Western culture, the Faust legend forms the basis for many later works in many media. Notable in literature are Christopher Marlowe's morality play *Doctor Faustus* (1593), Thomas Mann's response to Nazism in the novel *Doktor Faustus* (1947), and Mikhail Bulgakov's response to Stalinism in his magical realist novel *The Master and Margarita* (1966–67).

↬ Johann Wolfgang von Goethe, *Faust.* Part I (1808); Part II (1832)

(*Recommended translations:* Walter Arndt (Norton, 2000) or Stuart Atkins [Princeton University Press, 1994]. *Recommended commentary:* Jane K. Brown, *Faust: Theater of the World* [Twayne, 1992].)

Based on the popular versions of the Faust legend, Goethe's (1749–1832) magnum opus, composed over the course of sixty years, radically transforms the legend into a drama of human conflict. The devil is no longer purely evil, nor the Lord purely good. The Faustian pact becomes a wager according to which Mephistopheles agrees to help Faust so long as Faust continues to strive—should Faust ever tarry, he will belong to Mephistopheles.

Because of *Faust II*'s length and difficulty, *Faust I* is often read alone; it depicts a narrow social order, whose moral pretensions destroy the innocent. *Faust II* does reward those who rise to its challenge, both for its expansive probing of philosophical and social problems and for its verbal performance. More darkly than the first part, *Faust II* presents a world where unseen forces manipulate the newly emerging political and economic orders. The history of Goethe's drama, its symbolic status in German and Western culture, its reinterpretation in connection with the fortunes and failings of modern Germany, and its explorations of individual power and modern institutions, human strivings and human errors, continue to make it a compelling drama.

↬ Mary Shelley, *Frankenstein* (1818; ed. Paul J. Hunter [Norton, 1995])

Focused on a scholar-scientist who, not unlike Faust, strives to unlock the mystery of nature—only now in order to create life—Mary Shelley's novel traces the consequences of Victor Frankenstein's actions within a complex narrative framework. A feminist critique of male romantics' indenture to imaginative power, *Frankenstein* is also more: in mapping the effects of Frankenstein's defiance of conventional knowledge, the novel itself performs a similar act. It does so by positioning us as readers beyond the boundaries of middle-class convention, showing us the world from the creature's perspective, and showing how the middle-class world creates the outsider it despises. Frankenstein's flaw consists not in his invention per se, but in his decision to deny and repress the meanings of his own actions, which—in good gothic fashion—nonetheless return to haunt him.

⊷ H. Leivick [Leivick Halpern], *The Golem* (1921; trans. Joachim Neugroschel [Norton, 2006])

Like *Faust*, H. Leivick's Yiddish drama *The Golem* explores the world of magic, while, as in *Frankenstein*, its protagonist defies the boundaries of convention to create a living creature—a kind of "robot" made of clay. The idea of the golem derived from Kabbala, a Jewish mystical branch of study that existed at the margins of a people themselves at the margins of society. Yudl Rosenberg's 1913 chapbook, *The Golem*, popularized this figure, and Leivick's modernist drama takes up that work's plotline, depicting how a golem created by the great Rabbi Loew to protect the Jewish community eventually runs amok. Yet, Leivick's drama takes a darker turn, his golem acquiring a dark inner life, plagued by fears, premonitions, and apocalyptic visions spiraling out of control. Leivick's *Golem* links up with other modernist works from central and eastern Europe, exploring how the pursuit of knowledge leads not to enlightenment but to a sense of angst and of a world ruled by powers beyond our understanding and control. The Norton edition also contains the Rosenberg chapbook and several other tales of the golem.

⊷ Franz Kafka, *The Castle* (1926; trans. Mark Harman [Schocken, 1998])

A land surveyor, known only by the initial K., is summoned to a town to fulfill a task, the nature of which he has not been told. To make sense of things and discover his task, K. seeks to penetrate the castle bureaucracy, but his efforts lead not to clarification, but only to a wearying (and at times comical) proliferation of stories, rumors, myths, and legends about the castle, its inner workings, and the people who may or may not run it. To read *The Castle* is to enter into the disorienting world that gave rise to the term "Kafkaesque." Devoid of magic, mysticism, Faustian scholars, rabbis, demons, and inventors, *The Castle* suggests the debilitating effects wrought by an overflow of information and messages, especially when they issue from concealed and desacralized powers. The 1998 translation by Harman, based on a new edition of the text, is preferable to the earlier translation by Edwin and Willa Muir. The Muir edition is, however, worth consulting if one wants to see what was for many years the standard English language edition.

JEFFREY A. GROSSMAN, Associate Professor in the German Department, teaches German, comparative literature, and Jewish studies. His first book, *The Discourse on Yiddish in Germany from the Enlightenment to the Second Empire* (Camden House, 2000), explores transformations of German and German Jewish culture and writing in the age of nationalism and empire. He is the author of numerous articles, and his current research explores the impact of the poet and cultural critic Heinrich Heine on Yiddish, American, and German culture. He was named the Professor Bernard Choseed Memorial Fellow by the YIVO Institute for Jewish Research for 2006–7.

BRUCE HOLSINGER

Tolling the Bells: Liturgy and English Literature

From its recorded beginnings through the early decades of the Reformation, English literature coexisted intimately, enduringly, and creatively with the liturgy of the Church. The Venerable Bede's *Ecclesiastical History of the English People,* written in the early eighth century, records the famous story of a rustic named Caedmon, an illiterate cowherd who wakens from a dream miraculously invested with the capacity to create religious poetry in his native tongue—poetry that the monastic community of Whitby absorbs seamlessly into the rhythms of its daily ritual life. The lyric that our literary tradition has dubbed "Caedmon's *Hymn,*" perhaps the earliest surviving English poem, comes down to us most likely as a translation of Bede's own Latin paraphrase, and it survives as a kind of marginal notation to the massive Latin text in which its inspiration is narrated.

Despite its humble origins and its seemingly chance survival as English verse, Caedmon's *Hymn* speaks powerfully to a deep-seated and fascinating relationship between the making of English literature and the liturgy. A word of definition is in order here. Liturgy is generally understood as the forms prescribed by the Church for public or institutional religious worship. A group of monks living in a Benedictine monastery like Wearmouth-Jarrow (Bede's own institution), for example, would sing the Daily Office over the entire day, arising in the middle of the night to the bell at Matins (about 2 or 3 a.m.) and progressing through a number of other services of major or minor importance throughout the liturgical day (and this is not counting the performance of Mass, which, depending on the relative solemnity of feast days, could take up several hours of the monks' time). Most prominent lay worshippers—for example, Henry V, who invested greatly in his royal chapel and probably composed musical settings for several Mass movements—spent considerably less time at prayer. Yet their elaborate investments in liturgical worship led to the making of great artifacts such as the Old Hall Manuscript, an early fifteenth-century music book that represents one of the richest collections of multivoiced liturgical music to survive from this era.

Thus medieval liturgy should never be understood simply as the words of praise that constitute the rituals of Mass or Daily Office. Liturgy resides in books and ceremony, in cathedral naves and household chapels, in the conventions of music, gesture, drama, dance, and dress. The protocols entailed in its daily performance determined the most basic architectural decisions in the planning of monasteries, friaries, priories, and household chapels. Liturgy also influenced the most intimate daily, weekly, seasonal, and yearly choices believers could make about the structures of their own lives.

Liturgy was truly an industry during this period, and it is no accident that the religious orders were responsible for writing down and, in many cases, authoring a surprisingly large proportion of the surviving vernacular writing from the period in question. Throughout the Middle Ages, liturgy provided one of the most powerful forces inspiring the invention and writing of new literary forms. Those readers who want a challenge might take a look at some Anglo-Saxon writings (many available in modern translation) like the *Advent Lyrics,* which are based on particular antiphons used in the liturgies of Advent and Christmas. Modern editions of the English mystery cycles are more accessible. These plays, put on regularly by craft guilds in cities like York and Chester, build much of their dramatic tension around the liturgical actions they stage. They often exploit the earthy familiarity of liturgical Latin in English dialogue that plays with liturgy's official conventions. Chaucer's *Canterbury Tales* are filled with subversive, even bawdy allusions to liturgy, while the poetry of John Skelton constantly integrates liturgical tags or formulas into the rhythmical structures of his verse.

While my own research focuses on the liturgical history of medieval literature, I am continually fascinated by what we might call the after-effects of liturgy in post-Renaissance English literature. For this reason I've included several novels in the list below, though I'd encourage readers to open them only after perusing the less familiar and considerably more difficult books preceding them. The study of liturgy can occupy a lifetime, and I hope this list inspires reflection on its profound impact upon the origins and nature of English literature.

↬ *The Sarum Missal in English,* trans. A. H. Pearson (1911; Wipf and Stock, 2004)

This is the real deal: an English translation of an important part of the so-called Sarum Rite, the dominant liturgical tradition in England from the thirteenth century until the Reformation. The *Missal* contains the rubrics and texts (though unfortunately not the music) for a large majority of the Mass ceremonies throughout the liturgical year. This is not light reading, though after a few hours of paging around and learning how the various elements of the Mass fit together (and the distinction between the Proper and the Common, for example), users of this volume will begin to get a sense of the massive enterprise that liturgy represented for medieval culture.

↬ David Mills, ed., *The Chester Mystery Cycle: A New Edition with Modernised Spelling* (Colleagues Press, 1991)

This accessible cycle of mystery plays, performed in the city of Chester during the medieval and early modern periods, demonstrates the extent to which English drama was indebted to the ritual character of liturgy for much of its structure, its themes, and its narrative energy. Notice the number of Latin "tags" from the liturgy throughout the plays, particularly in the *Play of the Shepherds*, which constructs a lengthy exchange by playing with the words and syllables of the *Gloria in excelsis Deo*. Mills's long and informative introduction also contains a good discussion of liturgy and its importance to medieval drama.

↬ Eamon Duffy, *The Stripping of the Altars: Traditional Religion in England, 1400–1580*, 2nd ed. (Yale University Press, 2005)

Duffy's magisterial treatment of lay devotion in medieval and early Reformation England includes the most compelling discussion I have read of the role of liturgy in the shaping of everyday life. Duffy's treatment of liturgy embraces everything from books of hours and prayer beads to carvings on pews and the nature of funeral services. The first edition of *The Stripping of the Altars*, published in 1992, has proved enormously influential and quite controversial in the recent reassessment of the Reformation; Duffy responds to his critics in the second edition. Though the tone of the book can be nostalgic at times, Duffy's portrait of late medieval religion is convincing and often riveting.

↬ Anthony Trollope, *The Chronicles of Barset* (Penguin, 1983–91)

The Barset Chronicles are composed of a sequence of six novels (including Trollope's most beloved, *Barchester Towers*), all of them set in the environs of a fictional English cathedral city. What's interesting here are the ways in which the characters and plotlines in these nineteenth-century novels seem designed precisely to *avoid* the liturgical culture of the cathedral that surrounds them—a measure of the distance English literary writing has traveled since works like the *Canterbury Tales* and the Chester Cycle. The most vivid example here is Reverend Harding, kindly protagonist of *The Warden* (the first and shortest novel in the series), whose enthusiasm for amateur music-making at home seems to exceed his commitment to the liturgical music of the cathedral.

↭ Iris Murdoch, *The Bell* (Penguin, 2001)

The setting for this quietly gorgeous novel is a lay community on the grounds of Imber Abbey, which houses an enclosed order of Anglican nuns. While the laypeople in the community work, fight, hate, love, and otherwise interact with one another, the liturgical culture of the abbey serves as both backdrop and aspiration for their foibles—and, in the form of a bell lost since the Middle Ages yet miraculously uncovered by two central characters, as a source of mixed redemption by the end of the novel.

For further reading:

Thomas J. Heffernan and E. Ann Matter, eds., *The Liturgy of the Medieval Church*, 2nd ed. (Medieval Institute Publications, 2005).
Margot E. Fassler and Rebecca A. Baltzer, eds., *The Divine Office in the Latin Middle Ages: Methodology and Source Studies, Regional Developments, Hagiography* (Oxford University Press, 2000).

BRUCE HOLSINGER is Professor of English and Music. Much of his work concerns the relationship between music and literature in the Western Middle Ages. His first book, *Music, Body, and Desire in Medieval Culture* (Stanford University Press, 2001), won awards from the Modern Language Association, the Medieval Academy of America, and the American Musicological Society. His work on liturgy has been supported by grants from the NEH, the ACLS, and, in 2004, by a fellowship from the John Simon Guggenheim Memorial Foundation.

ELIZABETH FOWLER

Return to the Word Hoard

Who hasn't heard of Beowulf's painful victories, Chaucer's jolly pilgrimage, Shakespeare's sad kings, or Milton's grieving Satan? Each of us who reads English inherits this rich and powerful treasure trove—what the poets call a "word hoard." Strangely, though its early creators have been dead and gone for centuries, their legacy seems magically to transform every time we return to it. It looks very different to scholars now than it did when I first read Middle English in the 1970s, and as I continue to study, it shimmers and stretches and shape-shifts in my hands.

I was scheduled to teach *Sir Gawain and the Green Knight* to three hundred students of the history of literature in English on the morning after September 11, 2001. I was tempted to cancel, but I e-mailed my students instead and asked them to bring in readings that they found helpful in our distress. Many of my colleagues feared that the immediate tragedy made classes pointless, but my students and I were enormously moved as dozens of young women and men stood up to take the microphone in that cavernous place, bravely offering old poems to one another.

I was surprised to see *Sir Gawain* leap up and speak in a loud voice *to us* as we were during that morning. I had known it as a brittle, gorgeous poem, so refined as to be slight—a poem about the cruelties and gratifications of manners and the painful sensitivities of the famous—and it is all that. But it came to us then as a poem that places itself behind the images of that day, "behind" in a resonant palimpsest that the wars of the early twentieth century caused W. B. Yeats to see engendered in Leda, "The broken wall, the burning roof and tower," and T. S. Eliot to see in *The Waste Land:* "Falling towers / Jerusalem Athens Alexandria / Vienna London / Unreal." This is how *Sir Gawain* begins:

> Since the siege and the assault was ceased at Troy,
> The walls breached and burnt down to brands and ashes . . .

Here are the burning towers that recall us to the tragedy of empire; the post-tragic story then persistently invites us to consider the work of government (of the kingdom, of the landscape, of the self).

In the archives of English literature, that striking image is joined by so many others: the golden hall Heorot, emblem of all the fruits of achieved peace, burning and ravaged by the jealous terrorist Grendel; the huge tournament arena commissioned by the refined tyrant Theseus, who subdues by sports, religion, and rhetoric all the rebellious anger of the peoples he has brutally conquered; Arthur and his precarious, bountiful castle with its round table of "rightful brothers"; Milton's awesome Pandemonium, a hall built by greed to house Satan's parliament. The image of proud towers burning has a history evoked by the cruel terrorists that clear September day. In the word hoard, which is full of stories about the fates of nations, architecture is an emblem of the political constitution. How can we build and sustain a just polity? How should a good person respond to violence and its breaches of taste and of peace? Can empire be just? So much of the great writing of the Middle Ages and Renaissance is part of the struggle to establish principles and institutions in which a culture could find and trust itself.

For myself, I stick by what I said on September 12: when we are attacked, I pray that we respond by building up, rather than squandering, our most treasured legacies: the sense of alliance as life-giving and retribution as endless death in *Beowulf;* the superiority of earned consent to force and conquest that Chaucer and Spenser repeatedly explore; the English "mixed" constitution theorized in the late Middle Ages and developed by American history into the checks and balances I was taught to value in high school; the deference of leaders to law's restraints that was urgent for Shakespeare; the political freedoms that allow citizens to fall into error and therefore, as Milton argues, afford us a true opportunity to stand righteously.

What does the word hoard find you thinking now? Go back to read the old poets and their changing stories, wrestle with the images they salvaged for us from the wreckage of their times, set our near history into the long history of the language—and see what you think.

✤ *The Norton Anthology of English Literature,* 8th ed., vol. 1, ed. Stephen Greenblatt et al. (Norton, 2006)

If my ship, like Prospero's in *The Tempest,* were set adrift in the sea of modernity and I were allowed only one book, I might choose this one. It contains a moving translation of *Beowulf* by the Nobel Laureate Seamus Heaney, my favorite living poet. It also includes sound modern versions of many other medieval and early modern works, from *Caedmon's Hymn* to bits of legendary histories of ancient Britain, to William Langland's *The Vision of Piers Plowman,* to the rather wild and brilliant work of Margery Kempe and Julian of Norwich. The *Norton* is a tasting menu that amounts to a feast.

✤ *Penguin Book of Renaissance Verse, 1509–1659,* ed. David Norbrook and H. R. Woudhuysen (Penguin, 1993)

Favorite early modern poets are plentifully represented here in original spellings, together with tiny biographies. Look especially for the relative newcomers Mary Sidney, Countess of Pembroke (and Philip's sister), Mary Wroth, Isabella Whitney, Margaret Cavendish, and other thrilling canon-expanders. The volume includes more political verse than is usual, including a chilling lament for the shrine to the Virgin Mary at Walsingham, a major destination for medieval pilgrims that was destroyed in the Reformation:

> Bitter was it oh to vewe
> the sacred vyne,
> Whiles the gardeners plaied all close,
> rooted up by the swine

. . . .

Levell Levell with the ground
   the towres doe lye
Which with their golden glitteringe tops
   Pearsed once to the skye. (p. 531)

↬ *The Riverside Chaucer,* ed. Larry Benson (Houghton Mifflin, 1985)

Chaucer just gets better at an astonishing pace. He's the one poet I could happily teach every day of my life. The expanding canon hasn't demoted him a bit; instead, it has seemed to make him more interesting than ever. If you've only dipped into *The Canterbury Tales,* you might have missed the most curious and beautifully made saint's life in English, "The Second Nun's Tale." You might also be captivated by the eroticism, grief, intellectual engagement, and lush poetry of his dream visions, in which he flies on a ranting eagle to a twig house that whirls in the air (*The House of Fame*), visits a temple that enshrines a comically erect penis, and eventually overhears the enormous goddess of nature calming down a lot of quarreling birds (*The Parliament of Fowls*). The *Riverside* edition reigns in Chaucer studies, and is the best central place to go for texts, commentary, and a good gloss. A number of online Web sites (search for Chaucer) offer pronunciation tutorials; it's easier than ever to learn Middle English.

↬ Edmund Spenser, *The Faerie Queene,* ed. A. C. Hamilton (Longman, 2006)

↬ Edmund Spenser, *The Shorter Poems,* ed. Richard McCabe (Penguin, 2000)

With knights (of both sexes) in dirty armor, dragons, heartrending plots, and a politico-sexual-psycho-surrealism still difficult to dream of translating into film, *The Faerie Queene* is one of the most ambitious and fascinating poems in English. Hamilton's edition has the richest commentary on it; the copious shorter poems of Spenser are freshly admirable in Richard McCabe's paperback. A new edition of all of Spenser is currently under way for Oxford University Press.

↬ William Shakespeare, *William Shakespeare: The Complete Works,* ed. Stanley Wells and Gary Taylor (Oxford University Press, 1986)

↬ William Shakespeare, *Shakespeare's Sonnets,* ed. Stephen Booth (Yale University Press, 1978)

↬ Helen Vendler, *The Art of Shakespeare's Sonnets* (Harvard University Press, 1997)

Shakespeare can be happily read in more editions than seems possible, including copies of the quarto print editions of the plays at the British

Library (www.bl.uk/treasures/shakespeare/homepage.html). Wells and Taylor present probably the most authoritative complete texts, but Shakespeareans seem to let a thousand flowers bloom, and the classroom trade supports us in our heterogeneity. I still like Stephen Booth's edition of the sonnets with its facsimile of the early printed text facing each page of edited text. For scrupulous and responsive commentary to the sonnets' every move of thought, Helen Vendler's exquisite edition should not be missed, and can be browsed starting with any poem.

↬ Thomas Malory, *The Works of Sir Thomas Malory* (1947; ed. Eugene Vinaver [Clarendon Press, 1990])

Malory's charmless soldier's prose is strangely effective and seductive, and Vinaver's 1947 edition is appropriately naked of apparatus or commentary. It can be had cheaply in paper at used bookstores everywhere, or in a 1990 "reverified" third edition in the Oxford English Text series. The British Library's Web site (cited above for Shakespeare) is preparing an online copy of the entire Winchester manuscript in which Malory famously wove together many stories about King Arthur.

ELIZABETH FOWLER is Associate Professor of English, author of *Literary Character: The Human Figure in Early English Writing* (Cornell University Press, 2003), and a General Editor of the forthcoming *Oxford Collected Works of Edmund Spenser*. Her work lies in the intersection between literary fiction and other modes of representing the world, especially legal, philosophical, and economic.

J. PAUL HUNTER

Literature as Re-Viewing

Students often distinguish between Reading for Class and Reading for Pleasure, though teachers like me usually protest that in the best of all possible worlds—that is, in our own classes—there is no such distinction. A book like this depends on erasing the distinction entirely, assuming that readers have already decided to have fun and learn at the same time. That is pretty much what the Roman poet and critic Horace suggested two thousand years ago when he defined the aims of poetry as providing a combination of instruction and delight.

But "instruction," outside the classroom, has an ugly ring to it, as if delight were just sugar to make the medicine go down. We don't turn to imaginative literature mainly for knowledge or information, but literature does teach, usually in an unobtrusive way, mainly because it liberates us for a moment into an "as if" mode and frees us from our subjective limitations of perspective. Sometimes it offers temporary residence in places or eras or cultures we don't know, or exposes unfamiliar situations, or introduces the kinds of people we never meet—maybe even transporting us into a different mind-set or identity. The transportation is, to be sure, temporary (and less dangerous than most means of transportation), but sometimes we are quite different for the experience, perceiving something fresh about the world or ourselves. But sometimes the frontier is the familiar rather than the unknown or exotic; just as books can enlarge our perspective by taking us far away in space or time, so they can give us new eyes to see common, ordinary things in a new way. That's the way the books on this list work, reviewing the ordinary in ways that allow us to see the familiar anew.

One of the five books I've chosen, originally titled *Travels into Several Remote Nations of the World* and now usually called *Gulliver's Travels*, pretends at first to be taking us far away, into lands that have customs, histories, and probabilities very different from ours. In Lilliput (first voyage) everything is miniaturized; people and things are 1/1,728th normal size, and the traveler-narrator (Lemuel Gulliver) finds himself regarded as a clumsy monster among the natives in their fragile world, although capable of grand heroism because of his size. In Brobdingnag (second voyage) the telescopic and microscopic are reversed: everything is 1,728 times as large as normal, and the narrator is dwarfed and threatened everywhere. And so on into new lands peopled by talking horses, projecting philosophers who live entirely in the abstract, experimental farmers trying to extract sunbeams from cucumbers, etc. All very strange. But in every case, we are looking at ourselves, seen from a puzzled outside perspective; familiar institutions and human habits are there in all the visited societies, but refracted to make us self-conscious about what we see. The familiar never quite looks the same again.

Robinson Crusoe works in a more direct, novelistic way. Here the restless hero travels to real faraway places. But after a shipwreck leaves him on an uninhabited island off South America, he has to create a life from scratch. And we review what it takes to deal with basic issues—shelter, food, clothing, fear of uncertainty, solitude, relationships with other creatures, sense of self, purpose, destiny. Not taking the familiar for granted raises the ordinary into a self-conscious prominence, and we face, along with Crusoe, basic questions about life issues. In two other novels, *Tom*

Jones and *Persuasion*, we stay home (home in each case being England) and watch human relationships from familiar angles. Tom is a "foundling"— that is, an illegitimate child without social or legal status—and his story is the familiar boy-girl story of just deserts: How does justice work for figures outside "normal" living circumstances? But it is also a story of human imperfection, since the hero has personal *character* weaknesses too. The action here is filtered through an author-narrator whose style is facetious and ironic and who doesn't always evaluate straightforwardly or tell us the whole truth, so that we finally make the judgment calls ourselves. Similarly, the author's style is a major issue in Jane Austen's *Persuasion;* her voice too is teasing and ironic as she describes, with detached amusement, life and love in the English countryside in the early nineteenth century. Again, here is love triumphing belatedly, and the irony doesn't mislead us, just makes us ponder our judgments on people operating in common, habitual situations. The fifth book, *Strike Sparks,* is a contemporary collection of poems that deal with the issues of modern life: sickness, death, love, sex, marriage, neediness, betrayal, friendship—difficulties as well as triumphs—but the forthrightness of exploration of everyday experience is astonishing and brutally honest. New eyes again.

Literature doesn't always concentrate on Life's Big Questions, nor necessarily "review" in the sense of reminding, summarizing, or simplifying. More often it runs the familiar by us from angles that involve surprises, insights, re-viewings—defamiliarizing experience to bare the richness and stimulation in the most simple and habitual moments of ordinary life.

✎ Daniel Defoe, *The Life and Strange Surprizing Adventures of Robinson Crusoe* (1719; ed. John Richetti [Penguin, 2001])

> Daniel Defoe was a committed city-dweller who lived in London all his seventy years, and we have no evidence he ever traveled to the "New" World. But at age fifty-nine he wrote one of the world's great imaginative novels about a young man with "rambling thoughts" who became a castaway on what he calls his "Island of Despair." "Robinson Crusoe" tells his own story of twenty-eight years there, tracing both his struggle to tame his wilderness environment and to come to terms with himself. He isn't always clever—building boats too far from the water to launch them—but he wonderfully bares the basic issues of survival, self-discovery, and community-building in elemental form.

✎ Jonathan Swift. *Gulliver's Travels* (1726; ed. Albert J. Rivero [Norton, 2002])

> You may have first met this text as a "children's book," and it does work as an imaginative account of "discovering" worlds with different laws

and probabilities—especially the first two voyages, which depend on little/big contrasts that obsess children. Lemuel Gulliver is a wonderfully ineffectual narrator: he fails to observe the obvious, is easily impressed with other people's interpretations of customs and laws, and has an enormous, ill-deserved ego. And he's an unreliable judge, praising unpraiseworthy behavior and giving windy, lofty, undeserved compliments to practices he remembers from England. But his observations are as hilarious as they are ludicrous, leaving us to form our own judgments, which seem magically to coincide with those of the world's most articulate satirist. (Swift may have written *Gulliver's Travels* as a direct satiric response to *Robinson Crusoe;* you can give yourself extra points if you find parallels and parodies in the text.)

↤ Henry Fielding, *The History of Tom Jones* (1749; ed. John Bender and Simon Stern [Oxford University Press, 1996])

Henry Fielding was a playwright, journalist, and magistrate, and scored a huge popular success with this novel, which sold out before it was officially released and then was repeatedly reprinted, imitated, and adapted. It's a wonderful story as story—Coleridge called it one of the three most perfect plots ever conceived—but the star is the "voice" of Fielding himself, who jauntily reminds us repeatedly that he is in charge and entitled to make things happen as he pleases and mislead us about what exactly he is doing. He's a lovable narrator, but he does cheat, and we're therefore on our own to read characters by their actions rather than relying on opinions of others, including the narrator. What he's really doing is teaching us to *read*—actions as well as texts because that's what "readers" have to do in a real world without reliable narrators.

↤ Jane Austen, *Persuasion* (1818; ed. Patricia Meyer Spacks [Norton, 1995])

Jane Austen may have the best voice in all of English literature. She too builds brilliant plots and creates wonderfully vivid characters, but students of style just gush when they describe the narrator in her novels, especially this one. If you're already an Austen fan, *Persuasion* is the novel you really need. It is Austen at her mature best: a wonderful heroine from a comically dysfunctional family, a great plot about a stupidly delayed love connection, and a commenting voice that will double you up in its exquisite exposure of characters who are sometimes contemptible, sometimes pathetic, sometimes embarrassingly human, and always entertaining and educational in their mortal mistakes and failures. This is, I think, Austen's best novel, and if you haven't read all the rest, you might want to save this for last.

↭ Sharon Olds, *Strike Sparks: Selected Poems* (Knopf, 2004)

Readers are sometimes unnerved by Sharon Olds's poetry, and even if you are not easily shocked you may be surprised by her audacity and frankness. She is afraid of nothing human, and writes courageously about all kinds of human activities and emotions—most famously perhaps about sexual desire, but also about family issues of all kinds (affection, illness, alienation, divorce, parenthood, rivalry, loyalty, pain). Olds is ruthlessly committed to investigating what lies behind both external emotional expressions and moral pieties, and she writes about public figures and historical matters as well as personal issues and confrontations. The brutal honesty is contagious, and readers often see themselves much more clearly after reading her work. This book collects work from different periods of her life; if you can't find it, try any of her shorter books, which are equally varied and rewarding.

J. PAUL HUNTER has taught at Virginia since retiring as Barbara E. and Richard J. Franke Professor of Humanities at the University of Chicago in 2001. He is the author of a number of books, including *Before Novels* (Norton, 1990), which won the Louis Gottschalk Prize, and *The Norton Introduction to Poetry,* now in its ninth edition.

4

The Arts

FRANCESCA FIORANI

Art and Science in the Renaissance

To read about the relationships between art and science is to enter right at the center of the untidy, contradictory, and captivating world of the Renaissance. Indeed, this topic is uniquely suitable for considering the contradictory status of images in the construction and transmission of knowledge in the West: Do images contribute to the understanding of nature, people, and things? Or do they obscure knowledge, as Plato suggested long ago?

Today art and science are practiced as divergent forms of knowledge, but in the Renaissance they shared historical roots, methods of inquiry, and the belief in the cognitive power of images. Then, to re-create the ancient world and to investigate the secrets of nature were regarded as part and parcel of the same cultural project. Natural philosophy—to use the name that designated science in the Renaissance—studied nature alongside ancient works of art.

In fact, natural philosophers, scholars, artists, merchants, and craftsmen worked side by side in the utopian attempt to reconstruct the meaning and context of the ancient texts that were resurfacing, after centuries of neglect, from monastic libraries across Europe. Resourcefully, Renaissance scholars and artists shared their expertise in interpreting these fragmented texts in conjunction with whatever additional materials from the ancient world they had been able to gather. They unearthed ruins, discovered statues, measured buildings, excavated sarcophagi and reliefs, re-created ancient paintings from verbal descriptions, computed ancient measurements, mapped the ancient world, calculated terrestrial locations, observed the cosmos, collected plants and animals and matched them with ancient texts, designed astrological charts for ancient rulers, and interrogated the stars. In short, they took what we would call today an interdisciplinary approach to the ancient world, commingling mathematics and philology, science and humanism, measurements and antiquarianism, art and science. Along the way, they also redesigned the contours of the modern world.

In this joint process of rediscovering the ancient world and of inventing the modern one, images played a fundamental role. Images were among the most famous products of the period, especially the images created by such artists as Leonardo, Michelangelo, and Raphael, which became icons of Western culture. But, in the same period, images were also the undisputed protagonists of the investigation of the natural world. For instance, Leonardo da Vinci designed a treatise on the human body based predominantly on anatomical tables of body parts, which he never published, although it was instrumental for later authors. The natural philosopher Ulisse Aldrovandi envisaged the megalomaniac enterprise of reproducing the entire world's fauna and flora in colored prints and managed to assemble over three thousand drawings. Galileo Galilei himself drew the surface of the moon as he observed it through the telescope, while the Linceans, a group of Galileo's friends, published the first large-scale drawings representing an insect under the microscope.

Paradoxically, however, the status of images was far from fixed in this period. Neo-Platonic philosophers, who influenced greatly Renaissance art and science, adhered to Plato's teaching. He regarded images as doubly misleading in the acquisition of knowledge: they were copies of the natural world, which, in turn, was a pale copy of the ideal, superior world—the world of "Forms"—where true knowledge resided.

The books presented here offer engaging and penetrating reflections on the cognitive role of images through a series of compelling case studies relating to the rise of modern science. These books vary in genre and topics, while the different backgrounds of their authors, coming from the fields of geography, cognitive sciences, and art history, reflect the interdisciplinary intermingling of the Renaissance itself. These books succeed in bringing visual experience and visual evidence to the center of cultural history and the history of ideas. For too long considered as ancillary to verbal communication, communication through images, which dominates our modern world, rewards careful study. The authors below have, in exciting ways, done much to account for the specificity of images, that is, their materials, texture, scale, size, proportions, colors, and volumes. Here is a reading list to ponder on the cognitive power of images across time.

↪ Martin Kemp, *Leonardo* (Oxford University Press, 2005)

Trained as both a scientist and an art historian, Kemp enjoys a unique perspective on Leonardo's life and work. In this biography, which synthesizes thirty years of incessant scholarship on the artist, he demonstrates his intimate familiarity with Leonardo's mind. The book stands out among the immense literature on the artist for its unique focus on the reconstruction of Leonardo's thought processes. Rather than publishing every single scrap of evidence on Leonardo's life that we have discovered, Kemp aims to show with concrete examples how Leonardo's mind worked in combining visual observation with abstract diagrams, ancient authors with experience, art with science. In clear, incisive, and enjoyable prose, Kemp explains the intricate connections that Leonardo saw among art, machines, the human body, the earth, and the cosmos. A substantive contribution to the knowledge of Leonardo's biography, this is also a great introduction to the understanding of the relationship between art and science in the Renaissance.

↪ David Freedberg, *The Eye of the Lynx: Galileo, His Friends, and the Beginnings of Modern Natural History* (University of Chicago Press, 2003)

An expert on the power of images in Renaissance and baroque Europe, Freedberg narrates in this book the fascinating and little-known story of the Linceans, a small group of scholars who founded an academy in baroque Rome (Galileo Galilei was also a member). The work of the Linceans consisted primarily of recording minerals, fossils, plants, and animals in thousands of beautiful drawings, since they were convinced that the comprehensive visual record of the world would, one day, reveal the universal laws of nature. Freedberg, who discovered many of these drawings in European libraries, shows how the Linceans' resolute beliefs in the visual record of the world crumble under the sheer quantity of the drawings they produced. He also explains their role in contemporary debates on astronomy, especially their passionate defense of Galileo. Compellingly, Freedberg combines the intriguing microhistory of the Linceans with perceptive reflections on the status, function, and use of images created by direct observation either with the naked eye or through the telescope and the microscope.

↜ Roberto Casati, *Shadows: Unlocking Their Secrets from Plato to Our Time* (Vintage, 2004)

Written by a scholar who moves freely in the domains of the philosophy of perception, cognitive science, and the philosophy of the mind, this book holds more insights than one might expect from a work of popular science. Shadows are fundamental to perceiving the position of things in the world and to representing that position in painting illusionistically. And yet their usefulness has been questioned ever since Plato regarded them as an obstacle to knowledge. Casati asks whether Plato was unfair to shadows and then proceeds with a stringent analysis of the conscious use of shadows in the construction of knowledge, with a special emphasis on their role in the history of science and astronomy. The book is full of thought-provoking remarks on the mysterious status of shadows in philosophy, perception, folklore, mythology, science, and Renaissance painting.

↜ Horst Bredekamp, *The Lure of Antiquity and the Cult of the Machine: The Kunstkammer and the Evolution of Nature, Art, and Technology*, trans. Allison Brown (Marcus Wiener, 1995)

As a historian of art trained in the grand tradition of German iconography and history of ideas, Bredekamp has the talent of combining the close analysis of images and texts with wide-ranging conclusions. This concise, superb essay stands out among art historical writing, especially the vast literature on the history of early museums, as a uniquely illuminating contribution on the role of visual experience in fundamental shifts in the investigation of the natural world. Places of delight, refuge, intellectual entertainment, and political prestige, the cabinets of art and curiosities discussed in this book were indoor microscopic reproductions of the world that displayed natural objects and man-made artifacts side by side. Bredekamp argues convincingly that such a display trained the eye to visual autopsy, facilitated visual observations and analogies between different classes of objects, and ultimately contributed to the transition from the traditional, static view of nature to a dynamic view of natural history.

↜ Denis Cosgrove, *Apollo's Eye: A Cartographic Genealogy of the Earth in the Western Imagination* (John Hopkins University Press, 2001)

A geographer by training, Cosgrove looks at the historical significance of the globe from ancient times to our days. His inquiry is particularly pertinent to remembering the historical roots of the world of globalization in which we live. By reconstructing the symbolic, political, scientific, and cartographic meanings of the globe over time, Cosgrove shows unmistakably the major role that cartographic and artistic images played in the affirmation of globalization.

FRANCESCA FIORANI, Associate Professor of Renaissance Art, has written on Leonardo, art theory, and Renaissance art and science. Her book *The Marvel of Maps: Art, Cartography, and Politics in Renaissance Italy* (Yale University Press, 2005) addresses the interaction of Renaissance mapping with other forms of knowledge and representation. The director of *Leonardo and His Treatise on Painting,* an electronic archive devoted to Leonardo's legacy to art theory, she is currently writing a book on Leonardo's shadows.

JOHANNA DRUCKER

Maps, Graphs, and Icons: The Art of Visual Knowledge Representation

Much of human knowledge is communicated in texts, and our education tends to bias us toward a familiarity with reading as a way of getting information. But an enormous amount of knowledge is best (or even *only*) communicated visually. Timetables, bar graphs, maps, even pictorial icons (on restroom doors and other signs) figure prominently in our routine activities. Though these are part of our daily landscape, we rarely stop to think about the way a clock face or calendar expresses historical and cultural values (Why does the week start on Sunday? Why is midnight at the top of the clock?). Information in images isn't expressed only in *what* they show, but in *how* they show it. The structure and style of graphical information (is it in blocks, columns, tables, aligned on an axis, or laid out in a scatter plot?) is a crucial part of its meaning. The books in this list help to shift our idea of "visual information" toward an understanding of graphical forms as part of the larger cultural legacy that we rely on for knowledge of the world and ourselves. Oddly enough, precious few books have been written on this topic. Usually, when images are the subject, art historians or cultural critics are the ones paying attention. But we have to look long and hard to find the handful of books that are shaping the study of graphical forms of information. Though no ideal book exists, this group contains a few starting points for reading in this area. They are works that increase our understanding of the formats of graphical information as *knowledge,* that is, expressions of culture and history, not just statistical data.

Production of visual representations is increasing through widespread use of computers to turn data into images. We learn how to read most of these common graph forms in elementary school. But we rarely pause to consider the *rhetorical* structure of these visual forms that makes an argument, a persuasive expression. Though diagrams often seem to be "just there," their conventions have a long history that is structured into the way they "show" us meaning.

Most "information visualizations" come from fields where quantitative data are an integral feature of the discipline, such as statistics in the natural sciences, engineering, technical drawing, and applied mathematics. The work of Edward Tufte comes directly out of that realm and does not necessarily attend to the cultural history of the graphical forms those disciplines use. Works by James Elkins and Alan MacEachren are beginning to synthesize a fascinating history of graphical knowledge.

This synthetic history exposes the lineage of visual forms of information. The familiar tree-form diagram, for instance, assumes a continuous, branching, relationship of the elements that mirrors concepts of organic evolution (incorporating genealogical charts with biblical antecedents). Gridded tables that make use of columns assume continuity of information types along the horizontal and/or vertical axes—and were developed for classification and calculation. Cartographic modes structure a point of view into their presentation—an omniscient bird's eye, a cultural bias (usually emphasizing the Northern Hemisphere), or recording the history of an exploration as it occurred. Iconic symbols draw on long-held beliefs about the power of images to be read directly by the eye, in the tradition of the "hieroglyphic" or "Chinese character" taken as self-evident signs. Bar charts often "chunk" their data according to very crude or reductive parameters such as age groups, income distribution, or other unsubtle statistical metrics.

Many graphical forms contain incidental information. The representation of a "typical" woman, farmer, or soldier speaks volumes about the culture in which such images are legible. A map containing mermaids, monsters, and personified figures of the winds shows a belief system that once projected its imagery upon the world. Even the simple diary makes many assumptions through the way it structures the hours of the day into same-sized units. These information structures impose their expectations and shape attitudes. The study of cognition has led to the development of an information-processing version of visual experience, and away from earlier mechanistic models of stimulus-response through eye to brain. In such a systems-dependent analysis, graphical forms of knowledge become part of a set of exchanges in which the ability to know as well as the content of knowledge is formed by these structures.

Each of the books in this list offers some useful thoughts on this topic. But the best and most interesting work in this field? It lies ahead!

↪ Martin Gardner, *Logic Machines and Diagrams,* 2nd ed. (University of Chicago Press, 1982)

> This gem of a book, lucid and clear, is filled with information about Venn diagrams and the work of the fabulous Raymond Lull (the medieval visionary who created a system of revolving wheels to describe everything in the universe and compute God's capabilities), and others. This book is small and short, but it is a great introduction to thinking about graphical forms as machines capable of doing something, not only showing it. This distinction between generative methods of visualization and presentation of data already calculated is crucial, and though Gardner doesn't state it explicitly, his emphasis on the productive capacity of visualizations makes a strong contribution to this argument.

↪ Edward R. Tufte, *The Visual Display of Quantitative Information,* 2nd ed. (Graphics Press, 2001)

> Tufte is among the most elegant and sophisticated information designers in current practice. His first book on this topic is still the most engaging and striking. Its design embodies his beliefs that clarity and economy are essential to the graphical presentation of information. Tufte's approach is classical in its rigor, but is premised on a belief in the empirical credibility of data. For all his power as a designer, he stresses continually that the information exists independently of its presentation and that the designer's task is to make as clear a graphic image of it as possible. He never addresses the assumptions inherent in hierarchical structures, grids, or other formats, though he does present a series of "greatest hits" from the history of diagrams, beginning with work designed by the equally elegant eighteenth-century figure William Playfair.

↪ Alan M. MacEachren, *How Maps Work: Representation, Visualization, and Design,* 2nd ed. (Guilford Press, 2004)

> Simply the smartest book on vision, visuality, and theories of cognition that I have come across. MacEachren is a cartographer, but his introductory chapters in this book are thorough reviews of the history of models of vision from physiological and philosophical perspectives. His work is current, and contains an information-processing theory of vision that is attentive to the way images function to shape, constrain,

and generate knowledge. Though MacEachren is not a historian of graphical forms, he makes a significant contribution to our understanding of the history of visuality.

⊷ James Elkins, *The Domain of Images* (Cornell University Press, 2001)

Elkins has a creative and original mind and is one of the few writers trained in art history looking beyond the confines of the art historical canon to the broader history and use of visual images. This fascinating book raises many issues about the way the aesthetic properties of images work in the communication of information in medical imaging, scientific illustration, and other visual forms. Elkins is conversant with philosophical traditions and synthesizes notions of realism, empiricism, idealism, and functionalism across disciplines in a useful and tractable way. His writing is dense but unjargoned, his thinking is complex but he communicates well, and the book is finely designed so that captions and images and commentary are all in proximity (which should be the norm!).

⊷ William Mills Ivins, *Prints and Visual Communication* (1953; MIT Press, 1969)

A classic in the field of art history, Ivins's book is still extremely useful for thinking about the way print reproduction stabilized knowledge. Though he has been criticized by later art and cultural historians as mechanistic in his emphasis on the impact of technology, Ivins's analysis of the effects of standardized reproduction and circulation of knowledge in natural and physical sciences is valid. Ivins's premise is that print technology allowed visual forms to circulate widely and thus to function as a shared foundation of knowledge in emerging disciplines. Printed reference works that used imagery gave rise to conventions for representing natural processes as well as objects. Ivins's discussion of the "syntax" of printed images remains another useful contribution to the discussion of graphical knowledge. Ivins, like other art historians of his generation and training, wrote with generous clarity and erudition.

JOHANNA DRUCKER's scholarly interest in visual forms of knowledge—or *graphesis*—is an extension of her work in art history and in digital media. She is Robertson Professor of Media Studies and also has taught at Harvard, Yale, the University of Texas at Dallas, SUNY at Purchase, and Columbia University. She is a practicing artist and cofounder of the Speculative Computing Lab at the University of Virginia.

LISA REILLY

A Pilgrim's Guide: The Visual World of Medieval Art

Art historians deal primarily with objects and visual experience. Perhaps more than with other cultures, an understanding of the visual culture of the Middle Ages requires a knowledge of how visual experience at the time integrated many types of objects. A visit to a shrine or chapel exposed a viewer to metalwork, stone sculpture, painting, stained glass, mosaic, architecture, and textiles. All worked together to convey meaning and particular kinds of spiritual experience because medieval art always performs a function, whether symbolic or actual. In order to understand how the object works, its meaning for viewers, and medieval aesthetic sensibilities, the art historian, regardless of his or her specialty—in painting or architecture, for example—needs to consider how the ensemble worked together and how it functioned liturgically, politically, or otherwise. This analysis involves a close consultation of primary sources, an understanding of historical context and religious practice, and an understanding of the objects themselves.

The texts I've selected highlight the interdisciplinary practice of medieval cultural studies. They draw on primary sources not written for modern art historians, but commonly consulted by them. The art historical readings show the field's interest in both the micro and macro spheres of visual experience. The essays in *Reading Medieval Images* begin with objects as small as textile fragments and move on to discuss large-scale sculptures and buildings. Marvin Trachtenberg's volume on Florence expands the scale further to establish how the builders of pre-Renaissance Florence created the city's medieval urban setting according to deliberate design principles. Art history has generally shifted from a more narrow focus on the object itself, an approach popular for much of the last century, to a broader consideration of the audience (to include marginalized social groups), as well as a broader conception of an object's meaning and function. These texts reflect this broader and more contextual approach in medieval art history while remaining directly engaged with the object itself. Peter Brown's *Cult of the Saints,* though not, strictly speaking, an example of art historical scholarship, exemplifies the interdisciplinary nature of medieval studies in its integrated examination of the art, liturgy, and politics that combined to create a cult practice at the core of medieval Christian life.

Primary sources such as Ibn Jubayr's travels and *The Pilgrim's Guide* rarely include direct discussion of art in terms with which modern readers are familiar. Their descriptions are seldom precise and do not allow a reconstruction of the original object. Rather, the accounts dealing with art tend to be experiential, describing the overpowering scale, brilliant light, or jewel-like quality of the object. These descriptions provide modern readers with a sense of what medieval audiences valued in their art. At the same time, these accounts of travel and cultural difference provide a picture of cultural identity and confrontation that is useful for understanding medieval perspectives about the self and others. Ibn Jubayr, for example, is clearly perplexed when the Christian king of Sicily saves a group of shipwrecked Muslim travelers from slavery. He is equally astonished to see Christian women in Palermo wearing Muslim dress. In some passages, the medieval world seen in these texts seems immediate and familiar, and in others, overwhelmingly alien. Either way, this world has contributed significantly to the emergence of European-based modern cultures as well as current cross-cultural conflicts.

✎ Elizabeth Sears and Thelma K. Thomas, eds. *Reading Medieval Images: The Art Historian and the Object* (University of Michigan Press, 2002)

One can find much of the key scholarship in the field of art history in articles rather than in books. In this exemplary selection of essays chosen by leading medieval art scholars Elizabeth Sears and Thelma K. Thomas, the reader can see the vital nature of the field and the multiplicity of approaches, types of objects, and questions raised. Sears and Thomas are admirable for the clarity of their own essays and the judiciousness of their selections. The articles cover objects that range chronologically from late antiquity through the late Middle Ages and culturally across Byzantine, Islamic, and Latin Christian settings, demonstrating the diversity of medieval art history. The essays analyze a variety of media including architecture, textiles, sculpture, manuscripts, mosaics, and paintings using a wide range of methods. This volume offers a fascinating glimpse into the wide array of approaches and objects that constitute medieval art history.

✎ Marvin Trachtenberg, *Dominion of the Eye: Urbanism, Art, and Power in Early Modern Florence* (Cambridge University Press, 1997)

Dominion of the Eye revolutionizes our understanding of the creation of public space. Scholars now know that sophisticated, rational urban planning using principles of geometric perspective and contemporary ideas about optical science was a critical part of medieval design practice in Florence. These principles were long thought to be the provenance of the Renaissance. Trachtenberg's dazzling analysis provides a fascinating account that addresses how the residents and visitors of

Florence visually experienced its buildings, paintings, and sculpture. The placement of monumental buildings such as the Palazzo Vecchio or Florence Duomo, as well as the creation of urban spaces such as the Piazza della Signoria, is the product of careful and deliberate calculation of the spectator's position. In addition to articulating the principles of trecento planning in Florence, Trachtenberg uncovers how the creation of these public monuments and spaces contributed to the state's establishment of its identity and role in Florentine life.

⊕ Peter Brown, *The Cult of the Saints: Its Rise and Function in Latin Christianity* (University of Chicago Press, 1982)

Peter Brown is one of the great scholars in medieval studies. His examination of the cult of saints looks at texts, relics, tombs, and pilgrimages to explore the cult's creation in late antiquity. This brilliant and eloquent study reverses earlier assumptions about the connection between the lower class and pre-Christian religion and superstitions to chart the cult's development under the guidance of the clerical elite. Through a multidisciplinary approach, Brown articulates the changing dynamic between the dead and the living as well as the cult's multiple roles in late antiquity. His engaging writing brings to life the creation of a cult that contravenes pre-Christian attitudes toward the dead and ultimately promotes the followers' active presence in society as healers, dispensers of justice, and patrons.

⊕ Paula Gerson, Annie Shaver-Crandell, and Alison Stones, with the assistance of Jeanne Krochalis, trans. and eds., *The Pilgrim's Guide to Santiago de Compostela: A Critical Edition* (Harvey Miller, 1998)

One of the best-known of medieval primary sources, *The Pilgrim's Guide* has recently been published in a new and highly accessible English translation complete with extensive annotations and the Latin text. This marvelous text provides directions for those undertaking the pilgrimage to the church of St. James (Santiago) de Compostela in northern Spain. Analogous in some ways to modern guidebooks, the *Guide* describes various routes through France to Compostela with possible stopping points and offers advice on safety during travel, local customs, and sources of food and fresh water. Akin to a phrase book, some sections provide translations of useful words in various languages. The *Guide* has a profoundly spiritual component underscoring the integration of sacred and profane life in medieval society. The *Guide's* author tells the pilgrim what benefits to expect from each shrine and how to behave. Many of the descriptions suggest the medieval viewer's aesthetic values and capacity for close visual observation.

↦ Ibn Jubayr, *The Travels of Ibn Jubayr,* trans. R. J. C. Broadhurst (Jonathan Cape, 1952)

> Ibn Jubayr recorded his journey around the Mediterranean in 1183–85 from his home in Spain to Mecca and back. The compelling immediacy of his firsthand account brings to life the complexity of Muslim-Christian relations during the Middle Ages and Jubayr's own struggle to understand those relations. His account of his travel through Sicily is particularly vivid. Jubayr is blunt about his expectations concerning the treatment of Muslims in the Christian society of twelfth-century Sicily and his discomfort at what he actually finds in this multicultural society. His observations of successful personal connections between members of the two cultures as well as his more hostile rhetoric echo many of the current difficulties in understanding these complex relationships.

LISA REILLY is currently researching Norman visual culture in England, France, and Italy. Associate Professor in the Department of Architectural History and on the faculty of the graduate program in art and architectural history, she held the NEH/Horace Goldsmith Distinguished Teaching Chair of Art and Architectural History from 1999 to 2002. She is currently a fellow at the Institute for Advanced Technology in the Humanities at the University of Virginia. Reilly is on the board of directors of the International Center for Medieval Art and chair of its publications committee.

SCOTT DEVEAUX

"One, Two, Three, Four": One Hundred Years of Jazz and Counting

More than a century has passed since jazz first slouched onto the national scene with Buddy Bolden's success playing to prostitutes in New Orleans. Jazz may still be popular among the lowlifes, but it has subsequently shed its brothel aura, climbing up the social ladder through concerts in Carnegie Hall and degree programs at major universities. Today, it is virtually awash in official recognition. Jazz has been cited by the U.S. Congress, supported by the NEA, broadcast over PBS, and programmed at Lincoln Center.

That is its triumph—and also its problem. If part of the appeal of jazz was always its outsider status, it is disarming to realize how thoroughly it has progressed toward becoming, in Billy Taylor's phrase, "America's classical music." To be sure, there are benefits. To the dismay of some old-timers, jazz has become an ideal conservatory music. It not only teaches the student to master an instrument, but also insists that technical mastery must lead to other things: jazz musicians must be active creators, shaping their own melodic and rhythmic lines. Jazz also grounds European music theory in basic African principles, such as the primacy of rhythmic groove.

Still, any music from the conservatory is necessarily distanced from the streets. There's a kind of music known as "school jazz" that sounds as bad as its name, as though musicians had to please no one but their teachers. Jazz today is peculiarly divided. A lot of it still exists in the real world—the clubs that once peppered every city keep closing, but there are enough "general business" gigs (weddings, bar mitzvahs) to keep musicians alive while giving them time to play for the small but dedicated jazz public. And it will continue to be supported as an academic music. As for the concert halls—well, they're not the Village Vanguard, but they're comfortable, acoustically perfect, and don't allow smoking.

The literature on jazz also has to do a balancing act—pleasing the casual fan while taking the music seriously. To do the latter requires delving into music theory, which for many is a big turn-off. Jazz musicians are notoriously inarticulate about what they do, but as anyone knows who has hung out where musicians practice, they are workaholics, endlessly practicing, recycling, and memorizing the thousands of bits of musical information that will go into an improvised solo. Jazz critics must similarly commit to the details of the art, which makes them strongly adept listeners.

Writers on jazz must also pay attention to the social aspects of jazz—which in practical terms means race. By now, it is common to characterize jazz as an African American music. And there's a lot of truth in this, especially in the area of musical language. Anyone trying to understand jazz by imposing European music theory will quickly discover that jazz musicians are trying to *swing*—which means that they are relying on a different kind of theory, one that comes from Africa. Yes, European and African music contribute to jazz; but the African elements are deeper, and shape the way in which European elements like harmonic structure are used. As Duke Ellington once said, "It don't mean a thing if it ain't got that swing"—which also means that if it *do* got that swing, you can get away with murder.

Most anyone will recognize that the chief creators of jazz are black: Louis Armstrong, Ellington, Charlie Parker, John Coltrane, Charles Mingus, Thelonious Monk—the list goes on and on. But the *audience* for jazz has been majority-white (including me); and the authors I cite below are all white. This leads to a peculiar quandary: whether we are musicians, fans, or critics, we are typically looking across the racial boundary. We may know who we are, but in typical American fashion, we're obsessed with what we could become. White critics have typically fallen into the pitfall called *primitivism:* the belief that the Other (in this case, black Americans) are valuable because they offer a purer, more "natural," and less educated view of life and art. Black musicians know that that's hogwash. They take a different view, aspiring toward middle-class notions of respectability—through art, through income, through educational attainment. This attitude has helped fuel the drive of jazz toward the university and the concert hall. At the same time, it has been kept from the general public, which naturally assumes that improvised music is simple and impulsive.

The writers I list below understand the score. They are intelligent observers of the current scene, and their writings reflect and clarify all of its complications and contradictions.

⤙ Martin Williams, *The Jazz Tradition* (1970; Oxford, 1992)

We'll begin with Williams, who graduated from the University of Virginia in 1948. I met him in the 1980s and invited him for his first return visit to the university. He was difficult and moody in public, but warm and generous to his friends, and grateful to be accepted at home. For me, *The Jazz Tradition* defined a field. It is a closely argued, gracefully written critical discussion of great jazz musicians. It's not a history, but it made the writing of history possible. I took from him some central ideas—e.g., that jazz is entangled with the complex history of black Americans, a remarkable fact for a former southern aristocrat (full name: Martin Tudor Hansfield Williams) to discover. "Jazz is the music of a people who have been told by their circumstances that they are unworthy," he writes. "And in jazz, these people discover their own worthiness."

⤙ Eric Hobsbawm, *The Jazz Scene* (Pantheon, 1993)

Eric Hobsbawm is the distinguished English historian who also happens to be a jazz expert. His book *The Jazz Scene* was originally published in the 1950s under the pen name Francis Newton (a take-off on Frankie Newton, a swing-era trumpet player with communist sympathies). His approach to jazz is the opposite of Williams's: a vision of jazz informed by social politics, to say nothing of a Marxist sensibility. We learn, for example, that the music of New Orleans bears a striking resemblance to what he describes as "the professional entertainment of the 'working poor,'" which also produced the Parisian cabaret singer and flamenco. One doesn't go to Hobsbawm to learn about the music. Like his compatriot Philip Larkin, his passion for jazz was formed by incoherent reactions (a "grinning, giggling wordlessness") to overseas recordings in the 1930s. Instead, one takes away the sweeping, but deeply informed, generalizations that characterize his better-known historical books (*The Age of Extremes, Invention of Tradition*).

∽ Mark Tucker, ed., *The Duke Ellington Reader* (Oxford University Press, 1995)

In my own generation, I admired the work of Mark Tucker, whose life was cut short by cancer at age forty-six. Tucker was a skillful pianist and a meticulous scholar. *The Duke Ellington Reader* exemplifies to me what jazz scholarship is about. It's a portrait of the composer through primary source material, from his first review in 1923 to his funeral address a half century later. There are roughly one hundred musical examples, crammed into more than five hundred pages, carefully parsed by Tucker's introductions and footnotes. Ellington emerges as a canny figure, constrained by racial prejudice, but Tucker makes it clear that his music was the expression of intelligence—not just his own, but the black artistic intelligentsia he represented.

∽ Gary Giddins, *Visions of Jazz: The First Century* (Oxford University Press, 2000)

Gary Giddins is a critic who has followed in the footsteps of Williams to become one of the most prolific and influential writers on jazz. You may have seen him as the chief talking head in Ken Burns's documentary *Jazz* (he had more screen time than Wynton Marsalis), or have read his column in the *Village Voice*. I'm currently working with him as coauthor on a jazz history textbook, and to keep pace with the vast range of his ideas I find myself often leafing through his *Visions of Jazz*. Like *The Jazz Tradition*, it's a series of chapters on individual musicians; but instead of a handful of great figures, Giddins provides a sampling from the "thousand worthy angels" who have made jazz, from New Orleans cornetist Bunk Johnson to postmodern clarinetist Don Byron. The writing is engaging, even lapidary. In writing about Benny Goodman, for example, I've had trouble getting beyond his pithy observation of Goodman's breakthrough concert in 1935: "The swing era was born because on that night middle-class white kids said yes in thunder and hard currency." There are similar gems on every page.

∽ John Gennari, *Blowin' Hot and Cool: Jazz and Its Critics* (University of Chicago Press, 2006)

I've learned more about Giddins, Williams, and other great writers from John Gennari's incisive survey of jazz criticism, *Blowin' Hot and*

Cool. Another local connection: I met him during his several years as a post-doc at the University of Virginia's Carter G. Woodson Institute. His dissertation was so excellent I couldn't understand why someone hadn't pressured him to publish it right away. Ten years later, I see what patience can do. If you want to understand how jazz has functioned in the intellectual history of America, this is the place to start. As I said in the words printed on the back cover: "I can't think of a book on jazz that is more ambitious, more beautifully written, or more heartfelt."

SCOTT DEVEAUX, Associate Professor of Music, is a pianist who has taught about jazz for more than twenty years. His "History of Jazz" survey currently enrolls three hundred students per semester. He published *The Birth of Bebop: A Social and Musical History* (University of California Press, 1997), which won the ASCAP–Deems Taylor Award, the American Book Award, and the Kinkeldey Prize (for best book) from the American Musicological Society. He is currently working on a jazz textbook.

MAURIE MCINNIS

American Art and Material Culture

Americans are fascinated with America's past, and increasingly, it seems, there is a renewed interest in the colonial experience. How else can you explain a phenomenon like *Colonial House*—the PBS "experiential history" reality show where people volunteered to live life as if it were 1628? In addition to a surprising number of colonial history books topping the nonfiction best-seller list (such as David McCullough's *1776*), cultural tourism has become a major factor in the American economy. Each year millions visit historic sites like Colonial Williamsburg and Deerfield Village and historic houses such as Mount Vernon and Monticello.

Other than entertainment, what are people hoping to get when they watch such programs or visit such places? Most are hoping to come away with some understanding of what everyday life was like in the past, and being around old places and old things can bring that alive in the imagination even more vividly than can words on the page. Visitors, however, are seeking something more. Often they are seeking something personal—a link with the past as they imagine the experience of an ancestor, as they imagine an event important to their sense of self or country. Increasingly there are a number of sites and tours that tell a much wider range of stories encompassing the complexity and diversity of the American experience. Collectively these places go a long way toward shaping the modern "memory" of what the past was like. Consequently, those who study the material past and offer it for the public play a major role in shaping America's collective memory. The study of America's material past brings together scholars in universities and professionals from museums and historic houses, many of whom have trained as art and architectural historians.

American art history is, perhaps surprisingly, a relatively young field; it was only in the 1970s that many universities began offering courses in the subject. Perhaps because of its relative youth, or perhaps because of the fundamentally different nature of artistic production in what eventually became the United States (not much support from either church or state), the study of American art has differed quite a bit from its European counterparts. Even from the beginning, there has been a greater openness to considering everyday objects as part of the academic exercise. Thus, paintings are often studied alongside silver, architecture alongside furniture. American art historians—influenced by and working with anthropologists, folklorists, and cultural historians, among others—developed a much more flexible idea of "art." What grew out of this interdisciplinary collaboration is a field called "material culture." It takes as its general belief that anything transformed by man—from paintings and plows to buildings and bedsteads—provides essential information about America's past. Importantly, this information is often not available from the written documents. Thus objects have the potential to reveal unstated beliefs and cultural patterns that are central to an understanding of the way people lived and what they believed.

Because books about America's past material culture are written by people from different disciplines, they often have different emphases. I have chosen books that cover a range of topics in the eighteenth and nineteenth centuries written by scholars who would identify themselves as historians, art and architectural historians, and archaeologists. But all of them share a belief that the study of the material world can illuminate the past. In my choices, I wanted to give some sense of how studying the totality of the material past, not just buildings or paintings, can help open a new door on a past we thought we knew.

↪ Laurel Thatcher Ulrich, *Age of Homespun: Objects and Stories in the Creation of an American Myth* (Knopf, 2001)

Ulrich's beautifully written book animates the lives of individual women and demonstrates how the dusty objects in museums can open new doors on historical understanding. Trained as a historian interested in the lives of women, who are often scarce in the written records, Ulrich (whose second book, *A Midwife's Tale: The Life of Martha Ballard Based on Her Diary, 1785–1812,* won a Pulitzer Prize) turned her attention to material culture. Each chapter centers on an individual object (such as a cupboard, a counterpane, and a spinning wheel, among others), ranging from 1676 to 1837. Ulrich couples attentive reading of the objects with extensive documentary research to illuminate not only the lives of the objects, but also the lives of the women who made and created them, ultimately demonstrating the central role played by women in both the economic and social life of the early American family.

↬ James Deetz, *In Small Things Forgotten: An Archaeology of Early American Life* (Anchor, 1996)

What I love about this little book is the way that Deetz tells the story of early America through things many would regard as little more than trash, such as pottery shards, or things that people pass by every day without regard, such as doorways and gravestones. A pioneering historical archaeologist, Deetz was a leading light in the study of America's material culture. His lively prose tells the story of seventeenth-century New England's divergence from England, and then its convergence in the period leading up to the American Revolution. His book teaches all of us to think about new ways of understanding the past.

↬ Richard L. Bushman, *The Refinement of America: Persons, Houses, Cities* (Vintage, 1993)

In this wide-ranging book, Bushman explores how refinement came to America's upper class in the colonial period and generally spread downward, reaching the middle classes by the middle of the nineteenth century. While much of the story of refinement can be told through advice manuals and proscriptive literature, the tangible sense of its spread and acceptance is best seen through the proliferation of the goods of refinement. Bushman began his research at Winterthur Museum, where he was struck by the dramatic increase in the goods owned by Americans. Instead of the few stools, a bedstead, and a couple of knives and spoons that would have been found in the seventeenth-century household, by the nineteenth century, Americans had a huge array of specialized items—from cutlery to dining items to furniture. While ultimately Bushman avoids some sticky questions, particularly around race and gender, *The Refinement of America* remains an eloquent and at times witty exploration of the cultural significance of the stuff now preserved in historic houses and museums.

⮞ Kirk Savage, *Standing Soldiers, Kneeling Slaves: Race, War, and Monument in Nineteenth-Century America* (Princeton University Press, 1999)

A gem of a book and a model for demonstrating how the material world helps shape collective memory. Centered in the decades after the Civil War, this book explores the enthusiasm for monument building that transformed America's cities and towns. In this well-researched and beautifully written study, Savage explores a series of projects, both North and South, built and unbuilt, covering monuments to both common soldiers and famous generals, from Abraham Lincoln to former slaves. Savage investigates how struggles over race and gender played into what were often highly contested projects initially, but that have since their erection helped to shape a collective sense of the past.

⮞ Kenneth L. Ames, *Death in the Dining Room and Other Tales of Victorian Culture* (Temple University Press, 1992)

A witty and provocative book that explores the Victorian mind by focusing on some of the period's most particular material creations. Chapters center around object types—such as the hallstand, sideboard, or parlor organ—within a broader context of cultural concerns and conflicts. Not surprisingly, class and gender are major players in his discussion as he explores, for example, the male domain of the dining room, with its enormous sideboards groaning with the carved representations of the hunt, and the female realm of the parlor, where organs allowed women to demonstrate accomplishment as bourgeois Christian ladies.

MAURIE MCINNIS is Associate Professor of American Art and Material Culture and Director of the American Studies Program. Her work centers on the material culture of the American South in the colonial and antebellum periods. She has served on advisory committees for historic houses and helped curate several museum exhibitions. Her most recent book is *The Politics of Taste in Antebellum Charleston* (University of North Carolina Press, 2005).

JOHN FRICK

"Reading" Popular Entertainment

The immediacy and topicality of popular forms of entertainment make them convenient vehicles for exposing, and even examining, what is happening at any particular moment in society. This function of popular entertainment—its reflexivity—is on public display daily on such TV shows as *The Tonight Show with Jay Leno,* the *Late Show with David Letterman,* and *The Daily Show,* as well as at week's end on *Saturday Night Live.*

Popular entertainment's tendency to draw attention to contemporary issues isn't a phenomenon of just the last few decades. Throughout human history, popular entertainment forms such as mimes in ancient Greece, the Roman Atellan farce, Italian commedia dell'arte, Parisian Grand Guignol, British harlequinade and music hall have all served to introduce the vital, often controversial, issues of the day. Arguably, few times and places have been as rich in popular entertainments as nineteenth-century America. In their lifetimes, nineteenth-century Americans witnessed the rise (and in many cases, the fall) of a number of popular entertainments: the melodrama, the minstrel show, the concert saloon, the circus, vaudeville, the Toby (tricky servant) Show, the dime museum, living statuary, burlesque, the Wild West show, and the medicine show.

In America's earliest days, such a typology of "show business" was not possible, nor was a division of audiences into highbrow and lowbrow. Before the War of 1812, all classes crowded into the country's few theaters and enjoyed the same entertainments, mainly of play texts from England performed by actors from London. After the war, however, the aristocracy tired of the vile sounds, noxious smells, and unruly behavior of the lower-class audience members, while, at the same time, working-class patrons discovered performances and performers more to their liking. During the 1820s, American-born stars like Edwin Forrest and Charlotte Cushman became the darlings of lower-class audiences. They appeared in theaters like the Chatham that were becoming known as working-class venues, and attracted ever larger audiences from areas of New York like the Bowery and the Five Points.

With the increasing influx of people into America's cities during the 1830s and 1840s, both from rural areas and from abroad, the first signs of a mass audience appeared. With this influx came a proliferation of entertainments so simple that immigrants who were unfamiliar with American culture or the English language and the otherwise uneducated could readily comprehend them. By the middle of the nineteenth century, the popular entertainment "industry" had been born, and popular theaters sprouted along major city streets.

Sadly, until recently, scholars have often failed to consider popular entertainments as social documents. Why? Joyce Flynn theorizes that a puritan distaste for and suspicion of anything theatrical, with its taint of negative associations involving ethnicity and class, may have caused this neglect. Observing that theater was the "habitual sphere of outsiders in

American culture," Flynn suggests that "both literary and academic America have shared an aversion to the too-close scrutiny of art forms created in cooperation with democratic audiences." Flynn argues that prejudices about the nature of popular audiences led scholars to devalue popular entertainments by allowing social and political values to shape critical judgments of an art form. Susan Harris Smith likewise notes the absence of popular entertainments in studies of American expressive culture.

As a theater historian whose main interest is the cultural significance and influence of popular entertainments, I have found the books listed here to be of immeasurable help in my various inquiries. As recently as twenty-five years ago, it was possible for a theater historian to examine theatrical events in isolation from their host culture; but with the advent of new historical approaches (New Historicism, cultural studies, feminist theory and criticism, Latino/Latina studies, etc.), it has become virtually impossible to divorce theater from its cultural context. Therefore, it is incumbent upon the student of theater history to become knowledgeable about both entertainment forms *and* the culture that contains them.

You'll find in the books I've listed a variety of perspectives on popular entertainments and the people who enjoyed them, along with some pleasurable reading.

֍ John Fiske, *Understanding Popular Culture* (Routledge, 1989)

In the preface to this short, theoretical, yet commonsense approach to popular culture, John Fiske remarks that one of the benefits of *theory* is that it travels well from culture to culture and, one might add, from era to era. Thus, although he discusses primarily twentieth-century examples, his work gives his readers insights into such questions as: "What, exactly, *is* popular culture?" "What do popular texts reveal about some of the central dynamics (race, gender, class) of culture?" "Just how do texts become popular?" "What is the relationship between commodities and culture?" and "What, if any, is the difference between class culture and mass culture?" His subjects for study—blue jeans, the tabloids, TV game shows, and shopping malls—will be familiar to the average reader, making his theoretical work quite accessible.

֍ Lawrence W. Levine, *Highbrow/Lowbrow: The Emergence of Cultural Hierarchy in America* (Harvard University Press, 1990)

Today, three of the world's most prominent opera tenors perform in ballparks to mass audiences while every year a one-ring circus moves into quarters next to the Metropolitan Opera House. High culture invades low-culture venues to play to mixed-class crowds just as more popular forms appear in the temples of high culture. To many observers, this phenomenon may appear to be new. But as the historian Lawrence W. Levine demonstrates, high- and low-culture forms have always been in flux in America. Levine traces the journey of several art forms from their early days when they were considered *democratic* entertainments to their current "highbrow" status. He recounts how social elites, tired of sharing theater space with rowdy, unwashed spectators, appropriated, most notably, Shakespeare and opera for themselves over the course of the nineteenth century. *Highbrow/Lowbrow* is a marvelous study of how cultural transformation and the appropriation of cultural practices are active, rather than passive, phenomena.

↪ David Grimsted, *Melodrama Unveiled: American Theater and Culture, 1800–1850* (University of California Press, 1988)

Although vaudeville, the variety show (mounted in big-city concert saloons), and the minstrel show all achieved popularity in their own time, none was as ubiquitous and as long-lasting as the nineteenth-century melodrama. Analyzing this indigenous dramatic art of the nineteenth century, the historian David Grimsted theorizes that melodrama constituted the voice of the "historically voiceless" and became a truly democratic art form that was immensely popular in both its production and its reception. But *Melodrama Unveiled* is far more than a simple study of a single popular art form. Rather, it is a remarkably comprehensive overview of the entire nineteenth-century theatrical enterprise—its performers, managers, audiences, critics, and stage practices.

↪ Karen Halttunen, *Confidence Men and Painted Women: A Study of Middle-Class Culture in America, 1830–1870* (1982; Yale University Press, 1986)

During the nineteenth century, rural ministers and other moralists wrote hundreds of advice manuals for young men and women about to set off to the big city. In *Confidence Men and Painted Women*, the historian Karen Halttunen examines these manuals and the concern that America's youth would fall into the clutches of urban "sharpers" and female co-conspirators eager to capitalize upon the naiveté of "country bumpkins," leading them to ruin—an early grave for men and a life of prostitution for women.

To theater historians, *Confidence Men and Painted Women* offers both a graphic glimpse into the "nether world" of America's major cities and insight into the world of the nineteenth-century melodrama. Halttunen shows us that the urban con man, as he is described in the advice manuals, is remarkably similar to the standard representation of the melodramatic villain. Her study sheds considerable light upon the nature of evil in both nineteenth-century American society and the melodrama that so accurately (albeit symbolically) represented it.

⟿ Richard Butsch, *The Making of American Audiences: From Stage to Television, 1750–1990* (Cambridge University Press, 2000)

The sociologist Richard Butsch has undertaken a comprehensive survey of American audiences from the seventeenth century to the present with a special focus on audiences for popular entertainments. Butsch's work is unique in several respects: it confines itself to the "representational" arts of theater, film, TV, and their variations (video, DVD) while maintaining a focus on the receivers, rather than the producers, of these entertainments. *The Making of American Audiences* is an ambitious, well-researched, and thoroughly enjoyable study. Butsch dispels widely accepted myths about the active, disruptive nature of nineteenth-century audiences and the passivity of their twentieth-century counterparts. By locating audience behavior, taste, and ideology in a broad social context, he illustrates the exchanges among entertainments, their audiences, and the host culture.

JOHN FRICK, Professor of Theatre, is the author of *Theatre, Culture, and Temperance Reform in Nineteenth-Century America* (Cambridge University Press, 2003) and *New York's First Theatrical Center: The Rialto at Union Square* (UMI Research Press, 1985), and coeditor of *The Directory of Historic American Theatres* (Greenwood Press, 1987) and *Theatrical Directors: A Biographical Dictionary* (Greenwood Press, 1994). Frick is on the editorial board of the journal *Theatre Symposium* and President of the American Theatre and Drama Society.

MELVIN L. BUTLER

Music and Identity in the African Diaspora

Recent breakthroughs in digital technology have cooked up a sonic smorgasbord of songs virtually accessible at the mere click of a button. At the risk of romanticizing those uninitiated into the world of iPods and other MP3 players, I find it refreshing to note that while some of us cruise right along in cars or on jogging trails, consuming music primarily as an aesthetically pleasing form of passive entertainment, many others in the United States and around the world sense that there is something precious at stake in the live experience of musical sound. That "something" often entails spiritual, cultural, or national identities, which continue to be constructed and negotiated through active engagement with popular musics throughout the African diaspora. The books on this list examine the ways in which particular African American and African Caribbean groups use music to assert identities and engage with various forms of power.

Although the academic study of music is often assumed to involve some part of the Western classical canon, many music scholars focus their attention elsewhere, spending more time conducting fieldwork among specific communities of living human beings than perusing archived manuscripts. Borrowing theories and methods from anthropologists, ethnomusicologists tend to target non-Western musical practices rather than the elite "art" musics of Europe. Researchers of popular culture express a particular fascination with the "musicking" (to use the now-fashionable verbal form coined by Christopher Small) of everyday people.

What have ethnomusicologists found as they study the musicking of the African diaspora? In communities where musical participation allows for the expression of a self that is constructed in opposition to a perceived threat, issues of power and identity are inextricably linked. Each author on my list explores music whose nonelite practitioners aim to position themselves in creative and complex ways in relation to local and global power structures. For example, Stolzoff posits that Jamaican dancehall participants, who are often denigrated by transnational "uptown" elites, use provocative lyrics and dress to contest social boundaries of appropriateness, promote "downtown" forms of Jamaican identity, and maintain creative control over particular cultural spaces.

These authors also point out that power manifests itself in a variety of ways and that both the dominant and the oppressed appropriate music for political means. For example, Austerlitz argues that various social groups in the Dominican Republic have politicized merengue by wedding their particular versions of it to national identity. Hinson focuses more on spiritual power, describing how gospel singing among African Americans in the U.S. South builds group solidarity along both racial and religious lines. In a variety of services and programs, churchgoers sing and dance their identities as African American Pentecostal Christians. McAlister's treatment of Haitian rara also suggests the spiritual power of musical practice. In this case, however, music and dance are tied to the Haitian religious complex known as Vodou, and musical lyrics more explicitly chastise wealthy elites and governmental officials for actions deemed oppressive.

Both Hinson and McAlister deal with popular music forms that stand in contrast to the more commercial popular musics discussed by Guilbault, Stolzoff, and Austerlitz, who examine zouk, dancehall, and merengue, respectively. These five texts are, however, united by their emphasis on music as an *embodied* practice that reveals the perseverance and cultural creativity of marginalized groups. As Stolzoff suggests, for example, the symbolic power of dancehall derives as much from the gendered ways of movement within dancehall spaces as from the lyrics or musical sound. Thus ethnomusicologists now study closely how the physical body participates in the creation of a sense of self. These books thus represent continuing trends away from a reliance on purely textual analyses of musical meaning.

How do African diasporic peoples work out the "Creoleness" of zouk and the "Dominicanness" of merengue? In what ways do Haitians, Jamaicans, and African Americans develop, through the music they make, their cultural identities and moral-spiritual paradigms? These broad queries form the core of these authors' arguments as they combine fieldwork-based ethnographies of the present with narratives of the past. Each author shows how complex national identities are quite remarkably juxtaposed against a range of spiritual, racial, and cultural identities as music-makers vie for social and political advantage.

↝ Glenn Hinson, *Fire in My Bones: Transcendence and the Holy Spirit in African American Gospel* (University of Pennsylvania Press, 2000)

This book is a sensitive and well-written tribute to the musical and social lives of African American church folk in North Carolina. Hinson emphasizes the ways in which Pentecostal/Holiness believers *experience* their faith and the music that serves to articulate it. Steering clear of writing techniques that cast doubt on the validity of supernatural encounter, Hinson strives to embrace the worldview of Pentecostal believers—not simply as window dressing for a more "scholarly" anthropological analysis of black worship, but rather, as a key to what he regards as the fullest possible understanding of how spiritual power shapes musical expressions within the Holiness community of worshipers. He comments insightfully on the everyday struggles to experience the Spirit's transcendent touch within congregations that express a preference for authenticity and purity over the "form and fashion" of overly ritualized musical performance.

↝ Elizabeth McAlister, *Rara! Vodou, Power, and Performance in Haiti and Its Diaspora* (University of California Press, 2002)

Based on fieldwork conducted in Haiti from 1990 to 1995, McAlister's text, along with its accompanying compact disc, is a crucial contribution to the literature on Haitian expressive cultures. Both a Lenten festival and an often spontaneous processional music performed yearly in streets throughout the country, rara is a form of playful popular expression that is embraced most passionately by the poorer Haitian masses. McAlister sheds important light on some of rara's most underappreciated features, such as lyrics featuring *betiz* (vulgarities) and bawdy dance moves, to show that rara is also a vehicle of protest. Through it the underprivileged launch scathing critiques aimed at the conspicuous overconsumption and pious Catholic morality of Haitian elites. Most strikingly, we learn that this genre also constitutes a vital kind of "work" done to fulfill obligations to one or more of the *lwa* (Vodou spirits).

↜ Jocelyne Guilbault, *Zouk: World Music in the West Indies* (University of Chicago Press, 1993)

This book examines zouk, a popular dance music of the French West Indies. Drawing from fieldwork conducted mostly in the late 1980s, Guilbault considers this dance party music in relation to four distinct postcolonial societies in which a French-based Creole language is spoken: Martinique, Guadeloupe, St. Lucia, and Dominica. Ethnomusicologists Gage Averill, Edouard Benoit, and Gregory Rabess contribute important chapters that reveal zouk's strong historical ties to musical genres such as Haitian konpa, Guadeloupean biguine, and Dominican cadence, respectively. Through analyses of lyrics and musical features such as instrumentation, rhythmic patterns, and song forms, the authors show how zouk participants use this music to express localized identities. Guilbault posits that while national identity often holds sway within Caribbean nation-states, zouk plays a critical role in the negotiation of a transnational Antillean identity that unifies French Creole speakers—and singers—around the globe.

↜ Norman C. Stolzoff, *Wake the Town and Tell the People: Dancehall Culture in Jamaica* (Duke University Press, 2000)

This eye-opening monograph explores Jamaican dancehall, deftly situating this misunderstood genre of popular music within Jamaica's moral order and sociopolitical history. The author surveys dancehall's legacy of political appropriation, ties to gang violence, and role in nationalist projects in the decades leading up to Independence in 1962. Dancehall's oppositional stance toward "uptown" respectability consistently engenders the disdain of Jamaican elites, who generally see dancehall as contributing to the island's cultural decline. Although Stolzoff strongly critiques the homophobic and misogynist lyrics of some dancehall music, he highlights the ways in which dancehall is deeply entrenched in ongoing political struggles and negotiations of

Jamaican national identity. Offering a "cross-generational perspective" on dancehall culture, Stolzoff shows us how lower-class Jamaican youth use it in their attempts "to deal with endemic problems of poverty, racism, and violence."

↫ Paul Austerlitz, *Merengue: Dominican Music and Dominican Identity* (Temple University Press, 1997)

How has merengue been able to endure as a powerful symbol of Dominican national identity since the nineteenth century? The answer, says Austerlitz, lies in the fact that it crystallizes the contradictions inherent in the lives of Dominicans at home and abroad. Discomfort with merengue's perceived African origins have led Eurocentric Dominicans to gravitate toward variants from the Republic's Cibao region, where African cultural retentions are less obvious, even as the elite celebrate merengue for its "folk" qualities. Merengue is thus the ideal sonic representation of Dominican national character. Drawing upon early 1990s fieldwork in the Dominican Republic and New York, as well as his extensive experience as a merengue saxophonist, Austerlitz offers a succinct social history of this commercial dance music. The author's most impressive accomplishment is that he wades through the murky waters of merengue's origins, teasing out historical narratives tied to politicized racial and national identifications.

MELVIN L. BUTLER is an ethnomusicologist, professional saxophonist, and Assistant Professor in the McIntire Department of Music. His research encompasses music, identity, and religious practice in Caribbean and African American communities. He is currently working on a book manuscript on music, identity, and Pentecostal power in Haiti.

JUDITH REAGAN

The Pleasures and Terrors of Speaking (and Reading) Aloud

Many of us prefer to keep words safely confined to print and the page, rather than released into sound and air. Written text is not inert; it can enter brain and soul, sometimes deeply. But spoken text has the potential to move many simultaneously, to provide a compelling group experience. Perhaps it is that potential power of speech that makes us wary from at least two angles. As *listeners* we sense we may be fooled, be sold a bill of goods by a silver-tongued charlatan. As *speakers* we may feel we are inept, unnerved and disabled by terror of public presentation.

I teach oral interpretation and public speaking to undergraduates and to adult professionals. Because my training and experience are in theater, I begin sessions explaining that although we're going to use exercises originally developed for actor training, our purpose is different. No one will be asked to characterize, to become someone else, or to pretend. Rather we aim for comfortable and effective oral delivery of one's own ideas. We do exercises inviting relaxation and concentration in order to develop a voice and body ready for public communication. Many of us have forgotten or never explicitly realized that speaking is a *physical* act. Signs a talk is going badly include knocking knees, sweaty palms, clenched jaw, churning stomach. That's the body saying, "Wait a minute, pal, I need to be warmed up and engaged. This isn't a brain-only activity." It's amazing what remembering to breathe and reestablishing blood flow to the extremities can accomplish.

Among many reasons why fear of public speaking can be so strong is that speech and self-concept seem to be tightly intertwined. We sense that we will be judged quickly and harshly by listeners. But this near hyper-awareness of ourselves as speakers can also be an advantage in that we already know a ton about ourselves as speakers. We've received feedback ("Stand up straight"; "I can't hear you"; "You've got a funny accent") all our lives. And we've absorbed lessons from watching others—teachers, meeting and conference speakers, candidates for office. It's productive to pull this knowledge to the fore and examine it, rather than concluding that we're incapable of improving. In fact, none of the concepts surrounding oral communication are intellectually difficult. A considerable degree of difficulty does pertain, though, when we set about trying to change a lifetime habit.

(Speaking of changing habits . . . try reading the remainder of this essay aloud. Really. There are only a few paragraphs left. If you enjoy it, read more of these pieces out loud. I'm quite sure the authors won't object.)

Why undertake the quest to improve as a speaker? For positive motivation, contemplate this passage from *Touching the Rock: An Experience of Blindness* (Vintage, 1992). The author, John M. Hull, who went blind at age forty-eight, reports: "I find that all the emotion that would normally be expressed in the face is there in the voice: the tiredness, the anxiety, the suppressed excitement. . . . The capacity of the voice to reveal the self is truly amazing. Is the voice intelligent? Is it colorful? Is there light and shade? . . . Is it gentle, amusing and varied? Or, is the voice lazy? Is it flat, drab and monotonous? These are the things that matter to me now."

For inspiration from a negative slant, consider what passes for public discourse these days. Tune in talk radio, watch televised presidential debates, try to follow celebrity interviews in which the fillers "like" and "you know what I mean" are cruelly overused. Or endeavor to stay awake at conferences where there seems to be mutual agreement that speakers may bore listeners rather than venture clear, committed, engaged delivery.

A parting thought is that this "work" might more accurately be labeled "play." It should be FUN! The reading list takes an expansive approach to the topic, with the first three texts offering practical, creative vocal and physical exercises and the final two, a novel and a play, reflecting more on our strong personal and communal desire to tell our stories, find our voices, and be understood. In that effort we are often fighting both our individual fears and restrictions imposed by society. I wish you happy (and clearly audible!) reading.

⬦ Patsy Rodenburg, *The Need for Words: Voice and the Text* (Routledge, 1993)

> I use this book in teaching oral interpretation. It differs from more standard course texts in that Rodenburg first takes on the deteriorating state of oracy (speaking ability) in Western societies, then proceeds to offer strategies for effective delivery of all manner of texts, medieval to modern. She manages to both inspire and instruct, in part 1 igniting the desire to rebel against being a complacent citizen of this "age of cacophony and image saturation," and in part 2 providing tools and exercises to lead us toward confident, precise, effective speaking. You might also try Rodenburg's *The Right to Speak,* in which she writes: "Voice work is for everybody. . . . All of us would like to improve the sound of our voice and the way we speak. Doing voice and speech work can be, I think, as energizing and liberating as any other kind of physical exercise. There is no mystique about it. It is powerful and also very simple."

⬦ Stephanie Martin and Lyn Darnley, *The Teaching Voice,* 2nd ed. (Wiley, 2005)

> Martin, a speech and language therapist, and Darnley, head of voice at the Royal Shakespeare Company, offer a brisk, engaging march through the physical apparatus necessary to produce sound (I didn't even know I had an *oropharynx* or *arytenoid cartilage*!), the many factors that can negatively affect speaking health and ability, and solutions for many common vocal maladies. Case studies, used in every section, clearly illustrate problems and remedies. Although centered on observation of teachers, the recommended practices are applicable to any profession in which voice is essential. The authors are both creative ("The

arytenoids are the vocal gymnasts; they can in fact glide and rotate")
and practical, offering sections with headers such as "Suggestions for
Volume, Clarity and Distance." This is a very useful handbook for self-
diagnosis and improvement.

⊸ Uta Hagen, *Respect for Acting* (Wiley, 1973)

If you accept the premise that the study of acting and public speaking have fertile areas of overlap, walk with Ms. Hagen through her
powerful explication of how actors work to establish authentic communication. The aim in performing a role is always to be moment to
moment, to be in real time, the present, with the audience, offering the
character's experiences as if for the first time. Those are the same aims
for most speaking situations, so there is much here that nonactors can
learn, borrow, and adapt. For those who aren't aiming at a life on stage
or in film but want to improve as speakers, reading this book may be
akin to learning how marathon runners prepare, and taking from that
what is helpful to casual joggers.

⊸ Alan Paton, *Cry, the Beloved Country* (1948; Scribner, 2003)

This novel can be read as a meditation on language, expression, communication. The motif of voice, its liberation or strangulation, shifts
between background and foreground many times. Paton shows us
how the government's smothering of dissent, its imposition of restrictions on thoughts and rights, takes a great toll on individuals and
on society. Paton's concerns—finding one's voice, telling one's story,
shaping experience through speaking it—have resurfaced in the work
of South Africa's Truth and Reconciliation Commission. A key part of
its approach to acknowledging and rectifying the damage done during
apartheid is collecting oral testimonies. Paton describes voice, sound,
word, song, cries, breath, on almost every page.

⊸ William Gibson, *A Cry of Players* (1968; Dramatist's Play Service, 1998)

In an exhilarating leap of imagination, the playwright Will Gibson
details the dilemmas young Will Shakespeare may have faced when,
compelled by an ungovernable need to create/embody/communicate,
he tore himself away from the safe confines of Stratford to make his
way in London. Gibson posits that the life of a thespian then was even
more harrowing and uncertain than it is now, that throwing in his lot
with Will Kemp and other vagabond players was *not* a career move
likely to have been endorsed by his wife, Anne, or his comfortably
middle-class parents. The play vividly depicts an individual's struggle
to acknowledge, support, and follow the voice within.

JUDITH REAGAN's applied research is in transplanting communication techniques developed for and utilized by actors to other populations and professions. She is Associate Director of the Teaching Resource Center and Assistant Professor in the Department of Drama. Reagan has coached oral presentation for faculty at Cornell, Georgetown, and Tulane, and for professionals in law, business, and other civic and political groups. She is a professional actor, performing on stage when schedules allow.

5

Mind

Body

Spirit

MITCHELL S. GREEN

The Beginning of Wisdom: Self-Knowledge

The Temple of the Oracle at Delphi in ancient Greece bore, according to legend, two injunctions: "Nothing in Excess" and "Know Thyself." Priestesses controlled the temple, which was built over a fissure in the earth out of which an intoxicating gas occasionally escaped. Priestesses would inhale this gas and answer questions posed for them by visitors from all over the ancient world: Should I send my army into battle? Should I allow my daughter to wed this suitor? Will I die wealthy? etc. It was commonly believed that the priestesses' answers to these questions could not fail to be correct.

Obliged to defend himself in front of a jury of 501 of his peers against the charge of corrupting youth, Socrates remarks that he had once visited the Oracle with a friend and posed the following question: Is anyone wiser than Socrates? The answer he received was: NO. Socrates found this answer astonishing: surely *someone* in all of Greece's city-states knew more than he? After all, Socrates was famous for professing ignorance of the most essential matters: how best to live, and how best to organize a society.

Socrates goes on to tell his jurors that eventually he came to accept the Oracle's answer, for while he knows nothing, he at least is aware of that fact.

By contrast, others profess knowledge of virtue and the proper organization of society, but their alleged knowledge is a sham. Perhaps, then, the priestess had a point: the beginning of wisdom is acceptance of your own ignorance. Plato, through whom Socrates' speech to the jury comes down to us in *The Apology*, thus gives us what is perhaps the West's first written formulation of a connection between wisdom and self-knowledge.

Self-knowledge was not a topic of systematic study in the West for the next two millennia, perhaps because thinking during this time was so heavily dominated by theological concerns: if you're going to know anyone's mind, better it should be God's. However, in India, and then later in China and Japan, knowledge of the self was a major theme in contemplative rather than scholarly practice. Two centuries before Socrates, Buddha (563–483 BCE) preached and meditated in Nepal and India. Traveling the countryside to spread his teachings, he started what became one of the world's leading religions. Integral to the Zen tradition—one of many within Buddhism—is *contemplative practice:* sitting, walking, and other forms of meditation in which one aims for a *cessation* of conscious thought, a nonthinking. Yet how could such an activity have anything to do with knowledge, of the self or anything else?

Our answer lies in the fact that meditation aims at the cessation of *conscious* thought, not of thought. Archery, swordsmanship, and flower arrangement are also bound up with Zen practice, and all three of these require sophisticated cognitive and other skills. Cognitive, however, is not the same as conscious, and here is where Eastern contemplative practice and Western thought about the mind cross paths. A new consensus has begun to emerge in philosophy, experimental psychology, and related disciplines according to which much of our everyday intelligent behavior is produced by unconscious mechanisms: processing of language, recognition of faces and their emotional expressions, responses to danger, even much athletic activity are all largely carried out unconsciously. That's what athletes mean by being "in the zone," it's the source of our often powerful "gut feelings" about other people, and it's what enables those under severe stress, such as soldiers in combat, to survive by going on "autopilot."

This so-called *adaptive unconscious* differs strikingly from that posited by psychoanalysis. Freud's unconscious is largely bound up with repressed infantile urges toward sexuality and violence, yet the evidence adduced in its favor was strikingly thin. Psychoanalysis also tends to diagnose those who challenge its credentials as suffering from denial. By contrast, proponents of the adaptive unconscious are willing to subject any of their claims about the unconscious mind to experimental scrutiny. What's more, although the adaptive unconscious is more quotidian and less obsessed with sex and destruction, it's still pervasive enough to produce forms of prejudice that are not open to introspection, or to be the source of a debilitating anxiety.

By calling for a cessation of conscious thought in meditation and meditative activities such as archery, the Zen tradition emphasizes the extent of unconscious thinking and its centrality in self-understanding. Experimental psychology has finally caught up with that insight, and is now articulating and validating it empirically to offer an arresting picture of what makes us tick. The confluence of these two traditions also takes us full circle to Socrates: acknowledgment of the limitations of our conscious minds is the beginning of wisdom about ourselves.

The five works below are a mixture of classics of philosophy, spiritual journey, and contemporary research. All are accessible, relatively brief, and, while spanning 2,300 years, cohere into a striking image of the self and our knowledge of it.

↪ Plato, *Five Dialogues: Euthyphro, Apology, Crito, Meno, and Phaedo,* trans. G. M. A. Grube (Hackett, 2002)

Many agree that Plato is the greatest philosopher in the history of the West. In these dialogues, which ostensibly record discussions among his teacher Socrates and others, or speeches made by Socrates in public, Plato is at once imaginative, profound, witty, and poetic as he addresses issues of ethics, the soul, life after death, the proper organization of the state, and the nature of knowledge (including self-knowledge). *Apology* preserves Socrates' aforementioned discussion of self-knowledge, and his reasons for claiming that the unexamined life is not worth living; *Meno* contains Socrates' famous argument for the immortality of the soul; in *Phaedo,* Socrates' stirring depiction of the afterlife explains why he is unafraid of death. John Cooper's fine translation renders the Greek into idiomatic and elegant English.

↪ René Descartes, *Meditations, Objections, and Replies,* trans. Roger Ariew and Donald Cress (Hackett, 2006)

Not only did he cook up analytic geometry and (what would later be called) the Cartesian coordinate system, but Descartes is widely credited with ushering in the "modern" era of philosophy in the West. Descartes starts with the simple question: Which of my many beliefs can I know for sure to be true? His answer, starting with the famous *cogito, ergo sum,* is that he can be sure of those beliefs that he arrives at by the process he calls "clear and distinct perception." His answer lays the foundations for a new mode of scientific inquiry that enables those following him to break decisively with the medieval, "scholastic" systems dominating universities in his day. At the same time, he arrives at a definition of himself as essentially a "thinking thing" capable of surviving the destruction of his body. It was centuries before philosophers developed viable alternatives to Descartes' picture of the relation of mind and body. Roger Ariew and Donald Cress offer a fine translation of this classic, which also contains their translations of debates between Descartes and such distinguished contemporaries as Father Mersenne and Thomas Hobbes.

⟜ Tim Wilson, *Strangers to Ourselves: Discovering the Adaptive Unconscious* (Harvard University Press, 2004)

In this book, the social psychologist Tim Wilson synthesizes an explosion of new research in experimental psychology offering a radical yet experimentally supported picture of the unconscious mind. Descended but quite different from the unconscious posited by psychoanalysis, the "New Unconscious" is fast, automatic, hard to control, and modular. It accounts for a great deal, perhaps the majority, of our intelligent behavior. Wilson draws from this picture fascinating and sometimes disturbing implications for our emotional responses to situations, racial and sexual discrimination, and the power of so-called talk therapy to achieve genuine change.

⟜ Antonio Damasio, *Descartes' Error: Emotion, Reason, and the Human Brain* (1994; Penguin, 2005)

Damasio is a leading neuroscientist who offers, in what has become a classic, both clinical case studies and experimental evidence in support of a radical new hypothesis concerning how we make choices. This is the *somatic marker hypothesis,* according to which, in any given choice situation, certain options present themselves to normal humans with an emotional valency (attractive, fearful, etc.) that enables us to choose efficiently and, for the most part, accurately. Individuals with certain brain lesions or malfunctions, however, are unable to use somatic markers in their choices, often with devastating effects, in spite of their being otherwise intelligent. Damasio's work complements that of Wilson in emphasizing the importance of unconscious processes in helping us to negotiate the world, while providing more detail concerning the neural underpinnings of intelligent behavior.

⟜ Eugen Herrigel, *Zen in the Art of Archery* (1953; Knopf, 1999)

The author was a German professor of philosophy who taught at the University of Tokyo between the two World Wars. This brief, stirring book recounts Herrigel's rigorous six-year training under a Zen kyudo (archery) master. As his training progresses, the student finds his conscious mind giving way to unconsciousness, and comes to understand the dictum that in kyudo, the archer's target is himself. These insights are surprisingly consilient with the picture of the unconscious offered by Wilson and Damasio. Warning: once you've picked up this book, it will be nearly impossible to put it down until you've read all eighty-one pages!

MITCHELL S. GREEN is a Cavalier Distinguished Teaching Professor and Associate Professor of Philosophy. His research concerns the philosophy of mind, the philosophy of language, and aesthetics. His books include *Engaging Philosophy: A Brief Introduction* (Hackett, 2006); *Self-Expression* (Oxford University Press, 2007); and *Moore's Paradox: New Essays on Belief, Rationality, and the First Person,* coedited with John Williams (Oxford University Press, 2007).

JUDY DELOACHE

Babies, Toddlers, and Teens: How Children Develop

Have you ever gazed with fascination at an infant, wondering what in the world the baby could possibly be thinking, or whether thought is even possible so early in life? Been overwhelmed by the plethora of advice and products promising to make your child smart? Stared with astonishment at an adolescent, wondering what in the world the teen could possibly be thinking to have done something so stupid?

Never before has there been such demand for information about child development. Geographical mobility has resulted in many American families living far from relatives who were traditional sources of information about children and child rearing. In addition, enormous advances have been made in science-based knowledge about development. As a consequence of both factors, books describing development and offering advice to parents occupy shelf after shelf in most bookstores. Some of these books provide sound information, but far too many are inaccurate, and some are close to fraudulent in the claims they make.

One motivation for my selection of these particular books is to steer anyone who is interested in knowing more about child development toward excellent books offering up-to-date, correct information. All but one are written by researchers in the fields represented (several developmental psychologists, one anthropologist, and a science writer). These books are all remarkably well written—lively, entertaining, clear, and (even more importantly) accurate. Not only have I read and personally enjoyed them all, but students in some of my developmental psychology classes have also been enthusiastic about them.

This list is made possible by an amazing wealth of new information that has been amassed in recent years about development in the first few years of life. We know more than ever before about how infants think and what they think about, as well as how the most human of all abilities—language—develops in infants and young children. There have been veritable revolutions in scientific knowledge about brain development and the role of genes in development. Increased interest by anthropologists in early development has enriched our appreciation for the many varieties of reality experienced by babies around the world. A sampling of topics from the books on my list:

Right from birth, infants are attracted to human faces, although what they are actually drawn to is any oval shape that has more elements in the top third than in the bottom. (Look in the mirror and you'll see an oval shape with . . .) Newborns are also sensitive to virtually all the speech sounds in the languages of the world. With experience, they gradually focus on the sounds of their native language and become less sensitive to other sounds.

About half the genes in the human genome are expressed in the brain. The role of genes in the development of the brain is not just a matter of which variants of particular genes you possess. Rather, the infinite complexity of human minds results from the pattern in which those genes are turned on and off by other—"control"—genes. The switching on and off of genes occurs not just during development, but throughout life.

There are astonishing differences in what societies around the world believe about the nature of babies and how they should be treated. In Beng society (in West Africa), newborns are believed to need encouragement to make them want to stay in this world. At the birth of a baby, someone from every household in the village comes to pay respects and to welcome the newest member into the group.

The early development of infants requires interacting with people and the opportunity to explore a variety of objects. However, there is no need for the ever-increasing array of expensive, mass-marketed (and often abysmally designed) products claimed to foster cognitive development.

Teenage behavior has recently become somewhat less mysterious to us, thanks to scientific breakthroughs. Researchers have shown that extensive changes occur in the brain during this often tumultuous period of life, particularly in areas having to do with looking ahead and foreseeing the consequences of one's actions.

Your reward for reading any of these books will be fascinating facts, illuminating insights, and an enhanced regard for the complexity and wonder of human development.

⊷ Alison Gopnik, Andrew N. Meltzoff, and Patricia K. Kuhl, *The Scientist in the Crib: What Early Learning Tells Us about the Mind* (HarperCollins, 2001)

The title of this book reflects the authors' analogy between the strategies that infants employ to learn about the world and those used by scientists to learn about the world. Like scientists, babies generate simple hypotheses, conduct experiments to see what happens, draw conclusions from what they observe, and revise their beliefs accordingly.

All three authors—Gopnik of the University of California, Berkeley, and Meltzoff and Kuhl of the University of Washington—are prominent developmental scientists. In this lively, entertaining, and edifying book, they provide fascinating summaries of research with infants and toddlers demonstrating a surprising array of abilities that are present in the youngest minds. The research findings are always discussed with respect to the situations infants encounter every day. The authors repeatedly emphasize the theme that babies know a great deal to begin with and learn more through their interactions with the environment, including the other people who help to teach them.

⊷ Gary Marcus, *The Birth of the Mind: How a Tiny Number of Genes Creates the Complexities of Human Thought* (Basic, 2004)

Everyone knows that the development of any child is a joint function of nature—the genes that the child inherits from his or her parents—and nurture, the environment in which the child develops. This remarkably lucid and exciting book by the developmental scientist Gary Marcus of New York University will leave everyone who reads it with a much deeper sense of the inseparability of the roles of nature and nurture, as well as a better understanding of how the action of genes affects both the initial assembly of the human brain and its moment-to-moment activity throughout life.

Emphasizing the inextricability of genes and experience, Marcus points out that "children are born with sophisticated mental mechanisms (nature) that allow them to make the most of the information out there in the world (nurture)."

⊷ Alma Gottlieb, *The Afterlife Is Where We Come From: The Culture of Infancy in West Africa* (University of Chicago Press, 2004)

The title of this book refers to what the Beng people of Ivory Coast in West Africa believe about the origin of babies. A newborn is believed to be a reincarnated being just arrived from the afterlife, bringing along knowledge from that previous life, including the ability to understand any language. For some time the infant is tempted to return to the comfort of the afterlife, so it is necessary to treat the baby very well to make him or her want to stay in this world, to "lure the child into this life."

This beautifully written, moving, and mind-expanding book is based on ethnographic work in West Africa by the anthropologist Alma Gottlieb of the University of Illinois (who earned her Ph.D. at the University of Virginia). She frequently draws parallels between Beng and American parenting practices, emphasizing how cultural beliefs have profound effects on how people everywhere rear their children.

↩ Kathy Hirsh-Pasek and Roberta M. Golinkoff, *Einstein Never Used Flash Cards: How Our Children Really Learn—And Why They Need to Play More and Memorize Less* (Rodale, 2004)

Desiring to optimize their children's development, parents today fall prey to advertising touting a vast array of expensive products that supposedly promote infants' development. Psychologists Kathy Hirsh-Pasek of Temple University and Roberta Golinkoff of the University of Delaware take up arms against this hype, arguing forcefully that children learn best through everyday play. Piping Mozart into the crib or showing an infant flash cards cannot substitute for a parent talking to and playing with a baby.

Every chapter of this excellent book includes a brief, highly readable summary of what research has revealed about early development. Interspersed throughout are tips to help parents observe aspects of their children's behavior that they might otherwise miss and suggestions for simple play activities though which their children can learn. Reading this book should be a liberating experience for parents beleaguered by exaggerated advertising claims, as well as a benefit to their babies.

↩ Barbara Strauch, *The Primal Teen: What the New Discoveries about the Teenage Brain Tell Us about Our Kids* (Doubleday, 2004)

In this charming and fascinating book, Barbara Strauch (the health and medical science editor at the *New York Times*) offers a new view of the origins of many of the storms and dramas that typify the adolescent years for so many teens and their parents. This view is based on recent neuroscience investigations of the development of the human brain from early adolescence to early adulthood. Brain imaging of normally developing adolescents has revealed that, contrary to what had previously been assumed, the brain undergoes dramatic developmental changes during this period.

Strauch offers a readable review of this research, writing with re-markable clarity about what researchers have discovered and what those discoveries tell us. What makes this book so outstanding is her cogent integration of the breakthroughs in neuroscience with the daily struggles of parents coping with the sudden "mysterious, infuriating, and downright weird behavior" of their teenage children.

Judy DeLoache is William R. Kenan, Jr., Professor of Psychology. She studies cognitive development in infants and very young children, with a particular focus on the early development of symbol use. She is coauthor of a developmental psychology textbook and coeditor of *A World of Babies* (Cambridge University Press, 2000), a book about child care in seven different societies around the world. She recently published an article on her research in *Scientific American*.

DAVID B. MORRIS

Illness Narratives

Susan Sontag proposed that we all hold dual passports: in the kingdom of health and in the kingdom of the ill. The kingdom of illness is often a forgotten country. For laypeople, almost as soon as we enter the kingdom of the ill we begin looking around for exits or escape routes, and once out we rarely look back. Or, so it once was.

Today, best-seller lists almost always contain at least one memoir of illness, offering new and personal glimpses into the medicalized kingdom of the ill, from addiction and eating disorders to breast cancer and bereavement. This change is not really so surprising. Health care now accounts for some 14 percent of the U.S. total output of goods and services. A similar percentage of Americans has no health insurance—with uninsured rates much higher among Latinos and African Americans. Expenditure so vast and uneven suggests that matters of health radiate massively throughout our lives, visibly and invisibly, almost like the force of gravity.

What happens today when we pass into (or emerge out of) the kingdom of the ill? Subquestions proliferate, often attuned to the changes of postmodern, postindustrial cultures, where illness is a realm—at least for Americans—increasingly government-regulated, third party–funded, science-based, and lifestyle-inflected. Paranoia and discontent thrive. Many people ask if their maladies aren't directly related to job stress and to environmental toxins. Cancer survivors (a new postmodern category) often ask us to believe that illness, however unwanted, has made them better persons. In general, illness narratives are less testaments to personal strength—as in the paradox that what doesn't kill us makes us stronger, a self-evident falsehood—than explorations of changed values and of new perspectives. In addition to its status as an alien and threatening realm, illness now constitutes also a ground for wisdom, growth, and communal transformation.

The transit in and out of illness reinforces the difficult question of what happens (what social and individual changes occur) when we cross the line from well person to patient. Sontag reminds us that specific diseases change their significance over time. Moreover, certain illnesses seem to sum up nonmedical traits of the eras that they come to define or represent, such as black plague in the Middle Ages, TB in the nineteenth century, or, say, depression, Alzheimer's disease, and HIV/AIDS today. The social mythologies surrounding such illnesses inescapably affect the patient and thus alter the individual experience of illness. If the contemporary kingdom of the ill is defined in part through an impersonal gravitational field of caregivers, insurance companies, lawyers, advertisers, and policy makers, in what specific ways does our experience of illness differ from the experience of our parents or grandparents?

Illness is—despite the flood of writing by patients—the dark side of our cultural obsession with gym-fit, seductive, surgically enhanced, better-than-well bodies. Its complications grow only more tangled as medical consumers (the name we are learning to call ourselves) encounter tantalizing, largely unproven claims from the pharmacopeia of complementary and alternative medicine. (A famous study shows that Americans pay more for out-of-pocket alternative practitioners than for standard physicians, whom they also continue to consult.) Patients today, as they search beyond traditional biomedicine, sometimes come dangerously close to consulting snake-oil salesmen. Mind-body therapies seem to generate a guru on every corner, but with good reason. Our ideas are changing about the links between bodies and minds.

In this changed environment, when damaged bodies cannot be disentangled from toxic air and hurtful emotions, the physician Rita Charon in a groundbreaking 2001 article introduced the concept of "narrative medicine." Charon defines narrative medicine as medicine practiced with narrative "competence." ("Competencies" is a key term in current medical education.) *Narrative competence* is not the arcane feat of a few mandarin literary theorists but rather ultimately a knowledge that we all have access to, concerned with telling and understanding stories. For health and illness, stories (as Charon puts it elsewhere) matter. Here is a list of five texts by doctors and by patients that are meant to jump-start an introduction into the changed kingdoms of the ill. They offer a practical test of whether stories truly matter.

↬ Virginia Woolf, *On Being Ill* (Paris Press, 2002)

This slim volume reproduces the 1930 Hogarth Press edition of the famous essay that T. S. Eliot commissioned and published (with lukewarm interest) in the January 1926 issue of his highbrow literary journal, the *New Criterion*. Woolf republished the essay in various revisions, but this new version with Hermione Lee's insightful introduction and helpful notes is surely definitive. Woolf spent long periods as an invalid—a category inherited from the nineteenth century and largely given over to women—and here she inverts the traditional relation between the kingdoms of illness and health. She represents health, with its vast armies of the upright and its normalcy police, as an arena of convention and illusion, while it is the ill alone, in their inconsolable solitude, who pierce the veil and see life as it truly is.

↬ Jean-Dominique Bauby, *The Diving Bell and the Butterfly*, trans. Jeremy Leggatt (Knopf, 1998)

This little book—I trust it's becoming clear that I like short texts—was originally published in French in the same year as its English translation. The fashionable editor in chief of the giant French fashion magazine *Elle*, Bauby suffered a massive stroke (on the test drive for a new BMW he was considering buying). A month later, he awoke with the sense that someone was sewing his eyelid shut. "Locked-in syndrome" left him able to do little more than blink his one good eye. Blink by blink, as a speech therapist guided him through an alphabetic frequency table, he spelled out each letter of every single word in this astonishing account—as remarkable for its dry wit and wry insights into the social experience of illness as for its absence of self-pity, total lack of sentiment, and ironic disregard of traditional consolations. It is illness without a hint of transcendence except what the heart and mind, simultaneously damaged and enlightened, can muster in the face of extreme personal catastrophe.

↬ William Styron, *Darkness Visible: A Memoir of Madness* (1990; Random House, 2007)

A close friend, after the death of her husband, suffered a deep clinical depression. I was inexperienced enough to think that I could coach her out of depression by sheer cheerfulness or caring. Styron's brief account of the near-suicidal depression that struck him in his sixties— at the peak of his powers—gives outsiders a glimpse into an illness that defies coaching. Styron's narrative describes a descent into hell, which concludes by quoting Dante as he emerges from the Inferno: "And so we came forth, and once again beheld the stars." The turning point comes when Styron—ready for suicide after a series of preparations—hears "a sudden soaring passage from the Brahms *Alto Rhapsody.*" Readers who don't know it by heart should find a CD of the *Alto Rhapsody.* Research seems sure to confirm the link or narrative that, as here, connects music and healing.

↬ Audre Lorde, *The Cancer Journals,* 2nd ed. (1980; Aunt Lute Books, 2006)

Audre Lorde—who died in 1992 in her late fifties—calls herself a black lesbian feminist poet. The journal entries and occasional pieces that comprise this book together chart her experience with breast cancer. She embodies the liberationist spirit of the 1970s in her refusal of silence. Warriorlike resistance is her primary metaphor for women's relation to breast cancer, reinforced by the loving support of a female circle. She takes a provocative but principled stance in her refusal to wear a prosthesis—another form of silence, as she sees it—arguing that women with mastectomies must become visible to each other in order to creates a new sisterhood against victimhood and for social change. Cancer changes her in many ways. "I feel like I'm counting my days in milliseconds," she writes in her journal, "never mind hours. And it's a good thing, that particular consciousness of the way in which each hour passes, even if it is a boring hour. I want it to become permanent."

↬ Lori Arviso Alvord and Elizabeth Cohen Van Pelt, *The Scalpel and the Silver Bear* (Bantam, 2000)

"The first Navajo woman surgeon combines western medicine and traditional healing": so says the dust jacket. Lori Alvord grew up poor on a reservation in rural New Mexico, and this memoir recounts her journey from double-outsider (a half-blood within the Navajo community) to distinguished surgeon. As she negotiates the dividing line between two worlds, she sees herself as a Navajo weaver, for whom Western medicine and Navajo tradition constitute the warp and weft. Her book tells much about contemporary Navajo life—including its distinctive medical challenges, from alcoholism and diabetes to hantavirus. The link is clear between Indian suffering and white majority culture, but Alvord recounts a memoir full of hope for cross-cultural understanding and for wise medical change. A physician rather than a professional writer, she offers rare insight into the often closed or neglected Navajo community and into what it can teach us about health.

DAVID B. MORRIS published two prize-winning books—*The Religious Sublime* (University Press of Kentucky, 1972) and *Alexander Pope: The Genius of Sense* (Harvard University Press, 1984)—before leaving academia to write full-time. *The Culture of Pain* (University of California Press, 1991) won a PEN prize. *Earth Warrior* (Fulcrum, 1995) describes a voyage with the environmental activist Paul Watson. *Illness and Culture in the Postmodern Age* (University of California Press, 1998) proposes a biocultural approach to illness. He retired in July 2007 as University Professor.

LARRY MERKEL

Psychiatric Anthropology: Mental Illness and Cultural Difference

While at some basic level we are all the same, we are also intimately aware that there are deep cultural differences between people. Cultural differences in behavior might also manifest in differences in psychology and mental illness. Some of the most famous psychiatrists and anthropologists—Sigmund Freud, Carl Jung, Emil Kraepelin, Margaret Mead, Ruth Benedict, and many others—have taken an interest in this area. The field of psychiatric anthropology first came together in the years surrounding World War II as culture and personality studies. Early theorists built on the perceived juncture between psychoanalytic ideas about how the human psyche is shaped through early childhood experiences in the family and the anthropological observation that cultures are unique productions of human efforts to adapt to various environments. Unfortunately, the marriage of psychiatry and anthropology turned out to have an all-too-brief honeymoon. Although there was no divorce, it remained a marriage in name only, as psychiatrists became infatuated with neurobiology and the promises of psychopharmacology while anthropologists became fascinated with symbols, linguistics, and cultural change and complexity. It is no wonder that, since then, the field has traveled under different identities, struggling to find a new cohesion.

However, the initial concerns remained: Is mental illness, as we describe it in the West, universal? If cultures influence the way we think, do they also influence the way we become disturbed? Does culture merely change the content of mental illness, while the basic nature of a psychiatric illness remains the same? In other words, is it possible that though a person in the United States with schizophrenia may believe that he is being stalked by the Mafia and a person in Nigeria with schizophrenia believes that he is endangered by witches, the basic illness is the same? Are there forms of aberrant behavior that are unique to specific cultures—the so-called "culture-bound syndromes"? First brought back by European explorers as tales of exotic behavior, such things as amok (as in "running amok") were seen as manifestations of the primitiveness of the "darker races." Yet others have argued that these behaviors are really no different from phenomena known in the West, that is, amok is the same as "going postal." The attempt to answer these questions raises fundamental issues about the nature of the human psyche.

Given the massive migrations of people due to famine, war, and economic advantage, most societies today are multicultural. The clientele of your average psychiatrist may include people from most continents and members of various religious sects. Furthermore, the promises of neurobiology and drug treatment have not always lived up to expectations. American psychiatrists are consistently forced to defend themselves against questions from various governmental, political, and quasi-religious factions about electroconvulsive therapy, the use of psychoactive medications in children, and the insanity plea. To many, it appears that the time has again come for psychiatry to look beyond a person's basic biology and take into account his individuality and cultural context. These pressures have produced an increased need for some reconciliation between psychiatry and anthropology, despite their fundamental differences. This possibility is very exciting.

One hundred years of endeavor by many skilled clinicians and social scientists has produced a wealth of material that is both fascinating and challenging. I have tried to pick a few more recent examples that are either of fundamental importance or represent sensitive and valuable approaches to some critical issue within the field today. Each of these may then act as a springboard into a large and deep pool of further reading.

↪ Arthur Kleinman, *Rethinking Psychiatry: From Cultural Category to Personal Experience* (Free Press, 1988)

This book has become the corner piece for what Kleinman (a Harvard-based psychiatrist and anthropologist) has termed the "New Cross-Cultural Psychiatry." In this clear and easy-to-read book, Kleinman challenges the basic assumptions of modern psychiatry. He demonstrates the essential need for a cultural perspective to complement the established biological perspective in order to bring balance to the field. He does this by asking and striving to answer such fundamental questions as: *What is a psychiatric diagnosis? Do psychiatric disorders differ in different cultures? How do psychiatrists heal?* Most of the critical issues of the field are addressed in this book.

⇟ Roland Littlewood and Maurice Lipsedge, *Aliens and Alienists: Ethnic Minorities and Psychiatry,* 3rd ed. (Routledge, 1997)

This work by two British psychiatrists begins with the story of Calvin Johnson, a Jamaican immigrant to Great Britain whose Rastafarian beliefs and struggles with the police bring him to the attention of psychiatrists who believe he may be psychotic. The authors then proceed to explore in depth the circumstances of this not unusual case. Relying on their work with other immigrants to Britain—Irish, West African, South Asian, and others—they masterfully explore such issues as the fallibility of Western psychiatric diagnostic criteria, the effects of racism in medicine, and the process of migration and adaptation to a new culture. They end by exploring mental illness not only as the manifestation of a disorder but, more importantly, as a source of communication.

⇟ Robert L. Winzeler, *Latah in Southeast Asia: The History and Ethnography of a Culture-Bound Syndrome* (Cambridge University Press, 1995)

In this short but beautifully written book, Winzeler, an anthropologist, takes the reader along on an ethnographic detective story. Latah is one of the more well-studied, yet highly debated of the culture-bound syndromes, reports of which first came to the West from European travelers to various parts of Southeast Asia in the mid-nineteenth century. It is manifest by certain people who when startled appear to enter a trance, utter profanities, and mimic the behaviors of those around them. Questions have been raised as to whether or not it is truly culture-bound or even a syndrome (implying disease) or just exaggerated normal behavior. Winzeler, through his own extensive fieldwork and by sifting earlier reports and theories about Latah, presents an intriguing and enlightening glimpse into the cultural shaping of aberrant behavior.

⇟ Theresa DeLeane O'Nell, *Disciplined Hearts: History, Identity, and Depression in an American Indian Community* (University of California Press, 1998)

Ethnographic research, the process of living with a people and participating in their daily life, is at the heart of anthropological technique. In this extremely sensitive and powerful work, O'Nell uses this methodology, involving countless hours of interviewing and interaction, to explore the meaning of depression among the Flathead Indians of western Montana, where as many as 80 percent of the population consider themselves depressed. This journey of understanding results in both a richer sense of what this means for the Flatheads, and an effort to meld psychiatric and anthropological inquiry. The final product is a moving narrative of how the Flathead Indians have turned deprivation and domination into a morality of responsibility and connectedness.

⟜ James M. Glass, *Shattered Selves: Multiple Personality in a Postmodern World* (Cornell University Press, 1995)

As postmodern philosophy attacks rationality, the conceptual "isms," and the technological suffocation of modern society, it dismisses the existence of fundamental concepts as politically motivated efforts to hold power. This philosophy has strongly influenced modern anthropological theory. At its extreme, postmodernism denies the psychological concept of a unitary self and argues for multiplicity, even arguing for schizophrenia to be considered a modern heroic and revolutionary state. Glass, a political scientist, while accepting some postmodern premises, examines actual states of psychological multiplicity in those suffering from Multiple Personality Disorder (usually as the result of extreme childhood abuse). He departs from postmodernism, arguing, instead, for the importance of an inner concept of the self to mental functioning. The case histories are upsetting and heartrending, but make a strong case against an intellectual approach that loses touch with individual experience and the struggle for existence.

⟜ Giuseppe Mantovani, *Exploring Borders: Understanding Culture and Psychology* (Routledge, 2001)

At times witty and charming and at other times moving and challenging, Mantovani's short book, or narrative, as he calls it, is always skillfully written and highly entertaining. In it, he raises powerful arguments as to the centrality of culture to psychology. Drawing on a wide range of examples from anthropological fieldwork, *Robinson Crusoe, Alice's Adventures in Wonderland,* and recent headlines, he analyzes the psychological functions of culture and argues for the critical importance of encountering the Other at the cultural boundaries of our existence in order to know and understand ourselves. His purpose is more than academic; it involves an effort to raise a moral banner for understanding and an end to the violence and hatred that often accompany cross-border contacts.

Larry Merkel is Associate Professor of Psychiatric Medicine. He is a board-certified psychiatrist and has a Ph.D. in anthropology from the University of Pennsylvania, where he was on the faculty before coming to the University of Virginia. He has traveled and worked in Ethiopia and New Zealand. His research has examined the cultural construction of suicidal behavior among Vietnamese refugees and in Appalachia.

PETER METCALF

Exploring Human Diversity: An Entrée into Anthropology

What is anthropology? It's a fair question because the subject is not often taught as such in high schools, and so is unfamiliar to anyone who has not taken a course in it at college. The word itself translates as "people study," which doesn't get us very far since *all* the humanities study people in some way or other. Moreover, anthropology ranges over remarkably diverse issues and methods. What draws them together thematically is how humans differ from other species, and among themselves. But it is easier to grasp the discipline by listing its subfields as they emerged in the United States, and together constitute the famous "four-fields approach": *archaeology,* which uses methods of excavation to discover evidence of past societies; *cultural anthropology,* which compares those aspects of human beliefs and practices that are acquired by learning; *linguistic anthropology,* that is, linguistics with a comparative emphasis; and *physical anthropology,* which is concerned with hominid evolution and physical differences between human populations.

Of the four subfields, cultural anthropology has the most practitioners. It employs techniques of "fieldwork" developed in the early twentieth century as a response to the wild speculation on "primitive" peoples that had occurred previously. These techniques entail direct and prolonged participation in other peoples' ways of life, including the acquisition of indigenous languages. The results of such research are "ethnographies"— literally, writings on ethnicities. My list contains no ethnographies plain and simple, but that does not mean that they are in short supply. Any academic library can locate them for any place that is of interest to you personally. For present purposes, I chose Nigel Barley's lighthearted look behind the scenes of fieldwork in West Africa.

By contrast, the appeal of Patrick Kirch's book is that it synthesizes data from all four fields of anthropology in order to reconstruct Polynesian "prehistory," that is, Polynesians' ancient origins and subsequent diversification.

The whole phenomenon of language provides the starting point for Lévi-Strauss's theorizing. Throughout his long career, Lévi-Strauss argued that cultures manifest structure, just as languages do, so that cultural anthropologists had the same task of discovering structure as did linguists. To avoid confusion, let us be clear that language is itself cultural, since it is learned.

Marshall Sahlins's development of the concept of structure is to apply it to historical events. His examples are drawn from the encounters between Europeans and Polynesians. What he sees is not just a story of exploration and annexation, such as a historian might tell, but a collision of indigenous and alien modes of thinking—that is, structures—such that each is progressively modified by the other. What results is neither an amalgam nor a lowest common denominator, but something new and original.

The final volume on the list is noteworthy for initiating a discussion that goes far beyond technicalities. Nettle and Romaine describe how and why languages are disappearing at an appalling pace all over the world. There are examples from Europe, such as Cornish and Manx. But the majority of examples are in areas that were relatively isolated from major civilizations until recent centuries, such as Australia, New Guinea and adjacent islands, much of the Americas, sub-Saharan Africa, and Southeast Asia.

↢ Nigel Barley, *A Plague of Caterpillars* (Penguin, 1987)

Barley's slim book recounts his misadventures while conducting fieldwork in West Africa. Auberon Waugh described it as one of the "funniest book[s] to have come out of Africa." Barley has been criticized for making fun of his hosts, but most of the humor is in fact at his own expense. Meanwhile, by demystifying the process of fieldwork, his writing has drawn many readers to more serious ethnographic writing.

↢ Patrick Vinton Kirch, *The Evolution of Polynesian Chiefdoms* (1984; Cambridge University Press, 1989)

This is a scholarly account of the origins and diversity of the Polynesian peoples. Although it contains a great deal of data, it is nevertheless accessible to the interested layperson.

Since written records appear only with the arrival of the first Europeans, Polynesian prehistory ends in the eighteenth century. For previous epochs, we must rely primarily on archaeological data. But

linguistic evidence is also crucial in establishing the degree of related-
ness of different Polynesian populations. Knowledge of their development at the moment of Contact relies on ethnographic data, even
though the oldest records were collected by missionaries and administrators rather than by modern-day ethnographers. The common origins of the Polynesians are also apparent in their physical types, but
that is of limited interest given the clarity of the linguistic evidence.

↤ Claude Lévi-Strauss, *Myth and Meaning: Cracking the Code of Culture*
(1979; Schocken, 1995)

Another slim volume, written by one of the most famous anthropological theorists of the twentieth century. It provides a remarkably
clear and succinct introduction to his entire oeuvre. The aptitude for
language is a distinctive and universal feature of humankind, clearly
the result of a long process of evolution. At the same time, however,
languages vary enormously from one another, not only in vocabulary,
but also in grammatical structure. Most of us learn only European
languages—if indeed we learn any language other than English. You
would find Amerindian languages far more challenging, because they
operate in fundamentally different ways. In the same way, Amerindian
myths are incomprehensible unless one can crack their "code."

↤ Marshall Sahlins, *Islands of History* (1985; University of Chicago Press, 1987)

Sahlins's essays apply the concepts of anthropology to historical materials from the Pacific, and so make an interesting comparison with
Kirch's book. Technical jargon may be an obstacle, but can be largely
set aside, since the argument is plain enough. The most famous essay
in the collection concerns the tumultuous reception of Captain Cook
by the people of Hawaii in 1779, and his murder by the same people
only a few months later. Did Cook wear out his welcome? Did the Hawaiians presciently realize the danger that the Europeans presented?
Neither of these, argues Sahlins. Instead they incorporated Cook into
their own ritual calendar, treated him accordingly, and in the process
modified their religion. Cook's death was no mere accident, but an
intelligible sequence of implications and consequences.

↤ Daniel Nettle and Daniel and Suzanne Romaine, *Vanishing Voices: The
Extinction of the World's Languages* (Oxford University Press, 2000)

This book raises a puzzling issue. According to Nettle and Romaine,
90 percent of all the world's languages will be extinct by the end of
the century. How should we feel about that? A commonsense response
might be that it would be brilliant if everyone in the world spoke

English. Such barbarity might make a linguist wince, but why should the rest of us care? The answer, of course, is that language diversity implies cultural diversity, and anthropologists of all stripes are pretty sure that the sum total of human understanding is not contained in the currently dominant world languages. On the contrary, the industrialized world is already threatened by a lifeless uniformity. Whether the process of extinction can be reversed, or even slowed, is another difficult question, but the prospects do not seem good.

PETER METCALF has conducted fieldwork in central Borneo and written several ethnographies, including *Celebrations of Death: The Anthropology of Mortuary Ritual* (Cambridge University Press, 1979). His latest book is an introduction to anthropology, showing how the issues it explores are relevant to daily life. It is called *Anthropology: The Basics* (Routledge, 2002). Before that, he wrote an account of the dilemmas of fieldwork, entitled *They Lie, We Lie: Getting On with Anthropology* (Routledge, 2000).

JOHN PORTMANN

Sex and Morality

Undergraduates routinely jump at the chance to take a class on sexual ethics, to no one's surprise. Yet teaching the cultural history of sexuality, as well as reading about it, can make anyone a little uncomfortable. Studying sexual ethics involves yourself, specifically as you try to figure out your place in the conflict between a normative system and its deviants. Students in this seminar almost invariably come to see that sexual mores can and do change: what most people in a society at one time rejected (think of a sexually experienced bride) they may now accept.

Analyzing the history of sexual ethics from within the Judeo-Christian tradition, my seminar begins and ends in Judaism. A number of contemporary writers (for example, Gore Vidal) blame Judaism for spoiling the party. In the pagan era, so the story goes, sex was easier to find and enjoy. With the rise of Judaism, sex became thoroughly regulated, and the category of forbidden sex widened considerably. Once the Emperor Constantine formally protected the new sect of Christianity, it then promulgated the sexual ethic it had adapted from Judaism.

Almost at once, Christians distinguished themselves from Jews through a celebration of virginity and chastity. By the end of the second century

CE, celibacy had essentially become a state Christians revered. In praising life without sex, early Christians saw themselves following the example of Jesus and his mother (even though there had been pagan precedents). Well into the twentieth century, the Roman Catholic Church considered celibates morally superior to married people. This hierarchy is unthinkable in Judaism and Islam, faiths in which adults are pressured to marry (following the commandment to "go forth and multiply"). Jews, Muslims, and Protestants haven't opposed artificial birth control in the way Catholics have done. Yet two incendiary social issues have succeeded in uniting conservative Jews, Catholics, and Protestants: abortion and gay marriage.

In brief, sexuality has always roiled Western culture. The books I've chosen emphasize the importance of viewing recent sexual controversies in the United States through a Judeo-Christian lens, because cultural assumptions about sex rested on largely religious foundations. Indeed, religious groups derived some of their power from ruling over the domain of sexual activity. Americans continue to question whether the loosening of sexual strictures amounts to a good or bad thing, but no one doubts that an important set of cultural assumptions had been challenged by the late 1970s. Together these books reveal that debates over sex not only illuminate but also actively shape notions of morality and cultural value.

↩ David Biale, *Eros and the Jews: From Biblical Israel to Contemporary America* (University of California Press, 1997)

> Biale's comprehensive survey traces sexual mores in the United States to a pivotal ancient tribe in the Middle East. Hundreds of years ago, for example, many Jewish communities married off their children at the age of thirteen or fourteen. Although this is a practice that strikes us as bizarre, even repellent, a parent who today worries about the consequences of adolescent sex might for a moment see that ancient custom in a new light. Biale argues that erotic transgressions (think of, say, Ruth or Tamar) actually *advance* the political fate of ancient Israel, thus leaving us to ponder a remarkable flexibility in Hebrew Scriptures. Toward the end of this book, Biale usefully discusses Philip Roth's novel *Portnoy's Complaint* in order to make more explicit certain generalizations about Jews and sex. For Biale, Portnoy's plight nicely encapsulates the driving question of whether Judaism liberates or represses sexual activity.

↩ Angus McLaren, *Sexual Blackmail: A Modern History* (Harvard University Press, 2002)

> This study serves up a delicious history of hypocrisy. Sexual blackmail in eighteenth-century England began as a way to discredit and disarm homosexuals. The discovery that Alexander Hamilton was having an

adulterous affair with Maria Reynolds and paying for the silence of Mr. Reynolds marked the first widely recognized sex scandal on American soil. Blackmailers were able to make money, McLaren argues, only so long as Americans persisted in pretending they were all sexually upright Puritans, despite frequent evidence to the contrary. The freewheeling 1960s short-circuited extortionists for a time, as divorce, abortion, and gay sex largely ceased to shock Americans and Western Europeans. Since the advent of statutes to protect eighteenth-century Englishmen from being accused of sodomy, morality has been made the business of our legislators. Criminals, too, realized that they could make morality their business. This book drives home the point that a moral norm is not like a tree, something we can run into if we're not careful. We create moral norms, and we can undermine them at will.

⬧ Laura Kipnis, *Against Love: A Polemic* (Vintage, 2004)

Can any of us really choose not to desire love? What would the West look like if we could? The Cinderella myth prevails through assaults on it. The divorce rate may hover above 50 percent, but we continue to believe that someday our prince or princess will come. In a workaholic culture, we persist in the belief that we can make our dreams come true. Once we do find love, it all too often feels like work ("Relationships take a lot of work," we hear from married couples), which merely indicates that we're not working hard enough. Kipnis, a Northwestern University professor, recommends that we take whatever pleasure we can from sex and leave the love myths to medieval troubadours. Today, marriage is a social institution in transition; whether it will conform to Judeo-Christian ideals for long is anyone's guess.

⬧ Judith Levine, *Harmful to Minors: The Perils of Protecting Children from Sex* (Thunder's Mouth Press, 2003)

Levine attacks conservative attempts to forbid the teaching of sex education in American public schools. She argues against the idea that teaching teenagers about sex will get them thinking about sex: hormone-heavy teens already think about sex regularly, she insists, and they urgently need guidance. Moreover, and more controversially, she argues that even insinuating that consensual sex is dirty, or that the curious are deviant for desiring it, creates a stigma that can harm teens for decades to come. She urges tolerance, humor, and trust when tending to adolescents, all the while lamenting the damage Puritanism has allegedly wrought in countless American bedrooms. In an afterword to the paperback, Levine recounts the controversy surrounding the publication of her book, which attracted significant media attention.

↩ Alyce Mahon, *Eroticism and Art* (Oxford University Press, 2007)

Mahon's book explores the visual power of sexual images, while the other books on my list primarily involve words. Since sexual experiences often linger in the imagination as visual experiences, not necessarily verbal ones, this approach seems especially useful. Mahon's book follows the boundary between social orthodoxy and political transgression, the moving target that is sexual propriety in any given age. The fierce debate surrounding the artistic depiction of eroticism neatly parallels the controversy around sexual legislation (for example, birth control for minors or gay marriage) and especially the teaching of sex ed in public high schools. From a teacher's point of view, looking at erotic (or, some might object, pornographic) images carries much more risk than reading academic treatises about sexual conduct (treatises that, some might argue, often become pornographic).

JOHN PORTMANN, a graduate of Yale and Cambridge Universities, teaches religious studies. His first book, *When Bad Things Happen to Other People* (Routledge, 2000), probes the morality of schadenfreude, the pleasure we sometimes take in the misfortunes of others. He has also written, among other books, *Sex and Heaven: Catholics in Bed and at Prayer* (Palgrave Macmillan, 2003) and *A History of Sin* (Rowman and Littlefield, 2007).

IRA BASHKOW

For the Sake of Profit: Self-Interest, Self-Sacrifice, and Corporate Goals

One of the outstanding findings of my field, anthropology, in its long-running study of human cultures worldwide, is that no other society has ever encouraged people to pursue wealth and profit on a scale like our own. Formerly in Europe, greed was a sin, and only a few individuals in the aristocracy, clergy, and merchant guilds were positioned to indulge in gain-seeking to the point of attaining really significant wealth. But the religious attitude began to shift under Protestantism, which saw worldly success as a sign of God's favor. In Adam Smith's landmark 1776 book, *The Wealth of Nations*, greed was not only redeemed, it was set on a pedestal as the surest and best means for achieving collective well-being, since through the magic of the market, people trying to maximize their own profit would meet *everyone's* material needs most efficiently.

Smith's positive interpretation of greed as an incentive has been so influential that it is now common sense, and there is no doubt that it has proven a remarkably productive idea. The drive for profits, as everyone knows, has spurred innumerable innovations that helped bring into being the rich material culture of Western modernity, as exemplified in the unprecedented bounty of consumer goods we now enjoy every day. The profit motive is celebrated in every quarter of the business and finance worlds, and it serves as a foundational principle of the discipline of economics. As such it forms the basis for the economic prescriptions that have been urged upon poor nations the world over, generally as a condition for receiving foreign aid and loan money from the World Bank, the International Monetary Fund, and other multilateral banks.

Anthropologists do not question that self-interest plays a role in every society. But they recognize that individuals' actions are guided by different impulses depending on the situation. The ruthless self-interest that we associate with commercial trade is not appropriate in the family home, where even the most aggressively competitive bond traders behave toward their children in self-sacrificing ways, providing for them as communists are said to do: "from each according to their abilities; to each according to their needs." Not only are people's motivations responsive to different situations; they participate in the goals of organizations. Soldiers generally do not fight because they expect thereby to personally benefit (nor because they have violent impulses); they fight because the armies they have joined are engaged in war. Indeed, individual soldiers sacrifice themselves for the goals of their fighting groups and the governments of their nations.

So, too, do people sacrifice their own interests in the quest for profit. Most of us in the West today express our individual economic interests primarily through the choices we make as consumers, while in our productive lives, as producers, we work for organizations like companies. There is no systematic relationship between the strategic decisions of institutions and the self-interest of the people who work for them. If there were, companies would not need to spend so much on the quest to "align" these by employee training, benefits, and special incentives like stock options, gifts, and bonuses. In Adam Smith's day, when companies were still small, it was not so important to distinguish between the self-interest of individuals and that of organizations. But our economy today is dominated by large corporations that have far greater powers than do most individuals, and their institutionalized quest for ever greater profit raises social questions that were undreamed of in Adam Smith's time.

The five books in this list provide insights into how we in the West have arrived at this juncture and what it might mean for our well-being.

What is the cost to society of a pervasive concern with maximizing a narrow measure of value—the financial bottom line? How have ever more parts of our lives become structured by our own and others' profit-making activities? How do modern axioms of financial viability compare with the values that have organized other societies? While the books described here do not provide solutions to these problems, they do help us grasp their importance and scope.

⊷ Ruth Benedict, *Patterns of Culture* (1934; Mariner, 2006)

Arguably the all-time best general introduction to cultural anthropology, *Patterns of Culture* centers on three finely wrought case studies that reveal remarkable contrasts with the values and customs orienting the book's Western readers. Benedict argues that every society cultivates and honors only a small section of the "great arc" of possibilities allowed by human nature, which is highly plastic and thus culturally formed. How does our culture compare to the Zuñi Indian pueblo society that enshrined among its highest values even-temperedness and a submerging of self-interest in deference to the common good? Or to the Kwakiutl society of the American Northwest Coast, where individuals were encouraged to seek high rank and distinction by destroying their wealth, as well as by amassing it and giving it away? The answers to these questions are left for us to contemplate in light of the many implicit contrasts spread throughout the book.

⊷ James Scott, *Seeing Like a State: How Certain Schemes to Improve the Human Condition Have Failed* (Yale University Press, 1999)

This brilliant book, which is framed by the question of why state-sponsored development projects so often fail, arrives at a profound answer that applies to other diverse situations as well. In Scott's examples, which include eighteenth-century German scientific forestry, European city planning, Tanzanian village reform, and Soviet collectivization, the state's interests in maximizing revenue and efficient control lead it to construct and implement "thin" models of reality, like agricultural projects devoted to cultivating monocultures—single vulnerable species. The author argues that the risk of long-term failure arises intrinsically when a complex reality is simplified as a necessary concomitant of planning. However, his argument applies as well to any standardization of environments or social interactions undertaken in order to maximize simple quantifiable values. Scott explains why short-term success tends to give way to long-term failure, except where people supplement the simple planned structures with practical expertise, informal networks, and complex workarounds.

↵ Susan Linn, *Consuming Kids: Protecting Our Children from the Onslaught of Marketing and Advertising* (Anchor, 2005)

In this well-researched and engagingly written book on the $15 billion industry of marketing to children, Susan Linn documents how American children are confronted at every turn with images and messages brilliantly designed by richly rewarded marketers to exploit children's vulnerabilities and make them accomplices in companies' aim to sell products. Linn takes us behind the scenes to an industry conference where advertisers proudly share their expertise on how young children's maddening whining for desired objects—the "nag factor"—can be deliberately cultivated to break down parents' will to resist commodities like junk food that they know their children would be better off without. While parents are claimed to be "free" to help their children make responsible choices, they are undermined and beleaguered in their efforts to do so. The resulting harm to children and family life is an ethical issue the advertising industry is not obliged to confront; its only concerns are its profits. For another excellent book on this topic, see Juliet Schor's *Born to Buy: The Commercialized Child and the New Consumer Culture* (Scribner, 2005).

↵ Joel Bakan, *The Corporation: The Pathological Pursuit of Profit and Power* (Free Press, 2004)

Joel Bakan, a distinguished scholar of constitutional law, summarizes extensive legal research and numerous interviews with corporate insiders, CEOs, Wall Street traders, economists, critics, and industry spies to offer an informative and disturbing account of the dominant institutional form of our time: the business corporation. Bakan argues that since corporations are legal entities created with the single overriding purpose of maximizing their profit, we should not be surprised that they seek to shift their costs and liabilities onto workers, the environment, and society and government. Nor should we be surprised that they cover up product safety issues, interfere with democracy, and bend and break laws, since, after all, these are economically rational actions when the fines for misconduct are so small relative to the potential gain. Even though they have no morality or motivations apart from self-interest, corporations are granted the same rights and protections as human beings, a legal fiction they routinely and grossly abuse.

↵ Robert Jackall, *Moral Mazes: The World of Corporate Managers* (Oxford University Press, 1989)

The sociologist Robert Jackall conducted hundreds of interviews with corporate managers over five years of fieldwork in three public companies, resulting in a book full of interesting insights and anecdotes about the culture in which they work. What he found is that managers are constantly on probation, vulnerable and anxious, a situation they adapt to by elevating personal loyalties over moral principles and by acting in ways that minimize the possibility of being fired when things go wrong. Jackall shows that promotion and punishment are assumed to depend not upon one's achievements, but rather upon one's skill in positioning oneself and in successfully deflecting blame. This fosters a culture of nonaccountability in which managers recognize it as professional suicide to insist upon a clear principle, like the need to avoid injurious workplace practices, if it does not have preexisting support among managerial higher-ups. Instead of actually acting from principles, managers invent and promulgate "cover stories" that are carefully crafted to suit the interests of their audiences. So directors and stockholders receive messages about efficiency and the return on investment, while those on the outside hear only that the corporation serves the public good.

IRA BASHKOW, a cultural anthropologist, is Associate Professor of Anthropology. His *The Meaning of Whitemen: Race and Modernity in the Orokaiva Cultural World* (University of Chicago Press, 2006) examines how people in the Pacific Island nation Papua New Guinea conceptualize whites, the West, and development. Twice awarded fellowships by the National Endowment for the Humanities, Bashkow teaches and writes about globalization, intercultural relations, race, and the history of anthropology.

JOHN NEMEC

The Four Goals of Life in Classical Hinduism

Adherence to the law (*dharma*), pursuit of material well-being (*artha*), pleasure (*kāma*), and liberation (*mokṣa*)—these are the four legitimate goals of human existence in Hinduism. If one can identify a single, central tenet of the classical religion, it would involve the identity of all being with the universal, omnipotent divine, called Brahman, which is both infused into all of existence and yet lying beyond it, simultaneously. Given that the universe has such a nature, it follows that all things—and beings— are themselves in some sense divine. Each has its place in the landscape of an omnipresent divinity, and as such, all things have their value when engaged in the right way, in the right place, and at the right time. For this reason, the classical tradition legitimizes all sorts of human activity—the aforementioned four aims—in their appropriate contexts. With this in mind, I have selected primary texts in translation that speak to one or another of these four aims, this in an effort to offer something of a survey of classical Hindu literature.

It is, of course, impossible to present a comprehensive view of the religion given its scope. There are hundreds of thousands, if not millions, of Sanskrit texts—Sanskrit being the language of the literati—covering an impressive range of topics and showing incredible variations in style. Mathematics and architecture, astronomy and astrology, some historical works, manuals for governing the state, poetry and epic, music, art, philosophy, grammar, scriptural works, ritual texts, "secret" teachings aiming at enlightenment, books of spells—virtually every significant subject of human learning is represented in the canon.

The term "hindu" itself points, in a different way, to such diversity. Originally a Persian (and Greek) word, it first referred not to a religion but to the people of the Indian subcontinent. Derived from the name of a river, the Sindhu, which runs across contemporary Pakistan, the word "hindu" came to refer to *everyone* living east of the river. Reflecting the diversity implied by this etymology, Hinduism today (and in the classical period) includes a wonderful myriad of traditions, practices, and ideas, a variety that is perhaps unsurpassed by any other major religious tradition. There is no one sacred book or bible of Hinduism; there are many. Various gods gain ascendancy in various sects of the religion. Each geographic region manifests a unique form of the religion, which has developed over the course of some three and a half millennia. Indeed, the diversity of Hindu traditions is so great that it is sometimes suggested that nothing can be said about the religion without qualification.

The reading list offered below is therefore meant in no way to be comprehensive. Drawing from a variety of genres and including texts written across time and from around the subcontinent, the selections here are meant to give the reader a broad view of some of the most widely known works from what may be called classical Hinduism. The texts are presented below in roughly chronological order.

The first book is a translation of a part of the Vedic canon, the earliest set of sacred Hindu scriptures. Speaking primarily to the quest for liberation (*mokṣa*), the texts translated in the book are drawn from the "knowledge" portion of the Veda, as opposed to the ritual portion. The next two selections represent the epic tradition, the first being a condensation of the great epic, the *Mahābhārata*, composed by traveling bards between 400 BC and AD 400. The second, the Bhagavadgītā, was the first

Sanskrit text translated from the original into English, and it perhaps remains the most famous and most read of them all. Both speak to the need to conform to *dharma*, the law, though both also touch on theories and practices related and conducive to liberation (*mokṣa*). The fourth item, composed around AD 300, is concerned with practical wisdom and the pursuit of worldly well-being (*artha*). It is a sometimes humorous and regularly direct treatise on common sense. Finally, the last work was written in Bengal in the twelfth century, and though it deals with devotion to the divine, it speaks in the language of eroticism and love (*kāma*).

All are artfully translated, and all include useful introductions, notes, and/or indices to guide the reader further. Some of the best known and most loved of Sanskrit-language writings, these masterworks provide a window into a fascinating and elegantly described world. Enjoy!

↬ *Upaniṣads: Hindu Scriptures on Asceticism and Renunciation,* trans. Patrick Olivelle (Oxford University Press, 1998)

> Literally meaning to "sit down near," that is, close to the teacher, the word *upaniṣad* also refers to a "secret." The texts bearing the same name chronicle the teachings of gurus who reveal the nature of being, the divine Brahman, and its identity with the individual self, called the *ātman*. They recall the experiential nature of the search, the progressive deepening of insight through *yoga*, contemplation, and study. The *upaniṣadic* stories recount the processes one engages in coming to know one's own nature, which resides at a level beyond awareness of sense-objects, of fleeting thoughts, or even of the rhythm of one's own breath. "Not this" and "not that," the self (*ātman*) is utterly different from the ephemeral self, the body, thoughts, etc. In revealing this secret, the *Upaniṣads* also offer a wealth of insight into the culture and life of the ascetics, seekers, and kings who sought to know it.

↬ *The Mahābhārata,* trans. Chakravarthi V. Narasimhan (Columbia University Press, 1997)

> Some seven times larger than the *Iliad* and the *Odyssey* combined, the *Mahābhārata* is an epic story that aspires to omniety. "What appears here in the *Mahābhārata* exists elsewhere," we are told, and "if it is not in the *Mahābhārata*, then it simply does not exist." Narasimhan provides us with a faithfully translated, artfully redacted, book-length narrative of this struggle between the forces of good and evil. The battle scenes are plentiful, but they are presented with a great deal of moral context. The war marks the beginning of the *kali* age, the last and most decrepit of four Hindu eons. It is an era in which the moral order and law (the *dharma*) is fraying, and no single character is faultless. The

story is as inexhaustible as are human foibles, follies, and failures, and it explores the difficulties in deciding on the correct course of action in a morally suspect world.

↪ *The Bhagavad Gita*, trans. W. J. Johnson (Oxford University Press, 2005)

The "Song of the Lord" is the most famous of all Hindu scriptures. Formally a part of the *Mahābhārata*, it consists of a dialogue between the God Kṛṣṇa and his warrior-disciple, Arjuna. Two great armies stand ready to fight, and Arjuna leads one of them. The battle will determine everything: the future of the kingdom, victory for good or evil, the fate of the moral order. A member of the warrior (*kṣatriya*) caste, Arjuna is duty-bound to protect the kingdom, but those threatening it happen to be his cousins, his uncle, his teachers. Duty (*dharma*) also bars him from killing them. Paralyzed by the moral dilemma, Arjuna turns for council to Kṛṣṇa, who wonderfully instructs him to perform *dharma* for its own sake, and with devotion (*bhakti*) to God. In doing so, Arjuna not only discovers the right course of action, but also his own divinity and communion with God.

↪ Viṣṇu Śarma, *The Pañcatantra*, trans. Chandra Rajan (Penguin, 2007)

This manual of common sense concerns itself with *artha*. It teaches the practical wisdom that is vital for governance and the acquisition (and maintenance) of wealth and power. The narrative opens with a king's deep concern: his three sons are dull-witted and utterly uninterested in learning. No one, and no method, can awaken their interest and sharpen their minds. Enter Viṣṇu Śarma, a clever and learned Brahmin, or priest, who promises to produce three princes unsurpassed in learning, all within six months. What follows are a series of animal tales that were compiled in perhaps the fourth century AD, told for the benefit of the princes and teaching clever living. The cycle of five books tells one how to win friends, whom to trust, how to judge a man's character, etc., all in a narrative so clear that it profits even the most dim-witted among us, let alone the clever ones!

↪ *Love Song of the Dark Lord: Jayadeva's Gītagovinda*, trans. Barbara Stoler Miller (Columbia University Press, 1997)

In this classic poem, the author uses the language of erotic love to convey the power and emotion of devotion to God. The "Dark Lord" is Kṛṣṇa (whose name literally means "black"), and the *Gītagovinda* chronicles his back-and-forth romance with Rādhā, his favorite of many female cowherd lovers, called Gopīs in Sanskrit. The poetic narrative evokes the flavor of an absent lover, and the subsequent delight of an eventual reunion. Thus, the work conveys two forms of pleasure (*kāma*), that of erotic love and the pleasure of poetry, and in the end it points to the bliss associated with a personal and utterly intimate encounter with the divine.

For further reading:

Dominic Goodall, ed., *Hindu Scriptures* (University of California Press, 1996).

Thomas J. Hopkins, *The Hindu Religious Tradition* (Wadsworth, 1971).

A. L. Basham, *The Wonder That Was India: A Survey of the History and Culture of the Sub-continent before the Coming of the Muslims*, 3rd ed. (Picador, 2005).

JOHN NEMEC is Assistant Professor of Indian Religions and South Asian Studies and a member of the Religious Studies Department. He has studied Sanskrit and Indian religions at the University of Rochester, the University of California, Santa Barbara, Oxford University, the University of Pennsylvania, and, of course, in India.

R. S. KHARE

Differing Inequalities: Considering India, Europe, and America

Recently, the rising collaboration between India and the United States, already touted as a distinct twenty-first-century development, deeply involves these two peoples' different history, society, polity, and culture. Both are large plural societies, linked historically by encounters between Europe and India. These exchanges between India and Europe thus form a necessary backdrop to the challenges these two major democracies, India and America, face today. Both are challenged as much to tackle their own distinct racial/caste inequalities, socioeconomic disparities, and religious differences as to forge shared new initiatives enhancing global stability, peace, and prosperity. The five readings I suggest, read in any sequence, are meant to facilitate entry into this exciting old-yet-new (and fast reshaping) field of inquiry.

Since any effort at understanding the history and culture of India and America inevitably passes through Europe, our reliable guide on the encounters between India and Europe is Wilhelm Halbfass, a German philosopher. His book, *India and Europe,* in fact, renders Louis Dumont's *Homo Hierarchicus,* a book devoted to understanding India and its caste system, much more accessible. Dumont, a renowned French anthropologist, had found India and Europe "structurally opposed" fifty years ago, while Halbfass, following major German hermeneutical approaches, explored all major strands of India-Europe exchange. Though Dumont maintained "value oppositions" between "hierarchical India" and "equality-espousing modern Europe," Halbfass found encounters between "traditional India" and the "modern West" to be historically dynamic, with each impacting the other's philosophical, social, and political thought. Helpfully, Halbfass also connected many crucial historical and cultural dots for the reader, making the twists and turns of their discourses much more meaningful. Both indispensable, Dumont and Halbfass authoritatively illuminate major social and religious-philosophical differences between India and Europe.

Against this backdrop, India and modern Europe, in Dumont's view, have long displayed two clearly different systems of inequality. If India is the land of birth-based caste hierarchy, then Europe—and even America—is the land of entrenched class and racial inequalities. Lately, the debates on caste, class, and racial inequalities have politicized around international human and civil rights issues. Here, while caste-class inequalities challenge India's developing democracy, modern, affluent America must tackle its distinct race-class-poverty issues. If over 170 million Dalits (or the erstwhile "Untouchables"), "the lowest of the low," showcase the failures of democratic India, then tens of millions of poor and black Americans challenge the United States to deliver self-help. The view from the bottom of the society is always different than from the top. To Dalits, caste discrimination looks nothing less than "racial," while to African Americans, racism looks worse than caste. Learning about one today inevitably reveals something comparable about the other. So viewed, Bernestine Singley's volume, devoted to experiencing, expressing, and confronting racial discrimination in America, helps us reflect deeply on different inequalities.

Recently, my students and I explored the same issue in an undergraduate seminar on social inequality. We wrote and discussed *our* distinct "personal histories" on the racial/caste inequalities encountered in our lives. Singley's volume provided us a comparative text on the tragedy, fears, pain, and the self-accounting racism demands. Our exercise culminated in chasing the subtle language codes hidden in our personal languages "tackling" racial discrimination.

Given the deeply laid roots of inequalities across India, Europe, and America, we must continue our quest for ever more insightful, transparent, and inclusive cultural knowledge and expression. The fourth and fifth books, *In Light of India* and *The Argumentative Indian,* written respectively by two Nobel Prize winners, Octavio Paz (Mexican poet, diplomat, and thinker) and Amartya Sen (economist), move us in such a direction in their inimitable ways. Each author deftly leaves his own distinct intellectual, cultural, and humanistic signature on the issues and ideas that weave together India, modern Europe, and the world. As Paz soars to meditate on Indian history, philosophy, religion, polity, and current events vis-à-vis the West, he dazzles us with his poetic insights and commanding cultural and political observations. As Sen, an economist and social philosopher, magisterially explicates the social, economic, religious, and political inequalities facing India as they relate to the modern West (and China), he does so by helping us understand India's long inculcated ways of reasoning, debate, criticism, and skepticism. Thus, differing with Louis Dumont and agreeing with Halbfass, Sen emphasizes *similarity* and discourse dynamics over contrasts between India and the West. However, our quest for an unimpeded, reciprocal flow of global cultural knowledge must continue ever more.

The book list reflects the status of the changing multifaceted field of inquiry that seeks to understand America and India (via Europe) better, despite some enduring social, religious, and historical differences. The field now attracts some of the world's best intellects; it also exposes us to strikingly original scholarly work, debate, and reflection.

❧ Wilhelm Halbfass, *India and Europe: An Essay in Understanding* (State University of New York Press, 1988)

> This book, unique for its scope, approach, and scholarly erudition, explicates the history, breadth, and depth of Indian and European intellectual encounters, beginning with pre-Alexandrian antiquity to the early 1980s. Creditably, Halbfass examines, with an open mind, the reciprocal roles India and Europe have played in shaping each other's philosophical and cultural thought, and in shaping modern Indian thought. Relying on the German hermeneutical tradition rooted in Heidegger, Gadamer, and Habermas, Halbfass takes a dynamic and lively rather than an ideologically fixed view of India-West engagements. He adeptly mines original nineteenth- and early twentieth-century German sources, exploding many simplistic disciplinary conundrums.

❧ Louis Dumont, *Homo Hierarchicus: The Caste System and Its Implications,* complete rev. English ed. (University of Chicago Press, 1981)

> A "modern classic" in anthropology, this book continues to be unsurpassed in its breadth, depth, and very distinct "structural" approach

for understanding India through its caste system. To understand the "ideology" (value structure) of the caste system, Dumont maintained, was to understand the millennia-old Indian society, culture, and civilization. Dumont, however, considered his Indian study complete only when juxtaposed to his study of modern Western ideology: *Homo equalis*. In English, it was *From Mandeville to Marx: The Genesis and Triumph of Economic Ideology*.

↬ Bernestine Singley, ed., *When Race Becomes Real: Black and White Writers Confront Their Personal Histories* (Lawrence Hill, 2004)

This is a riveting and revealing collection of personal stories by a range of accomplished black and white American writers trying to account for the "racial question" in their own life experiences. The collection as a whole might be more significant for presenting vivid personal stories at one level, and becoming witness to the continuing racial divide at another. Either way, the racial issue causes suffering and angst in America, and reading personal histories most often involves a reader's preconceived notions. For a striking comparative parallel in the social profile and in reform movements, see Eleanor Zelliot's masterly study *From Untouchable to Dalit: Essays on the Ambedkar Movement*.

↬ Octavio Paz, *In Light of India*, trans. Eliot Weinberger (Harcourt Brace, 1997)

Octavio Paz, who spent six years as Mexico's ambassador to India (1962–68), first landed in India in November 1951 and developed, as this book records, a lifelong personal bond with the country. This work in prose and poetry packs "the reflections, impressions, and objections that India had provoked in [him]." As he effortlessly weaves his dazzling scholarly erudition into meditations on and criticisms of India and the West, the book yields many a philosophical, artistic, social, and poetic insight for the reader to ponder. Here, America comes lumped with the modern West and its exercise of power and influence.

↬ Amartya Sen, *The Argumentative Indian: Writings on Indian History, Culture, and Identity* (Picador, 2006)

Highlighting the long-preserved ways of Indian dialogue, dialectics, and skepticism, Sen's essays strike out in several directions to show how important this Indian reasoning stance (comparable to modern Western ways of reasoning) remains not only for Indian democracy and its secular politics, but also for tackling Indian caste-class-gender inequalities, the politics of deprivation, the problems of social injustice, and the challenges of a nuclear-armed subcontinent. Sen, like Paz, shows a distinct perspective on what India, China, and the West were in the past and what they could be in dialogue in the future.

For further reading:

W. Norman Brown, *The United States and India, Pakistan, Bangladesh,* 3rd ed. (Harvard University Press, 1972).

R. S. KHARE's interest in India, modern Europe, and America grew out of his anthropological research on both the top (i.e., the Brahmans) and bottom (Dalits) of Indian society, and his teaching in America. He is Professor of Anthropology and has visited as faculty at L'École des hautes études en sciences sociales, Paris, and the University of Chicago, and as a fellow at the Institute for Advanced Study, Princeton, and the Wissenschaftskolleg, Berlin.

PETER OCHS

Islam, Christianity, Judaism: Reading across a Difference

The book list you are about to read concerns reading itself: in particular, what it means to read across two significant differences. One is the difference between heaven and earth, or between literatures that describe themselves as having individual human authors and those that describe themselves as having "sacred" origins outside this world as we know it. Another is the difference between one intensely religious group and another. In this case, we are dealing with the different ways that members of the three Abrahamic traditions of Judaism, Christianity, and Islam read one another's sacred texts.

I have chosen these books from several course syllabi that address religious and political relations among the Abrahamic traditions. The University of Virginia is a leader in the study of such relations. We offer a Ph.D. in what we call "Scripture, Interpretation, and Practice," focusing on comparative studies in religious traditions. We also offer related undergraduate courses in such topics as "Abrahamic Religions in Conflict" and "Scriptural Reasoning," our name for what happens when religious scholars from the three traditions meet in small groups to study scriptural texts together for hours and even days.

I have gathered a sampling of readings to help students encounter this kind of reading and reflect on what may be learned from the encounter. There are of course the primary scriptures. There is the TaNaKh: an acronym for the Hebrew Bible, which combines books of the Torah, the

Prophets (*neviim* in Hebrew), and the Writings (*khetuvim* in Hebrew). There is the New Testament, with the Gospels and the Acts and Letters of the Apostles. And there is the Qur'an, whose name means "Reading" itself, or "Recitation": that is, the book of words that came down from God to the Prophet Muhammad.

The reading list below also includes texts that display similarities and differences and mutual relations among each of the three scriptures. And there are texts that narrate how these traditions have interacted over the often difficult centuries and texts that reflect on what it means to read scripture across such differences.

As a philosopher of Judaism, I examine how modern Jewish thinkers read and interpret Judaism's vast literature of commentaries on the classic sources: the Bible and the Talmud, the vast literature of the rabbinic sages who fashioned what we know of Judaism in the years after the destruction of the Jews' Second Temple in 70 CE and the creation of the diaspora that began in the second century CE. Over the years, I got interested in how the cousins of the Jews—Christians and Muslims—read their own traditions of commentary and reflect on what it means to read and interpret sacred texts. This interest has led to a "comparative philosophy of reading": a study of similarities and differences in the ways that Muslims, Jews, and Christians think about how and why they read and interpret their sacred traditions. Over the years, I found other scholars with similar interests, and, in 1995, a group of us formed a society for such things: The Society for Scriptural Reasoning. Academic subgroups now meet regularly at Cambridge University, the University of Virginia, Princeton's Center of Theological Inquiry, and five other places internationally. Several public outreach centers have been set up as well, the largest at the St. Ethelburga's Center for Peace and Reconciliation in London.

Some remarkable lessons have come out of the meetings of these various groups. Here is a sampling: (*a*) *Reading together* can serve as a primary instrument for nurturing peace and understanding across differences; (*b*) One helpful method is to have folks sit around a table, place a brief set of their traditions' texts on the table, and have all of them agree that everyone has equal access to the texts and equal right to offer different readings, but that the texts alone hold final authority. To say "the texts hold authority" means that whatever reading I offer, someone else can always return to the words of the text and derive from them a different reading; (*c*) Every time any one of our groups has conducted such a discussion for two to four days, lengthy discussion has always increased mutual respect and understanding, not decreased it. Whenever sharp differences have raised the "heat" of the room, someone has been able to reach deeply into the texts and draw up some fresh insight that, like water drawn from a deep pool, brought a cooling relief to us all; (*d*) In discussions like these, the texts appear to serve as impartial mediators among all who sit around the table. No individuals' inner thoughts and beliefs serve as hidden judges of what is right and wrong; the words are the judges, and they are always out there for all of us to see and to consult and consult again.

The three sacred scriptures:

Tanakh: The Holy Scriptures (Jewish Publication Society of America, 2007).
The New Oxford Annotated Bible with the Apocrypha, 3rd ed. (Oxford University Press, 2001).
The Message of the Qur'an, trans. Muhammad Asad (Book Foundation, 2003).

✧ F. E. Peters, *The Monotheists: Jews, Christians, and Muslims in Conflict and Competition,* 2 vols. (Princeton University Press, 2003)

For the sake of peace among the three Abrahamic religions, there is urgent need for the kind of books F. E. Peters has been composing for the past three decades. This two-volume set is his best yet. Volume 1 narrates the origins of the three scriptural traditions. Volume 2 introduces the more complex story of how, in his view, each tradition has interpreted and embodied the message of its scriptures. This is a great way to study the three Abrahamic traditions side by side, as teachings of the One God that are as interrelated as they are conflictual, as intimate one to the other as they claim to be separate and exclusive.

✧ Barry W. Holtz, ed. *Back to the Sources: Reading the Classic Jewish Texts* (Simon and Schuster, 1986)

While Peters tries to stand alongside all three traditions, Barry Holtz's best-selling collection is designed to draw out the inside story of one tradition. Holtz gathers some of the best scholars of Judaism and asks them to teach us how to enter the different genres of classic Jewish literature, such as Bible, Talmud, Prayer Book, Legal Codes, Kabbalah, Philosophy, and more. So many different ways to read! Entering one tradition this way will also help you enter the others. For me, there are two central lessons to learn from Jewish reading. The first is not to read (only) alone, but to learn to read in direct dialogue with others as well as with the text and its author(s). The second is to read so carefully that each word and even letter reveals its own inner universe of possibilities. This kind of reading explodes conventional understandings at the same time that it honors the text and its traditions.

↪ Jane Dammen McAuliffe, Barry D. Walfish, and Joseph W. Goering, eds., *With Reverence for the Word: Medieval Scriptural Exegesis in Judaism, Christianity, and Islam* (Oxford University Press, 2003)

> This selection and the next bring us inside the contemporary academic disciplines. *With Reverence* illustrates the perspectives of historians and literary scholars. How did the great medieval scholars and theologians read and interpret scripture? Twenty-nine scholars analyze twenty-nine different ways of answering this question, from studies of "literary exegesis" to "mystical allegories." This collection stretches my imagination to unanticipated ways of reading.

↪ David F. Ford and C. C. Pecknold, eds., *The Promise of Scriptural Reasoning* (Blackwell, 2006)

> In this volume, scholars of scriptural reasoning reflect on what happens when Muslims, Jews, and Christians read across their differences: how this reading affects what philosophers say about "reading as noticing other people's suffering," or what social scientists say about "how the world gets re-enchanted," or what literary theorists say about the scripture's "heavenly semantics." Perhaps you will sense, as I do, how years of reading together has drawn the scholars who contributed to this book into a level of community that reaches across their great differences.

For further reading:

Conceived at the University of Virginia and published by its Electronic Text Center, the *Journal of Scriptural Reasoning* displays the fruits of long sessions of study and dialogue among scholars of the three scriptural traditions. Each issue addresses a single topic, such as "Pharaoh's Hardened Heart" or "Poverty and Debt-Release." Essays examine brief selections of scripture, leaving space for many levels of interaction among different styles of reading. Once you get the swing of these essays, you'll be sharing in the process of scriptural reasoning. Perhaps, like me, you will discover that this kind of reading strengthens one's own tradition of knowledge and belief at the same time that it brings this tradition into intimate relation with two others. (http://etext.virginia.edu/journals/ssr)

PETER OCHS is Edgar Bronfman Professor of Modern Judaic Studies and co-founder of the Society for Scriptural Reasoning and the Society for Textual Reasoning. His graduate degrees are in philosophy and in rabbinic literature, and most of his writings relate one to the other (as well as recent Muslim and Christian theologies). Among his books are *Peirce, Pragmatism, and the Logic of Scripture* (Cambridge University Press, 1998); *Postliberal Christianity and the*

Jews (Brazos, 2008); *Textual Reasonings* (coedited; Eerdmans, 2003), and *Reasoning after Revelation* (coauthored; Westview Press, 1998).

ABDULAZIZ SACHEDINA

The Need to Know Islam and Muslims

The need to know Islam and Muslims: perhaps no other subject today has received so much attention. I am a regular traveler and deeply interested in what the bookstores at the airport carry for the average educated American to read while they are traveling or waiting to catch their next flight out. Only five years ago you would have found few, if any, titles on Islam and Muslims in these bookstores. Today, they carry numerous titles by academicians as well as politicians and journalists.

In the age of globalization when information about other cultures and peoples is readily accessible, one would have thought that books about Muslims and Islam would be free of political bias and cultural prejudice. And yet, after a long-term engagement with the academic study of Islam, I have come to this conclusion: it is not the lack of materials that is the source of misinformation and dehumanization of the cultural and religious "other" in our midst and in the Muslim world. It is the glut of books and articles that has served, intentionally and sometimes inadvertently, to distort the Muslim image today.

For instance, the idea of jihad, which is "struggle" and "striving" to improve one's life and environment, is always depicted as "holy war" against infidels. Such a distortion makes Muslims appear religiously militant and politically terrorist. More insidious is the media presentation of Muslim women as being oppressed by Islam through institutionalized gender inequality in the religious law of Islam—the Sharia. Whereas women in patriarchal Muslim culture suffer from violation of their human rights, to single out Muslim women's treatment cannot be without a political agenda to ridicule Islamic tradition.

Most readers lack a sufficient way of evaluating hundreds of books on these topics and choosing the right one to educate themselves. Usually, the books that make it to the weekly *New York Times Book Review* get added to the list of "Must Read." Ironically, however, books selected for journalistic reviews are no different than journalistic representations of Islam. Hence, a reader's quest to get to the heart of the matter remains unfulfilled. However, it is worth keeping in mind that even a specialist like me cannot in reality read all that is on the market. For many readers the problem is one of selection.

Having taught Islam for more than thirty-five years, I meticulously select the books for the course keeping in mind my young educated readers. Moreover, since my readers come with a number of preconceived notions, largely gathered from the media, about Muslims and their beliefs, my efforts are geared toward neutralizing the hastily concocted negative media images through some well-researched and balanced studies of Islam.

Given the fact that our engagement with Muslims in North America and abroad is going to be a permanent and important part of our domestic and foreign policies, I have identified the following books as my list of recommended readings about the people we expect to influence and to learn from in ways that would make this world a peaceful and secure place for all of humanity.

▻ Sachiko Murata and William C. Chittick, *The Vision of Islam* (Paragon House, 1995)

This book is published under the series Visions of Reality: A Series on Religions as Worldview. Any worldview consists of three basic elements: fundamental beliefs, religious practices, and attitudes toward peoples and cultures of the world. The authors have lucidly outlined the major components of an Islamic worldview, taking care to give the reader a thorough understanding of Islam as a religion that continues to inform Muslim understanding of God's purposes for humanity and their role in advancing the world community to create a just public order. The most significant aspect of the book is its success in weaving together beliefs, practices, and history to underscore the relationship between what is professed and what is operative in actual history, so that the spiritual and political configuration of Muslim religion becomes accessible to the reader.

▻ Abdulaziz Sachedina, *The Islamic Roots of Democratic Pluralism* (2001; Oxford University Press, 2007)

The subject of the role of Islam in the public square is important for several reasons. As Muslims struggle to make sense of their religious heritage and its relevance today, they are confronted with autocratic political systems in their countries that deny their citizens the basic freedoms guaranteed in the UN Charter of Human Rights. To add to this political injustice, the extremist religious elements in Muslim societies have prescribed violence as a means of change, threatening the well-being of the civilians caught in the crossfire. This book is a journey in search of Islam in the context of modernity and its trappings in secularism and rationalism. It asks this question: Can a classical faith provide solutions to the quandaries faced by modern men and women in Islam?

⇌ Jane Howard, *Inside Iran: Women's Lives* (Mage, 2002)

The author, a former BBC correspondent, traveled and lived in Iran. She provides a vivid account of the challenges faced by women under the Islamic government and what it means to be a Muslim woman in Iran today. The narrative aspect of the book affords a fascinating account of the ways in which Iranian women, who are deeply religious and yet modern in their outlook, assert their rights in an essentially patriarchal culture. This book serves to remind the reader that without fieldwork—that is, more direct engagement with women's lives in their social, political, and cultural settings—analyzing and judging attitudes about Muslim women remain at the most tentative.

⇌ Seyyed Hossein Nasr, *Islamic Art and Spirituality* (State University of New York Press, 1987)

In Islamic civilization visual arts, whether in places of worship or in palaces, were created by Muslim mystics. As such, there is a deep spiritual symbolism connected with Islamic art. My choice of this book is based on a course I've taught, "Mystical Dimensions of Islam." This mystical quest is the soul of Islam that speaks universally to all human beings. The author shows us that Islamic visual arts capture the inner dimensions of the artist's existence and evoke the observer's response by speaking to her innermost feelings. Religious art and architecture are even more powerful in imploring a spiritual response. The author, a prominent scholar of Islamic spirituality, shows us in this inspiring study that world religions have created visual arts to kindle devotion and love of the divine.

ABDULAZIZ SACHEDINA is Frances Myers Ball Professor of Religious Studies. He has studied in India, Iraq, Iran, and Canada, and has written about Islamic law and theology for more than two decades. His recent publications include *Islamic Messianism* (State University of New York Press, 1981); *The Just Ruler in Shiite Islam* (Oxford University Press, 1988); *Human Rights and Conflict of Cultures: Freedom of Religion and Conscience in Western and Islamic Traditions* (coauthor of Islamic sections; University of South Carolina Press, 1988); and *The Islamic Roots of Democratic Pluralism* (Oxford University Press, 2001).

Index